DREAM·HOVSES

By the same author

EDWIN LUTYENS: ARCHITECT LAUREATE

DREAM·HOVSES
THE·EDWARDIAN·IDEAL

∷

Roderick Gradidge

∷

*With twenty photographs
by André Goulancourt*

Braziller · New York

For information address the publisher:

George Braziller, Inc.
One Park Avenue
New York, N. Y. 10016

Library of Congress Cataloging in Publication Data

Gradidge, Roderick
Dream Houses, the Edwardian ideal
Bibliography: p.
Includes index.
1. Architecture, Domestic—Great Britain
2. Architecture, Edwardian—Great Britain
3. Architecture, Domestic—South Africa
4. Architecture, Edwardian—South Africa
I. Title.
NA7328.G78   728.8'3'09034   80–17866
ISBN 0–8076–0988–9

Set in Monotype Fournier 12pt
Printed in Great Britain by The Anchor Press Ltd,
at Tiptree, Essex

'To my friends pictured within'

CONTENTS

ILLUSTRATIONS

PREFACE

JUST three years before the Great War the German architect Hermann Muthesius published in Berlin *Das Englische Haus* (The English House), concluding a love affair with English architecture which eleven years earlier had been celebrated with two vast folios on *Die Englische Baukunst der Gegenwart* (English Architecture of the Present Day). The publication of these two books appropriately symbolizes the high-water mark of foreign admiration for British architecture, which began in the 1840s but hardly survived the 1914–18 War. But during those years the influence was immense and for good or ill international twentieth-century architecture would not be as it is without the designs of the English architects who flourished at the close of Queen Victoria's reign.

It was another German, Nikolaus Pevsner, who in more recent times first recognized the importance of this period of English architecture, by publishing in 1936 *Pioneers of the Modern Movement from William Morris to Walter Gropius*. P. Morton Shand underlined this when in a contemporary review of the book he remarked that it was 'a period that will ultimately be regarded as the most crucial in the whole of architectural history'.[1] This perhaps is going a little far and reflects the single-minded approach to history by committed modernists of the thirties; none the less in his book Pevsner revolutionized our attitudes to modern architectural history, and by so doing forced the history of English architecture of the last century into a Prussian corset from which we have not yet escaped.

Although no one would wish to suggest that Pevsner's book was not important, it was clearly intended to be used as a weapon in the war that was at that time being waged by 'advanced' Germans against what they thought to be reactionary architecture. Unfortunately what began as polemic has now become received truth. Since that time numberless books have been written on the 'pioneers' that Pevsner canonized, but little has been said about the other magnificent (but perhaps more traditional) architects who flourished just before the reign of Edward VII. Particularly disgraceful has been the neglect of two of the greatest of

English masters, Ernest Newton and Edwin Lutyens; even those approved architects, such as Voysey and Baillie Scott, have been looked at only through Pevsner-approved Bauhaus-tinted spectacles. This is particularly absurd in Voysey's case since as early as 1935 he was repudiating just these ideas (see page 75). At the same time if one compares the buildings that Voysey or Baillie Scott actually built with those of say Lutyens or Newton, it will not be hard to see that there is very little to choose between them, except in one important matter— neither Voysey nor Baillie Scott designed in the Classical style whereas Lutyens and Newton sometimes did. This would seem to be the only reason why one group of architects is praised while the other is rejected. Unfortunately Pevsner, fresh from Germany, did not realize that by the 1920s at least the English Vernacular Revival had reached such a degree of sophistication that it was able to take local styles of any period and combine them, creating an architecture that had little to do with the Beaux-Arts Schools or any of the other traditional styles that were still at that time flourishing on the Continent.

If the *Pioneers* had been merely a book of architectural history this discussion might perhaps have been of little importance, but it was so successful that, with followers like Siegfried Giedion in *Space Time and Architecture* (1941), it succeeded in converting architectural thinking for a whole generation and in the process destroyed a flourishing English school of architecture. Recently, however, with the virtual collapse of the Modern Movement people have been again wondering whether there is more to architecture than the arid tenets of functionalism, and have been turning back to a more vernacular style which more readily fits into the countryside or cityscape. For this reason, if for no other, it seems sensible to look at the last period when English architecture was flourishing and to see whether it has anything to offer us today.

We find in the 1890s a self-assured but unintellectual architecture. Nowadays it is academics like Nikolaus Pevsner or David Watkin who tell the architect how to design; in those days it was the architects (not trained in a school but in the office of fellow practising architects) who created the new architecture. They were men who knew their clients, who knew what they wanted and knew how to give what was wanted. The building type where this talent is most important is in the individually designed house and it was in this field that the turn-of-the-century architect flourished.

The English house has an architectural history of about a thousand years. For most of that time the important innovations were made for royal or aristocratic clients, new ideas only slowly seeping down the social scale. The late Victorian period is the first in which innovations were made in smaller houses designed for middle-class people. The masters of the middle-class house as it reached its full flowering were Newton, Voysey, Baillie Scott, Baker, Dawber, Frank Lloyd Wright and Lutyens. As it happens all of them started their careers in the 1890s, although there was a wide discrepancy of age between them, Newton, the eldest, being fourteen years older than Edwin Lutyens, the youngest. During the decade they created a style that was to serve them and their followers for two generations. While there were developments, particularly in the swing to Neo-Georgian by some of the architects (and in Lutyens's and Baker's case, at the end of their career, there was a further swing to Imperialist Neo-Classicism), it was the Vernacular style, itself a child of the Arts and Crafts Movement, which was to be the basis of all English (and a lot of American) design right up till the 1950s. For this reason the early buildings of these architects—seen together as a group—are worth careful consideration. While there have been monographs (some contemporary, some new) on most of the architects they have never before been considered as a 'school'. This book therefore concentrates on the early creative years in the 1890s and considers their houses in a strictly chronological order.

Like all creative people architects are affected by what is going on in the other arts at the same time, and this was never more true than in England in the 1890s, when all the arts seemed to be moving to a minor Renaissance creating in the process a distinct English style. In all the arts the English style was deeply imbued with the Gothic Revival/Arts and Crafts idiom, personified in the overpowering figure of William Morris, who was to die before the decade was out. For this reason if we are to put the architecture of the houses in context we must first consider what was going on in the rest of the artistic world in England at that time, both in the work of 'advanced' designers like Aubrey Beardsley, or more traditional artists like the second Mrs Watts, or Edward Elgar.

This 'English Renaissance' was not to last for very long. The dream was created in the last years of Victoria's reign and flourished during the short reign of her son, only to be destroyed by the machine guns on the Somme and their sequel in the late 1920s in the Bauhaus at Dessau. It was Robert Furneaux Jordan, another doctrinaire architectural historian of Pevsner's generation, who called the Lutyens houses of the 1890s 'dream houses'; he found them unreal like a dream leaving not a wrack behind. 'It all died' (he wrote in 1966 in his *Victorian Architecture*), 'as it should have died, in August 1914.' Perhaps now when we have seen what horrors have replaced the Edwardian ideal, we may ask why it had to die then and also whether it might not be possible to revive at least some of the integrity and humanity which made the architecture of this period so acceptable to ordinary people and so infinitely preferable to the architecture which replaced it.

Since this is the work of a practising architect rather than an architectural historian I have had to rely heavily on the work of others. The published works consulted are included in the Bibliography, but I have also consulted the many notes of tours and lectures given under the auspices of the Victorian Society. The following notes have been particularily useful: Alan Crawford's, 'Madresfield Court' (15 July 1967), 'Tour of Broadway and Chipping Campden' (15 September 1978) and 'Re-creation of Beauty's Awakening' (16 September 1978); Andrew Saint's 'Haslemere and District' (25 July 1975), 'Hampstead' (1977) and with David Ottewill 'Arts and Crafts in Berkshire and Hampshire' (5 August 1978); Gavin Stamp's contribution to 'Of the Soil Racey—Arts and Crafts Rogues in North Norfolk' (24 April 1971); Nicholas Taylor's William Morris Society Tour No. 3 'The New Forest' (29 July 1967) and 'Surrey Houses by Lutyens' (17–18 October 1970); and David Verey's 'Ernest Gimson' (29 June 1968). I am grateful to Messrs Longman and Co. for permission to quote at length from Gertrude Jekyll's *Home and Garden*.

I have over the years had many discussions with other members of the committee of the Victorian Society, in particular its Secretary Hermione Hobhouse, Peter Howell, Peter Miall, Alastair Service and Robert Thorne; and also many public and private discussions with my fellow members of the Art Workers' Guild, in particular the late Past Master Lawrence Bradshaw, whose fund of memories of many of the early guildsmen and Frank Brangwyn was immense. Other Guildsmen include my fellow Honorary Secretary, Anthony Ballantine, Past Master John Brandon-Jones, the Honorary Architect, Douglas Shepherd and the Honorary Librarian, Gavin Stamp. I have learnt a lot from the other members of the Arts Council Lutyens Exhibition who include, as well as people already mentioned, Colin Amery, Margaret Richardson, Mary Lutyens and David Watkin. Over the years I have had numberless discussions with other friends; particularly valuable have been those on music with Edward Greenfield, and Art Nouveau book design and the work of Jessie M. King with John Russell Taylor. I am particularly grateful to Andrew Saint, who has read this book at proof stage and made a number of valuable comments and corrections. I must also thank Gavin

Stamp for his delightful title page design, reminiscent of so many architectural books published at the turn of the century, and André Goulancourt for his magnificent 'portraits' of the houses.

Finally my special thanks must go to Andrew Best, Sarah Bunney and George Horner who between them have tried to pull together what must have seemed to them to be an intolerably muddled manuscript. But I fear in spite of all this help there will be many errors, and they are of course all mine.

S.A. *Vaal* and Chiswick 1978–80

Part I

THE·PERIOD

The education of the architect

In 1887, when Herbert Baker first met Edwin Luytens in the office of Ernest George, English architecture was flourishing—there were English architects whose work was admired throughout the world, and there were plenty of other men who, since there was a healthy freedom in their art, were able to contribute new and exciting ideas. Sometimes of course things got out of hand. Indeed Pugin himself, the great originator (like Brunel and Disraeli, a second generation Englishman) had died insane, when he was only forty, thirty-five years earlier; but the serious-minded Gothic Revival that he had pioneered had over those years progressed and come to dominate English architecture, led by a group of architects of great genius, such as William Butterfield, James Brooks and the architect who was to have the strongest influence on later generations—both through his splendid architecture and the people that he had in his office—George Edmund Street. After them came in the next generation, who were still very active in the 1880s—people such as G. F. Bodley and Richard Norman Shaw who treated the Gothic style in a lighter vein. Ernest George belonged to this group, though he was perhaps not in quite the same class as the leaders. He was the architect who built Pont Street and other streets in London in an entirely credible Dutch style and also a number of country houses, honestly built and in various styles, but always carefully designed to fit in with the countryside.

In England at that time there were no full-time schools of architecture. The young architect-to-be, or his parents, chose an architect as a master, and while working on the day-to-day work of the office the pupil learnt his trade by seeing all the problems of the practical business of building. He learnt little of theory, but a lot from practice. In this way Baker and Lutyens were trained, as were all the other architects whose work we shall be considering in this book. George's pupils did not expect to build palaces or great government buildings; they were house architects, architects as little concerned with big buildings as they were with the intellectual ideas of clever Frenchmen. They had not been trained to build great buildings or to handle the orders with the clarity and deadly exactitude that were the stock-in-trade of French or French-trained American architects.

Lutyens's generation of architects was taught by their masters to go out and sketch and to look at buildings in the round, especially to look at large Gothic buildings, cathedrals and abbeys. It was these buildings that showed them the three-dimensional nature of architecture, something that they would have difficulty in learning in any *atelier*. From looking at these buildings they learnt about archi-tectural balance and about the relationship between horizontal masses and soaring vertical towers and pinnacles. They learnt how, as one walks around a building one form starts to dominate as another recedes. They learnt too to delight in the texture of building materials, new and old, and to take pleasure in the history of buildings. So often different parts built in different periods in an old building seem to lie together without any offensive clash. As they learnt this they began to delight in good manners in architecture.

In the 1880s three offices predominated in the training of architects, that of Norman Shaw, Ernest George and J. D. Sedding, and each of them developed its own kind of architect. Shaw's office produced many successful house architects of the second grade such as J. M. Brydon, G. C. Horsley, Mervyn Macartney and E. J. May, all of whom followed their great predecessor Newton's lead. But it also produced a group of extreme Arts and Crafts leaders, such as Prior and Weir Schultz who, following Lethaby (in spite of their having helped to found the Art Workers' Guild) more often gave themselves to mystical fancy than to the serious business of building. Yet it must be said that Weir Schultz at least had a very successful, though largely unpublicized, house practice.

Ernest George's office produced Herbert Baker, Guy Dawber, Edwin Lutyens, Stanley Adshead, Arnold Mitchell and Herbert Reid. Weir Schultz worked in both offices and he no doubt brought some of the intense passion from the Shaw office but learnt at George's a great deal about the day-to-day work of getting and keeping clients, something that the George pupils seem to have developed to a high degree. Certainly this group of architects seemed more able to combine the Arts and Crafts Movement's High Romanticism with the more practical business of getting a building built, something that the Shaw product never seemed able to combine in one person. Again it was George's pupils who displayed more genius when they followed Newton's lead into Neo-Georgian; Macartney and May seem strangely uninspired when compared with Lutyens and Dawber.

In an earlier generation both Philip Webb and Norman Shaw were trained, as indeed was William Morris for a short time, in the office of G. E. Street. Although Street himself seems to have understood, at least in metalwork, the craftsman's sensitivity, he was never able to achieve this in his brick and stonework, which is always harsh. Morris recognized this and set out to remedy it, in particular in his founding of the Society for the Protection of Ancient Buildings, which was as much concerned with the texture of craftsmanship as it was in the restoration of buildings, something little appreciated today. But Shaw, in spite of his magnificent romantic vision and his wonderful ability to draw this vision, seems never to have understood this; most of his buildings are a grave disappiontment on the ground, none of them comes up to the vision. This is borne out in Shaw's pupils; none had the sensitivity of the Sedding or the George pupils. Webb on the other hand, close friend and co-founder of SPAB with Morris, understood more of this problem but somehow was only rarely able to achieve it in his buildings.

It is difficult to see why George's pupils turned out so well. George himself, who lived to a great age and ran through three partners, does not seem to have been much different from most architects of his generation. His work displays as much imagination as Shaw's but there is never that final spark that gives his architecture the undeniable glamour that Shaw had, and at the same time there is none of Philip Webb's intensity. His pupils and assistants, also, do not seem to have been much influenced by him and when they were, as Lutyens was at the first part of Crooksbury, or Baker was in the early Groote Schuur, the result gives little suggestion of future greatness. Much the same may be said of Guy Dawber. Batsford Park, where Dawber was Clerk of Works for most of the time that Lutyens was in George's office, is a splendid re-creation of an Elizabethan manor house, but there is little here to suggest George's later sensitive architecture, any more than Flete, where Newton was Clerk of Works, suggests much of what Newton was to do later. Yet within just a few years, Lutyens was building his dream houses in Surrey, Dawber was creating Cotswold manor houses almost indistinguishable from the real thing, Schultz was building in a styleless vernacular manner and Baker in South Africa was almost single-handedly creating an Arts and Crafts Movement of his own on the other side of the world. No doubt it was the Shaw pupils who gave the intellectual basis to the movement, but one only has to consider the harshness of, say, Avon Tyrell with the sensitivity of Orchards, to realize that more than intellectual integrity is needed.

There was a third important office and this was J. D. Sedding's. Sedding was a highly refined late Gothic Revivalist but he was perfectly willing to design in the Classical style if he considered this to be suitable. The magnificently Italian Church of The Holy Redeemer in Clerkenwell, London testifies to this, but his partner and successor was H. Wilson, who was another strong supporter of highly romanticized Arts and Crafts work. Wilson's approach to Classicism was always heavily tinged with Art Nouveau Romanticism and this seems to have caused a reaction in Sedding's pupils who never had anything to do with either Classicism or Art Nouveau. They were Sidney Barnsley, Ernest Gimson and Alfred Powell. Sidney Barnsley's brother, Ernest, however, was in Shaw's office and he no doubt came under Lethaby's influence and was able to bring some of his puritanical enthusiasm to Gimson.

The late Victorians believed that the arts should not be separated, as they are today, into minute specialized self-admiring groups, but that they should be seen as an integrated whole. In this they were influenced by such universal men as William Morris, who not only trained as an architect with G. E. Street, and became an overpowering influence on printing, book design, fabric and wallpaper design, stained glass, interior decoration, the revival of handcraftsmanship and country crafts, but was also a poet and novelist, and in his later life a revolutionary socialist. Morris died in 1896 but his great influence is still with us today; in the period up to his death he was all pervasive.

Another major influence was the Art Workers' Guild. The Guild had been founded in 1884 by a group of young men who were Norman Shaw's assistants. They were: Gerald Horsley, W. R. Lethaby, Ernest Newton, Mervyn Macartney and Edward S. Prior—all architects who were to become successful in later life. They were inspired by the essentially Gothic Revival ideals of Street's pupils, such as Philip Webb, William Morris and Norman Shaw himself, but within a few years they had come to see that the Arts and Crafts Movement could not confine itself only to the Gothic and traditional. It was in the 1890s that they began to see that the Georgian style as practised in simple country buildings was as much part of the vernacular tradition, and within a few years they had all come to recognize the genius of Christopher Wren and the English contribution to the Renaissance style.

Although the Guild was founded by architects, the intention was that all artist-craftsmen, who were elected on the basis of their work, should meet together and get to know each other's work and hear lectures and have craft demonstrations on all aspects of art and their work. It did not believe in the professionalization which was at that time creeping into all the arts. In 1892 Norman Shaw and T. G. Jackson edited a book of essays entitled *Architecture, a Profession or an Art*, which contained essays by thirteen different architects and artists, most of whom were Guildsmen including all five of the founders of the Guild. All the writers were against the registration of architects and the attempts being made at that time by the Royal Institute of British Architects to bring everyone within their professional fold. It must have been very dispiriting for those in favour of professionalism to find so many distinguished architects—all the architects most admired by the younger generation—against them. At this time the Guild's influence was at its strongest; practically every architect and craftsman, and most artists, of any importance were members, and they used the Guild to publicize their ideas. The Guild still exists and still holds to its ideals. It is now discovering a new membership in the young who find the standards that the establishment architects of the present day work to unappetizing.

Between 1890 and 1898, a fresh breeze was blowing through all the arts and was creating a new style. In architecture and most of the other arts it was profoundly Anti-Victorian, but it also combined an understanding of traditional building techniques and materials, with a dream of an ordered and settled society which was to become—albeit briefly—the Edwardian experience. It was this understanding and dream that Lutyens and Baker brought to Classicism and the rules of the Beaux-Arts schools when it fell to them to design the buildings of the Empire. It was perhaps inevitable, given the climate of the time, that they should turn to Rome, but it was equally inevitable that they would never be able to accept the Roman rules just as they stood, as they had been codified by Palladio and Vitruvius. It was inevitable that in their hands Rome would be just a little touched with the Gothic Revival and with its offspring, the Arts and Crafts Movement.

New Delhi is the great monument to all that had gone before in the 100 years since Pugin had destroyed for ever in England the absolute rule of the Classical ideal. However in the second half of the century, in the years between 1880 and 1930, the world had changed and changed again. Any young man interested in architecture in England in the 1880s would have accepted the precepts and accomplishments of the Gothic Revival as the norm. He would, with Street and his pupil Morris and all those who followed Morris in the Arts and Crafts Movement, have believed in 'truth to materials' and honesty in planning. He would have rejected symmetry and pure Classicism, but he would probably have accepted the Georgian buildings of the countryside, with their Classical cornices and sash windows, as part of the vernacular tradition of England. He would have learnt to care little about any style in particular, to him style in the end did not matter; what mattered was the way in which building materials were handled and above all their use in architectural form.

By the 1930s all this had largely gone. The young no longer believed in these ideals, in this sophisticated styleless architecture. Suddenly once again they now passionately believed in style, a style that rejected all the ideals of the unintellectual architecture of the post-Gothic Revival. Now architecture had to be an intellectual affair, an affair largely invented by Frenchmen and Germans, products of the Beaux-Arts schools, who had not unreasonably rejected that teaching as being too academic and too little related to modern use. These Continentals did not turn to the English solution, or rather not after their first steps in the creation of their new style; they propounded a solution of their own devising, which made the architecture of Lutyens and his contemporaries seem as irrelevant as say Garnier's flamboyant Paris Opera House. It is only today fifty years later, after modern architecture has proved itself to be such a disastrous disappointment, both in visual and human terms, that we can readily turn back to look at the architecture being created in England at the end of the nineteenth century, to look at it again with less doctrinaire eyes and to consider what it has to offer us today.

Architecture in the 1890s

In 1890 the work of the house architects was just one facet in a multi-faceted world of art. If any field seemed to dominate it was the churches with their great potential for commissioning many different artists to do the best in their own particular field. In a short compass of years, however, all this seems to have changed, and by 1898 churches and even commercial buildings are considerably less interesting than the houses which were being produced by a whole galaxy of young architects. In this year the oldest of the new leaders E. S. Prior was 46, Mervyn Macartney and E. J. May were 45, Ernest Newton, 42, W. R. Lethaby and C. F. A. Voysey, 41; those under forty included Weir Schultz, 37, Herbert Baker and Gerald Horsley, 35, Ernest Barnsley, 34, and Ernest Gimson and Baillie Scott, 33. Detmar Blow and Frank Lloyd Wright were 31, Charles Rennie Mackintosh was just 30 and Edwin Lutyens, already with an important corpus of work under his belt, was not yet 30! Only Philip Webb and Norman Shaw, both 67, were older.

In architecture there have never been such opportunities for younger men as there were at the turn of the century. Suddenly it seemed everyone was building what they thought of as small houses, mostly in what is now called the stockbroker belt in Surrey, Sussex and Kent. So often these rich middle-class clients turned to the new young men who were able to create a softer and more acceptable house than those of the earlier generations, who thought too often in terms of vast mansions only. The houses were, though, still built for a leisured society. This was the great period of house parties and the bigger houses were designed to cope with an influx of guests and their servants. It was important that these house guests were not all thrown together in one great room the whole time. If possible there should be a number of small areas where just a few people could meet for conversation, an art much cultivated at this time. So it is that there seems in so many of these houses to be numerous rooms with bays and ingles, and wide corridors which suddenly develop into spaces often the size of small rooms. In planning like this, Lutyens was the master, but as the architect for the free-thinking artistic, Voysey also provided these areas. Only Frank Lloyd Wright, evolving a completely different style of house for a different type of living, did not have to supply these nooks, and the result is that his plans soon become much more open than the romantic work of his English contemporaries.

Baillie Scott on the other hand, although his plans have often been compared to those of Frank Lloyd Wright—by those who would like to find in his work the origins of the 'open plan'—was always most careful to provide plenty of ingles and enclosed talking spaces. The difference in the plans of these two architects can be directly attributed to the different climates. In the hot summers on the Chicago prairies it was a positive advantage to have great open rooms with porches, which were neither inside nor out, but which caught every breath of fresh air going. In the cool damp climate of England cosiness is a very real necessity. The sense of enclosure given by a small room within a room, warmed with a great wood fire, womb-like and protective while outside the storms howl or the fog drips is one of the greatest pleasures to be had from an English house. No amount of Palladian elegance can compensate for this warmth and enclosure.

Most of the house architects who started their practice in the 1890s were involved, one might almost say, involuntarily involved, in the Arts and Crafts Movement. Oddly none of them came from Norman Shaw's office, with its direct link through Street with William Morris. None of these younger men had anything to do with the foundation of the Art Workers' Guild, though two of them, Voysey and

Lutyens, were destined to become Masters of the Guild. None of them was much involved with the practice of craftswork, for although all of them designed sound craftsman-like furniture, none of them made it.

However, there were other architects who were more directly concerned with the crafts, sometimes to the detriment of their careers as architects, and the leader of these was without a doubt Ernest Gimson. In 1890 he exhibited one of his first pieces of furniture at the Arts and Crafts Exhibition Society's show in London. This Society, founded in 1888, was an offshoot of the Art Workers' Guild. The Guild, reflecting Morris's and Walter Crane's socialism, refused to lend its name to any form of advertisement and so a separate society had to be formed merely to mount exhibitions.

In 1890 Gimson and a similar group of architects, Lethaby, Mervyn Macartney and Reginald Blomfield, all Guildsmen and two of them, Lethaby and Macartney, from Shaw's office and founders of the Guild, formed Kenton and Co. to make and sell handcrafted furniture. Although the project was not a commercial success (it collapsed after only three years), its furniture was much illustrated and admired. It is interesting to see how the careers of this group diverged in later life. Lethaby built little but took to architectural writing and mysticism becoming at the end of his life Surveyor to the Fabric of Westminster Abbey. Macartney went on to edit *The Architectural Review* during its great days at the turn of the century. He, as much as Lutyens, was responsible for the swing to Neo-Georgian, which he created both by the example of his own architecture and the many measured details and articles on Georgian architecture that appeared in the *Review* at this time. Blomfield soon moved from his Arts and Crafts origins towards French Classicism. He was responsible for the present look of the Quadrant at Regent's Street, following on from, but simplifying, Shaw's original design. He was a great admirer of Shaw and wrote the first biography of him. By 1900 he already had a large country house practice. Although these large houses, usually very well built, were almost always Neo-Georgian in the early days, they seem to lack real style and are often thoroughly out of scale, something that became less disturbing when Blomfield turned to the less sensitive French style.

Walter Brierley, later to be known as the 'Lutyens of the North'—although he was in fact seven years older than Lutyens—started his practice like so many others at the beginning of the 1890s, at the age of twenty-eight, with the rebuilding of Welburn Hall, Kirkdale in his native Yorkshire. He had been trained in his father's office and most of his practice was in the north of England, centred on

York. A deal of it seemed to comprise the rebuilding of eighteenth-century houses that had been destroyed by fire. However, he had a fine practice in country houses, and was able to design both in an Arts and Crafts Tudor style and in a refined Neo-Georgian. He was, in spite of his reputation, not much influenced by Lutyens, designing in an unobtrusive style entirely his own. His buildings today sit unnoticed in the countryside for which he designed them.

The same is true of the works of Guy Dawber, who might well be called the 'Lutyens of the West'. Just about the same age as Brierley, he was in Ernest George's office with Lutyens and Herbert Baker. He suffered from bad eyesight and so in 1887 he was sent into the country to become Clerk of Works to the building of Batsford, Lord Redesdale's new mansion, which was built in the hills above Moreton-in-the-Marsh in the Cotswolds. While working on Batsford he came so to love the Cotswolds, that he set up his practice in 1890 in the small Cotswold village of Bourton-on-the-Hill, just outside the gates of Batsford. This was twelve years before Ashbee moved to the nearby Chipping Campden in 1902 and ten years before the Barnsley brothers moved to Pinbury, near Cirencester in 1900. Within a few years Dawber had built up a considerable practice with the hunting upper classes in that part of the world. Designing like Brierley in a vernacular Tudor or a Neo-Georgian style, his best houses were built after the turn of the century. He kept to the same sort of clients throughout the forty years of his practice. In the late 1920s, when a later Lord Redesdale found that he had come to need a less pretentious house it was to Dawber that he turned for the Neo-Georgian Swinbrook house, Oxfordshire. It is this house which figures so often in the various books about and by the Mitfords.

Two architects of this period who approached the Arts and Crafts Movement not so much through architecture but through the founding of crafts guilds were C. R. Ashbee and A. H. Mackmurdo. C. R. Ashbee was the son of H. S. Ashbee, the self-styled 'pornographer royal', whose *Index of Forbidden Books* is one of the most important sourcebooks of pre-twentieth century obscenity. Charles Ashbee rejected his father's wealthy philistinism and was articled to that most upright of late Victorian architects G. F. Bodley, in 1886. There he imbibed the doctrines of Christian socialism which so influenced the young of this period. In Ashbee's case, the Christian part of the equation was soon dropped but he turned his socialism to good effect by going, as so many of his Christian contemporaries had done, to the East End of London, where in 1888 he founded The Guild of Handicraft, moving to Essex House in the Mile End Road, Whitechapel in 1890. Here he offered the full Arts and Crafts recipe to the East Enders, setting them to making hand-made furniture, hand-beaten silver, copper and iron, and all other forms of decorative and practical objects, alternating with lectures on art and socialism. In 1898 Ashbee took over two Albion presses from Morris and with the help of some Morris craftsmen he set up the Essex House Press, which over the next decade or so was to produce some of the finest of the privately printed books. Just as in his later silverwork, the Arts and Crafts design is slightly tinged with Art Nouveau. Ashbee always seemed to have his feet in both camps—the Morris socialist Arts and Crafts world, and the decadent sophistication of the aesthetes, who might have preached Morrisian socialism but had little understanding of its implications or little real wish to implement it.

In 1894, Ashbee built a house for himself and his mother, not in the East End, where he had originally been living in Toynbee Hall—an early university 'settlement'—but round the corner from the 'artistic' homes of Oscar Wilde and his circle, in Cheyne Walk. This, like Morris's houses, was meant as much to be an advertisement for his Guild (which also had a shop at 16a Brook Street), as it was a home, and Ashbee filled it with the products of the Guild. Some of Ashbee's later architecture was to be influenced by the work of Lutyens and Voysey, though in the process attenuating their forms, which both of his originals found distasteful. But 37 Cheyne Walk, which he named The Magpie and Stump after a pub that had been on the site, is a very different matter. He was clearly influenced by Shaw's tudory London work rather than Shaw's—or for that matter Ashbee's master Bodley's, Neo-Georgian designs. The inside was decorated in dark colours, with stamped leather, beaten copper and dark-red tiles glowing in a rather gloomy interior. A fireplace from the house, which has recently been unnecessarily demolished, can be seen in the Victoria and Albert Museum. All this contrasts with Ashbee's later lighter and more elegant style.

Never was there a career more designed to show up the hollow stuff on which the standard view of the English origins of the Modern Movement is based than that of A. H. Mackmurdo. In his long, and none too successful career, Mackmurdo seemed to essay all styles available at the time. He was trained in the office of James Brooks and started his career in 1882 by founding the Century Guild, the great precursor of the Arts and Crafts guilds. Here in the 1880s he was producing work that could easily fit into any survey of Continental Art Nouveau of a decade or so later. Then in his Guild magazine *The Hobby Horse*, still in the 1880s, he started illustrating architecture by his pupil, and later partner, Herbert P. Horne.

These buildings were in a semi-Neo-Classical style which had nothing to do with Neo-Georgian, then still hardly in existence, and odder still nothing to do with the Arts and Crafts Movement, which was then still in its Gothic-Tudor phase. One of the Neo-Classical houses was built in 1883 at 8 Private Road, Enfield, Essex, immediately beside an earlier Mackmurdo house built in the ordinary sub-Shaw 'Old English' style of the day. There is nothing in this latter house which would suggest anything but the most mediocre talent. Thus he went all through his life, and it cannot be suggested that he only built imaginatively when he found a good client since his own house which he built at Wickham Bishops, Essex in 1904 is in a surprisingly Italianate Queen Anne style. It was built, however, with such extravagance that he could not afford to live in it, and was forced to sell it and live in a much smaller cottage nearby. This cottage and other small houses that he built in the neighbourhood have much more style, and sometimes remind one of the *Hobby Horse* houses. All in all Mackmurdo is a mystery. What was the reason for the early designs, and why were they carried no further? What is the reason for the wild swings in his career? Why too did Herbert P. Horne desert architecture, first for poetry and then for book design, going on to become closely involved in the painters of the Renaissance and in particular Botticelli, on whom he wrote an important study?

While Mackmurdo's architecture was moving to a strange Classicism his fabric, book and furniture designs were also being influenced by Renaissance sources although the results may today seem somewhat surprising to us. Well before it became fashionable on the Continent he was using the Art Nouveau 'whip-lash line', though probably not in any 'forward-looking' way. To him no doubt this seemed a natural development of Eastern-influenced seventeenth-century Dutch fabric design. His furniture of the 1880s is certainly influenced by eighteenth-century models, which shows that he was well ahead of popular taste. But none of his work had much influence before the 1890s; indeed there is no record that any of his furniture was ever sold.

Between 1893 and 1895 Mackmurdo and Horne designed and built 25 Cadogan Gardens in Chelsea for Mortimer Menpes. Menpes was an excellent artist, an etcher, painter and illustrator of travel books about the East who seemed to be able to combine Brangwyn's colourful exoticism with Whistler's spareness of line. For him Mackmurdo built a very remarkable house. It is on a corner site, a square brick block, with an overhanging cornice under a dull mansard roof. The main body of the house is far from dull. Rising from the ground there are flat panels of

D.H.–B

windows, the lower panes lighting the basement, the upper the ground floor. Above these windows vertical strips of bays rise through two storeys, supported on curving bases which grow from the keystones of the lower windows. The lower windows are wood sashes but the tall bays are leaded, a combination of Tudor and Georgian which here produces a building that fits into the Shavian Dutch architecture of the Cadogan estate but is none the less an original design. It was this ability to be original yet not destructive to the environment which makes architects of this period seem so much better than those of the present day.

In Glasgow George Walton and C. R. Mackintosh, away from the main source of inspiration and relying on illustrations rather than seeing the buildings, were starting work. They collaborated in 1897 on the first of the Cranston tea rooms and Walton alone designed a café in Scarborough and the interior of a house in York. In the Cranston tea rooms at Buchanan Street, Glasgow, Mackintosh contributed only the murals—stencils of tall ladies entwined in roses with a horizontal halo of roses above their heads. Surely he must have seen an illustration of one of Gilbert's similarly entwined ladies, or perhaps he merely developed from the same source, Burne-Jones's *Briar Rose* murals at Buscot (painted only seven years earlier).

At Rosebank in York, Walton's rooms are largely lost to us but here he also designed a mural with flowing rose bows. This is an enchanting panel, still in the house, a mosaic of marble glass and silver, designed to fit over the fireplace. Its border is large squares of green mosaic, divided by white strips which end in squares of formalized roses, and on the outside there is a thin purple border. White, purple and green, being a favourite colour combination of this period, it is not surprising that these were the colours later adopted by the suffragettes. Within the border in the centre stands a rose tree from the base of which two branches spring, and these curve off to either side sweeping up to the top of the tree forming a heart shape. From the branches tight rose buds grow, alternating with a sprinkling of green leaves. Within the branches are two doves, one flies and the other is perched upon the centre in front of a silvery oval. To the left the figure of Eros, not more than four times the size of the doves elegantly walks over a field of shells. As well as *Briar Rose*, the obvious influence on this design is Botticelli's *Birth of Venus*. However, neither of these paintings formalizes nature in such a manner as does Walton's where there is no attempt in any way to suggest a really existing scene; this is purely decorative art, and as such it and similar designs were to have a considerable influence during the next few years—not just in decoration but also in book designs. The rose bush forming itself into a heart shape was to become almost a cliché in the hands of such people as Talwin Morris, and even talented illustrators such as Catherine Cameron and the incomparable Jessie M. King of the Glasgow School.

The first stage of the Arts and Crafts Movement can be seen to run roughly from the early career of Street in the 1840s through the work of William Morris to Philip Webb at Standen. It was an inward-looking rather parochial affair, which developed directly, and exclusively, from the Gothic Revival. Its whole history could be written round the employees of Street's small office. Neither Webb nor Morris would have anything to do with Classicism, and although they in the end came to recognize Georgian architecture as being within the vernacular tradition, they would certainly have never looked abroad for anything but Gothic precedents. For the next generation the Arts and Crafts Movement had become more important than Gothic and so they were able to look to other styles for their precedents. The first place that they turned to was Byzantium. This was not surprising in a period, rather like our own, which seemed passionately to need romance, colour and mystery, which was searching for the orthodoxy of Classicism, but was unwilling to accept the dogma of Rome.

In 1892 Sancta Sophia, Lower Kingswood was commissioned of Sydney Barnsley by Dr Edwin Freshfield who had 'travelled much abroad'. Barnsley, who was twenty-seven in 1892, was one of a group of young men who, having made a study of Venice as it were through Ruskin's eyes, had moved on to the source of the Venetian Gothic style—Byzantium. With his friend from George's office, Weir Schultz, he had toured Turkey and Greece, where he had probably met Freshfield. In Byzantium they had discovered a style which combined the freshness of Gothic with the order of Classicism and in Freshfield Barnsley found the perfect client—rich, knowledgeable and as obsessive about the Byzantine style as they were. He also, a spiritual heir to Lord Elgin, had continued an ancient English tradition by collecting unappreciated antiquities and bringing them back to England for safety: these included a group of ancient capitals from the church of S. John of the Stadium at Constantinople. We are told by the church *Guide* that: 'When Dr. E. H. Freshfield and his son remonstrated with the Turkish priests at the use of [one of these capitals] as a target for revolver practice, they were told they could have them if they liked. Accordingly they paid a pound for each capital and took them away at once.' Having got the capitals he decided to build a church to house them. In spite of all this Barnsley's church is far from being a Byzantine pastiche; it is in many ways a typically English Arts and Crafts building. On the exterior the red stone dressings contrast with soft red brickwork which is laid in a complex herringbone pattern in the tympana which are formed of relieving arches of tiles over the pairs of small arched windows. The materials are chosen and laid with an obsessive care in the smallest details which is typical of English Arts and Crafts work. The exterior has a polish which would look odd beside the rather ramshackle buildings of Greece.

The interior, perhaps more Mediterranean and more sensuous, is lined in sheets of marble quarried in Rome. There is an apsed chancel, the walls faced with marbles taken from Roman columns of Tiberius's time. Above, the walls are covered with a splendid mosaic designed by Barnsley: floral trees glitter on a dark-blue background above the great apse in gold mosaic inset with a tall Greek cross in scarlet. The roof trusses are painted with spring flowers. At the end of the beautifully made priests' stalls are domed ambos made of ebony with mother-of-pearl inlay. Barnsley's friend Gimson worked on these and they are not dissimilar to the magnificent Gimson stalls which Weir Schultz designed for St. Andrew's Chapel in Westminster Cathedral. In the middle of the church there hang two enormous rings of metal suspended on wires threaded with golden balls and holding eighteen tall candles on candlesticks. Bentley used a more elaborate version of this design when he came to design his candelabra, or rather electroliers, in Westminster Cathedral.

The church of Sancta Sophia deserves to be better known if only because it was in so many ways a precursor of infinitely the greatest ecclesiastical building built in the last hundred years—the great culmination of the Gothic Revival, if not in the Gothic style, Westminster Cathedral. Westminster Cathedral was commissioned of J. F. Bentley. It is this building, with its Byzantine splendours, which seems to embody the best of the Decadence, and at the same time is probably the most successful of the late Victorian monuments. Between the time of the building of the Palace of Westminster and the Cenotaph no building has been more completely accepted by the public, to such a degree that it is difficult for us now to appreciate the brilliance with which Bentley handled this commission, and the Byzantine style that he chose.

In the 1890s it was a bold step for the Roman Catholic hierarchy to decide to build a cathedral right in the heart of the capital, with one of the most revered Gothic masterpieces, Westminster Abbey, just down the road. The Gothic Revival had been a very Anglican affair, in spite of the fact that Pugin, the proselytizer of

Gothic as the only Catholic style, had been a Roman Catholic. Cardinal Vaughan's choice of Bentley as his architect was surprising for Bentley had always been an adventurous Gothic Revival stylist. But St. Peter's at Rome was Classical, and in that period of triumphalism Vaughan believed that a good Catholic should build in the Classical style, leaning as near to the Baroque of the Brompton Oratory as was possible. In this way no one could believe that the church had anything to do with the establishment down the road.

In a re-enactment of an earlier skirmish in the 'Battle of the Styles' (when Palmerston routed Sir George Gilbert Scott over the style of the Foreign Office), Cardinal Vaughan squared up to Bentley. But this time instead of Bentley 'purchasing some expensive books' as Scott had done, he made a tour accompanied at least some of the way by Vaughan himself, to Italy and the old Byzantium. He came back with a new appreciation of buildings like St. Mark's, and a new understanding of the essentially Gothic, or at least post-Classical, nature of the Byzantine Romanesque style.

While the style was approved by the leaders of the Arts and Crafts Movement for its catholicity, the church approved of the style because it was untainted by any suggestion of later heresies—the reasons for the Great Schism being at this time no doubt forgotten. It is interesting that the solution found should have been so similar to the Romanesque designs used by the German intellectuals of the 1840s or for that matter George Gilbert Scott's so-called Classical work at the Foreign Office. But now all was different: whereas before, the Gothic Revivalists had considered the Romanesque style at best a compromise, now the Arts and Crafts men suddenly realized that the Byzantine was a truly functional and Gothic style. There were snags of course. In the first place the style used domes, always much disapproved of by the true Goth, but the Byzantines, unlike the architects of the domes of St. Peter's and St. Paul's, displayed the structure of their domes honestly. Not for them the false dome work supported on a cone, of a Wren or a Bramante. True, the walls were faced in an unstructural material, and many were the purists who said that they preferred the bare brick walls of Westminster Cathedral before they were clad. However, marble and glittering mosaics were clearly cladding, for no one could be expected to imagine that, in England at least, the walls were entirely made of costly marbles. And then most splendid of all, were those icons and the great hanging lanterns, all so decorative and as highly wrought as the most romantic imagination could conceive, suggesting as they did a holier and even more mystical religion than that even of the Middle Ages.

Finally, unlike Classical architecture, the Byzantine style allowed full range for the sculptor. Although Classicism has always used sculpture for such things as the capitals of columns, there is little opportunity for the sculptor to display his originality. Each capital must be exactly like its neighbour; sculptured panels must remain within a straitjacket of style and shape. However, in the Byzantine style each capital is individual, giving every opportunity to the sculptor to create, though the style did demand a tightly controlled approach to decoration which later sculptors like Eric Gill, who created the Stations of the Cross at Westminster as a sort of war work between 1913 and 1918, were able to respond to. No wonder then that Harry Wilson, Barnsley, Lethaby, Weir Schultz and Bentley all took to this style.

Why then are there so few monuments in the Byzantine taste; why did it disappear so quickly? One of the reasons was Bentley himself. In Westminster Cathedral he produced an overwhelming masterpiece which few architects could hope to emulate. Secondly, of course, the Gothic Revival was dying, and so many of the younger architects were turning to Neo-Classicism or to an almost completely styleless Arts and Crafts architecture or to the style that led from that, Neo-Georgian. Sometimes Lutyens in the 1920s seemed to be hankering after the style of Westminster in such things as the Temple of Music at Tyringham. The fashionable Art Deco interiors, distantly related to the Stoclet house, Brussels, which was designed by Joseph Hoffmann in 1905–11, with an interior by Klimt in a kind of Byzantine style seen through ancient Cypriot eyes, had something of this exoticism. But after the Great War, this kind of extravagance was not fashionable and the new chaste Neo-Classic style approved by both those really go-ahead countries, the United States of America and Nazi Germany, rapidly took its place.

The only young church architect of importance in this period was Ninian Comper who, at the age of thirty-one in 1895, had a growing practice, though his work so often comprised the making of alterations to churches built by other architects. 1895 saw one of the finest of these early Comper designs for the crypt of one of Street's finest London churches, St. Mary Magdalene, Paddington. The church stands proudly overlooking the Paddington canal, a great monument to the first 'high and dry' period of the Catholic movement. It is a church in a cool and elegant, though none the less passionate, Gothic which only Street seems to have been able to handle. Into Street's barren crypt Comper inserted a chapel to house the Blessed Sacrament, which in those days of Anglo-Catholic persecution it was wise to keep from the prying eyes of the followers of Mr Kensit. For this Holy

House he transformed part of the crypt 'into a sumptuous late medieval dream-world, where the wealth of gilded decoration is almost overpowering', as Peter F. Anson says in *Fashions in Church Furnishings*.[2]

The chapel is divided from the crypt by a delicate Gothic screen, and beyond are the great brick vaults of Street's basement—inside all is romance. At the back of the chapel there is a playful little organ which, with its miniature Gothic tracery decorated and gilded and its doors painted with saints, looks for all the world as if it could be carried away and used as a portative organ by a singing angel in a late Gothic painting. The windows are filled with stained glass shining in brilliant blue and red, and the dark blue vaulted ceiling is a mass of stars formed from little convex mirrors. The Pyx, holding the Blessed Sacrament, hangs, covered in a lace cloth, before the altar, whose reredos has alabaster figures of elegant saints standing under gilded Gothic canopies.

The whole is a riot of colour and delight, but beneath the surface glitter is the firm line of Comper's exquisite draughtsmanship, for Comper did everything himself here. He painted windows and carved figures, the whole being a personal act of piety by a young man who dreamed wistfully of a medieval past but none the less had the talent and tenacity to give it reality. It is all the more surprising to find this glittering medieval dream contrasting with the crypt of Street's High Victorian church which had only been opened twenty years earlier. It reflects the move by Anglo-Catholics as well as architects, to a lighter and more elegant religion, which in its turn reflects a return to a lighter style in house design. Here too it suddenly seemed possible to turn the dream into reality.

Not just houses and churches but even public buildings started to take on an elegance that could not have been imagined in the 1870s. In 1895, the young partnership of Dunbar Smith (aged 24) and Cecil Brewer (aged 26) won the competition for a social settlement house in Tavistock Street in London. In the main elevations of the Mary Ward Settlement, as it became known, everything was done to reduce the institutional quality and to emphasize the domestic. Two staircase towers, capped by flat-pitched roofs, jut forward between the central block, the staircases being expressed by small sash windows that run up diagonally on both bays. In the centre there is a low-pitched roof in which there are three long dormers, the central one arched, with leaded light windows to the hall. Below the heavily overhanging eaves there is a deep frieze of plain plaster, which expresses the floor level of the hall, and below this line there is a wide band of red brickwork. Below all this, and placed asymmetrically (it was still rare for an architect at this time to design a completely symmetrical building), is the stone entrance porch. Beside this there is a line of small sash windows with shutters. And below this, lighting the basement, are the arched windows.

The only use of stone on the facade is the porch, a delightful little piece. To each side, stone buttresses curve up to a thin overhanging cornice and above this two stone eggs are balanced upright. To either side of the main porch, in the staircase towers, there are two lesser porches with thin overhanging canopies, and below there are curved walls, which reflect the walls of the porch. Between these curves run normal area railings integrated to the pavement as it were by the sweeping curves. The porch itself, Gavin Stamp says, is 'in a proto-art nouveau sublime manner which may reflect . . . the influence of the American H. H. Richardson via that original talent James Maclaren',[3] and one might add Harrison Townsend. The entrance sweeps in under a flat arch, everything curving inwards to give a sense of intimacy and welcome. The interior is Classical, at least there are Doric pilasters and columns which support arches and cornices with a flat curve to them. Originally the rooms were furnished with ladderback chairs and simple country furniture, which all added to the cottage look. All in all this is a delightful attempt to bring the country virtues of warmth and welcome into a London institution, perhaps particularly surprising in the light of Dickens's descriptions of the cold charity of only forty years earlier.

In Great Britain 1896 might be called the year of the Art Institute. The Central School of Arts and Crafts (note the juxtaposition) was founded this year in London, after pressure from the Art Workers' Guild and Lethaby in particular. Originally, in the heated discussions at the Guild, he had opposed the teaching of arts and crafts in schools, believing, as did most of the Arts and Crafts men, that a sounder training can be given by apprenticeships. However, by even the end of the nineteenth century the apprenticeship system was breaking down and Lethaby came to see that if the ideals of the Guild were to be continued then it would have to be through official schools. In 1896 the London County Council was persuaded to found a school of arts and crafts; the building, however, was not completed until 1909. It was designed by an LCC architect, one A. Halcrow Verstage, but Lethaby as its first principal had a considerable influence on its rather dull design.

For a short time in the 1890s C. Harrison Townsend became the leading Art Institute architect. Although his beliefs were firmly wedded to the ideals of the Arts and Crafts Movement (he later became a Master of the Art Workers' Guild), he built a number of public buildings and churches in a style which would on the Continent have been called Art Nouveau—not a style much admired by Guildsmen. Born in 1851, after articles in Liverpool he set up in practice in London in 1877 but for the next fifteen years he did little of interest. He may have gone to America at some time and got to know the work of H. H. Richardson. It was not until 1892, however, that he was to produce the first of the buildings for which he is remembered. In that year he designed both the charming, and highly romantic, church of St. Martin, Blackheath in Surrey, and the Bishopsgate Institute in the City of London. Whereas the church is low, tucked into the side of the road with a great roof sweeping down almost to the ground, only the squat bellcote suggesting that it is a church, the Institute is tall and urban. This was the result of a successful competition so there is more Gothic trim than Townsend later essayed, and because of this there is less American influence; his later buildings suggest that he has looked closely at the work of Richardson in his forms, and Louis Sullivan in his use of pattern.

In 1896 Townsend was commissioned to build the Whitechapel Art Gallery in east London and he exhibited his designs in the Royal Academy. They were very different from the building that we now know, which was finally built between 1899 and 1901. In the 1896 design the Richardson influence is clear, in particular in the central arch in a blank banded wall; above there is a balcony and over it there is a line of arched voussoired windows and above that again a large frieze. To either side there are square towers with rounded corners, and at the top of these a wide arch from which projects a curving balcony. Above this the curved corners become turrets, which in turn support a larger turret with a cupola. This is the first time we see Harrison Townsend up to his favourite tricks—playing a three-dimensional game with seemingly unrelated forms.

In the Horniman Museum, Forest Hill, Lewisham, which was also started in 1896, though it was not completed until 1901, Townsend plays similar tricks. This habit of forcing different forms into each other was a trick much liked by the Gothic Revivalists of the 'Vigorous' school of the 1850s and 1860s. The architect's attitude to form has never been the same since the work of G. E. Street and his followers. The tower of the Horniman Museum is probably the most extreme example of this Victorian 'vigour', not in any way reduced in quality because it is so late and designed in an alien style. From a square base the tower rises, a great semicircular voussoired arch punched into it at its bottom, but from this it rises sheer to the top, the corners again chamfered in a curve. At the top, the large circular face of a clock with a frame is punched into each side, the corners of the tower now rising in columns beside it. Above the clock faces the flat plane is cut back to reveal a circular turret carved with foliage within. This circular turret now rises, with the four turrets beside it, for a short distance only, when the carved tree forms curve outward to support a heavily dentilled ring, which cuts into the smaller turrets, which in turn at this point are carved with tree forms. Above the main tower is stopped with a parapet, the turrets rising a little further to be capped with miniature cupolas. The delight in as it were discovering decoration within a form, when it has been cut back, was a particular habit of Street.

Without a doubt the most important building of the 1890s to be concerned with art and possibly the most influential art school ever built, was the over-exposed Glasgow School of Art. It was the first product of a number of competitions of the period won by young men, the most sensational of these being the Liverpool Cathedral competition of 1903 which was won by the 21-year-old Giles Gilbert Scott. The Glasgow competition was a limited one and was set up for Mackintosh to win. He was still working for a firm of architects in Glasgow called Honeyman and Keppie at the time and submitted his design under their name. However, everyone knew that the chief assessor and the framer of the conditions was Fra. Newberry (as he was affectedly called) and that he was hoping that his favourite, but still only 28-year-old, prize student would be successful. Mackintosh won his competition and took the job with him when he set up practice on his own.

Like so much of Mackintosh's work the surface eccentricities of the school disguise what is essentially a very traditional building. Throughout his life Mackintosh believed himself to be working within the traditions of architecture, and was always strongly influenced by his own Scottish background. Thus, while the studio lights on the main facade are strictly functional, factory-type studio windows, which would have been seen in any artistic quarter in the world for the last half century, the most remarkable part of the facade, the entrance doorway, with to one side of it a pair of bay windows, finally topped by a small turret, is a reinterpretation of Scottish baronial motifs mixed with the Scottish urban tradition of bay windows precariously hanging to the blank flanks of tenements. Robert Macleod, in his brilliant biography of Charles Rennie Mackintosh, has pointed out[4] the resemblance, in its forced asymmetry, to Norman Shaw's New Zealand Chambers, but here once again there is also the influence of Street's 'Vigorous style': the mouldings are cut off the wall plane and the octagonal turret grows out of the face of the building, which on one side is set back just an inch or so and to the other is cut back in a sweeping curve of the balcony front, to display a window set well back into the wall surface. Where Mackintosh really differs from the earlier masters is in his use of ornament, but in this building there is little on the facade to startle, even the knots of iron at the studio windows look at first glance as no more than functional bolt ends to the ironwork. Inside there is a little more excitement. The balusters of the staircase running up to a high horizontal band are merely a further development of one of Voysey's more unfunctional ideas but, since Mackintosh's staircase rises up through the centre of the building, whereas Voysey's stairs always cling round the sides, the spatial effect is far more exciting.

Both the board room and the directors' room in the earlier part of the building contain details that were to crop up continuously in Mackintosh's work and were to have a considerable influence on the Continent, but at the time seemed to Englishmen to be commonplace. Most important is the use of a very deep frieze, which is not unique to him, but with Mackintosh and Frank Lloyd Wright the frieze line becomes a plate rail which is carried across all the various breaks in the wall surface, becoming a mantelshelf at the fireplace. Only the very tall windows break through this horizontal line. These windows protrude out from the wall to form vertical bays, an idea originally used by Shaw in the Old Swan house in Chelsea, but also used, as we have seen, by Mackmurdo in his Chelsea house. Mackintosh, like Mackmurdo, also mixes leaded lights with rectangular panes and wooden mullions. Here in Scotland he does not use sash windows, which were becoming popular in England at this time. Whether this is because he believed them to be foreign, that is English, importations, or whether he was just being old-fashioned and rejecting all things that were not acceptable to Ruskin, is not obvious.

Magazines

However good they are the architect and the artist need publicity if they are to bring their work before the public. The best way to do this is through a magazine, which while it is sympathetic to their art none the less appeals to a wide public. In the 1890s two such magazines were founded and both became instantly successful: both were helpful in getting young designers established; both in their own ways were remarkably catholic in their approach; and both helped to spread the idea to the English-speaking world and to the rest of Europe that there was at that time a specifically English style. They were *The Studio*, which was founded in 1893, and *Country Life* which was founded four years later in 1897.

The Studio, with Charles Holme as its editor, was to have a profound effect on all the arts throughout the world for the next twenty years. New printing techniques meant that it was possible, using photolithography, to reproduce works of art, both in colour and black and white much more accurately than could the wood engravings that the Victorian art magazines were forced to use. However delightful wood engravings may have been as works of art in their own right, they rarely gave any impression of the true quality of the original painting.

However *The Studio* did not limit itself to the illustration of fine arts only for it called itself 'An Illustrated Magazine of Fine and Applied Arts'. It was a magazine that had little time for theories, for it was not written for intellectuals. It was a show-case designed for artists to display what they had done; it did not attempt to tell them what they ought to be doing. Right from the beginning it concerned itself with all the visual arts; with architecture and furniture, fabric and wallpapers, craftwork in metal and clay, book design and illustration, as much as it did with painting and sculpture. Even here, following the beliefs of the Art Workers' Guild, it was as much concerned with mural painting and architectural sculpture as it was with the work of the easel painters and the 'fine' artists. It was this catholic attitude to arts and crafts which was to have such a profound influence for good or ill when the magazine was disseminated throughout Europe and America—for it had an enormous overseas sale, turning a whole generation of Continental artists away from fine art to an appreciation of the applied arts. But since it was not a magazine given to intellectual discussion, the Continental designers, coming to English design for the first time, had some difficulty in understanding what the nature of this 'English style' really was. For instance, the first number, as well as having an 'advanced', though still heavily Morrisian, cover by Beardsley and illustrating work by Voysey, made great play of the Anglo-Dutch painter Jan Toorop's symbolist painting, *The Three Brides*. This is a painting of three ladies of widely differing character, dressed in white, surrounded by naked maidens whose immensely long hair sways around the picture in swirling patterns. In the next numbers there were articles on wallpaper, furniture design and metal-work by such designers as A. S. Benson, Mackmurdo and Voysey, all of whom seemed, quite by chance and in fact taking precedents from many very different sources, to echo these swirling curves.

As well as *The Studio* there were other strong English influences; not least was the overpowering influence of John Ruskin. No one would call him un-intellectual, but his writings are by no means always clear and are constantly self-contradictory, which means that it is possible to read several different meanings into one statement. If, like Gaudí in Barcelona, you are approaching Gothic for the first time through the writings of Ruskin, it might not seem unreasonable to take his talk of the growing form of Gothic literally and translate this into patterns made up of growing plant stems. Ruskin is clearly as much responsible for the sudden appearance of Continental Art Nouveau at this time as were the designers illustrated in *The Studio*. Perhaps it was inevitable that Art Nouveau should be immediately disowned by the very men responsible for its birth, for it seemed to them that it had nothing to do with the ideals of the Arts and Crafts Movement. It was inevitable but unfortunate, for it meant that English designers turned their backs once again on Continental design, and so were not in a position to influence the next movement that grew out of Art Nouveau.

But *The Studio* and the English designers that it illustrated had another important effect on the Continent. The leading English artists of this period, with their profound sense of 'fitness for purpose', believed that there was as much a place for fine art as there was for applied art. To them Burne-Jones's great easel pictures with their complex symbolism were as important, but not better nor worse than, the delicate designs that he did for William Morris's stained glass windows. That great supporter of the Art Workers' Guild, Walter Crane, was also as much at home in the design of vast paintings, such as his *Neptune's Horses* painted in 1893, 'in which the horses' limbs and manes are forced into the lines of foam-curved waves'[5], as in the design of his rather naïve children's allegories or his many badges and cards which he designed for the myriad 'forward-thinking' groups to which he belonged. Or Frank Brangwyn, who could as well design mural paintings, rugs, furniture or crockery as he could paint easel paintings, a facile faculty which seems to have had a lasting and deleterious effect on his reputation, since his multi-faceted work cannot readily be catalogued and characterized.

But the Germans seemed unable to see this. When the Deutsche Werkbund was founded in 1907, as a direct result of the English guilds and *The Studio*, it, and its follower Walter Gropius's Bauhaus, rejected 'fine' art all together, thus forcing artists into a rigid and arid dogmatism totally at variance with English pragmatic good sense, replacing it with an art which Paul Klee was to characterize as 'taking a line for a walk'. It has been one of the disasters of the twentieth century that the beliefs of the Bauhaus should have triumphed everywhere.

Country Life unlike *The Studio* never had large sales abroad and so has had little influence outside Britain. However, in the British Isles it has probably been the most influential magazine concerned with the arts ever published. This, ironically, is because the paper has never concerned itself solely with the arts but, as its title suggests, with all aspects of country life. The origins hardly suggest the authoritative architectural journal that it was to become. Its bachelor perfectionist founder, Edward Hudson, inherited a printing works and realized in the early 1890s, like Charles Holme of *The Studio*, that with the development of the half-tone block it was now possible to produce a weekly magazine with much superior plates. So, since his printing works printed sporting magazines, he first produced *Racing Illustrated*, but this was not very successful. One day, while playing golf at Walton, he decided to expand the scope of his magazine into *Country Life Illustrated*. The first numbers in January 1897 were still largely concerned with hunting, golf and racing—the normal pursuits of the wealthy countrymen of the period—and took little notice of the houses in which they lived. Indeed this was still the time when it would have been considered discourteous to discuss a gentleman's home or his possessions.

Soon, however, there were articles about 'princely mansions and quaint old houses of long lineaged gentlemen'; there was no attempt at scholarship, just an interest in romantic exteriors, as parts of the garden. The first interior to be photographed was the library of Sledmere, Yorkshire; this was taken by a photographer who had been sent up to photograph the stud. It was published on 6 March 1897 and shows an interior cluttered with all sorts of pieces of furniture and bric-à-brac which related in no way to the cool Classicism of the vaulted interior of the 1790s. It turned out to be an important photographic record, for in 1911 Sledmere was burned down and this picture became valuable when Walter Brierley was commissioned to rebuild the house.

In 1898 the much more scholarly series of 'Country Houses—Gardens, Old and New' started, and they have continued to this day. At the same time Charles Latham became the architectural photographer and it was he and Hudson who together were to make a revolution in the furnishing of the ordinary English middle-class house. To quote Christopher Hussey writing in the Seventieth Anniversary Number of *Country Life*: 'Latham had a genius for the pictorial presentation of romantic atmosphere, the discriminating taste and the forceful personality to omit or eliminate the inappropriate . . . by 1903 Latham was . . . [denuding] historic interiors, as at Levens Hall, Westmorland . . . of all but a few perfectly placed and apposite furnishings. Indeed one chair, placed askew on the foreground facing a fireplace, virtually became his signature'.[6] Soon people seeing these aristocratic but underfurnished interiors began to believe that this was the way in which the really grand lived and so middle-class housewives soon took out most of the furniture from their drawing rooms and began to live in smartly uncluttered spaces.

It was not, however, only by its good example that *Country Life* had an influence. Very soon Hudson was illustrating new and quite small houses by architects of the younger generation. In particular he showed the work of Edwin Lutyens, an architect that he came to admire beyond all others. This admiration lasted all his life: when he went out to the opening of the Viceroy's House at New Delhi in 1929 he went around saying 'Poor old Christopher Wren, *he* could never have done this'. At the beginning, though, Hudson preferred gardens to houses. Hussey again: 'In 1900 William Robinson sold his interest in *The Garden*, the journal which he had founded and edited, to Hudson . . . After a visit to Munstead . . . Hudson persuaded Gertrude Jekyll to take on the editing of *The Garden* and to contribute garden notes to *Country Life*. And she had introduced Hudson to her young architect Ned Lutyens. This significant conjunction was the background to the appearance in *Country Life* (December 8, 1900) of a notably perceptive article on Munstead Wood . . . it contained this prescient phrase: "We do not hesitate to say that this modestly beautiful house, its wood and garden are clearly destined to become classical in the same sense as Gilbert White's at Selborne".'[7]

Directly Hudson discovered Lutyens he commissioned of him one of his finest houses, The Deanery Garden at Sonning, Berkshire which was built in 1901. This is a romantic house in red brick. The entrance is through an arch in an old garden wall from which a tunnel vault runs right through the house to arrive at a terrace at the other side which runs at right angles from the house. Under the terrace there is a small canal and beside the terrace there rises a tall bay window with plain, thick oak mullions glazed with multi-faceted leaded windows— possibly the finest of all Lutyens's Tudor elevations, and his most often illustrated house. 'So began the life-long association that was to be of such benefit to both men. Hudson worshipped Lutyens as the greatest British architect since Wren, and undoubtedly *Country Life*'s presentation of each successive masterpiece served to build up that reputation. But while Hudson loved to do so, it also seems to have been understood that Lutyens should design Hudson's own commissions for love too. The immediate outcome was the *Country Life* office building in Covent Garden . . . Aptly signalizing the firm's "arrival", the beautiful edifice was also the architect's first work in London, his first public building and the first display of his mastery of his matured style—which he called the "High Game" or "Wrennaisance".'[8]

The Country Life Building is a beautifully proportioned red-brick Neo-Georgian building with a stone rusticated ground floor and a grand entrance doorway taken from the dome arches of St. Paul's Cathedral. Above is a mezzanine line of small windows with semi-circular heads and sills; above are tall *piano-nobile* windows and above those just one row of square windows below the cornice and the great hipped pantiled roof on which tower two tall, red-brick chimneys. The whole thing looks more like a country house than an office block, and the fact that Lutyens was able to get away with completely different windows on each floor meant that the facade has none of the dreariness that we have come to associate with Neo-Georgian office blocks, though of course no attempt has been made to indicate on the facade the complex interior uses.

While the Country Life Building is a serious office building Lindisfarne is a very different matter. When in 1900 Hudson bought this castle perched on a rock off the coast of Northumberland, it was no more than a few decaying walls, which romantically followed the shape of the rock. Lutyens kept these shapes, slightly exaggerating them, and inside created a romantic fantasy, all passages and stone staircases seemingly forced through the living rock. The house was never intended for anything but holidays and cannot have been easy to live in, though Madame Suggia, the cellist, often stayed with Hudson here. It is, though, one of the last examples of the taste for old castles and 'the true rust of the barons' wars', as Horace Walpole had described his house Strawberry Hill 150 years earlier.

Finally in 1927 Hudson bought a sixteenth-century manor house in Sussex, called Plumpton Place, and here Lutyens added a delightful line of weatherboarded cottages and a brick bridge with a cantilevered wood balustrade. Lutyens's magic still worked with Hudson, ' "My dear Huddy [he said] lovely, lovely! Those millponds! You must have millions and millions of *roses*, d'you see? Reflected in the water—and water-falls—something like this." And out would come pencil and paper.'[9] Hudson was very typical of so many clients of Lutyens and other architects, such as Lord Curzon or Lord Kitchener—collectors and restorers of houses. Obsessed by the architecture of country houses and able to afford to restore them, many of the houses that are most popular with tourists today, like Montacute and Lindisfarne, we owe to the zeal and knowledge of these men—not architects themselves but bitten with an almost insatiable desire for good architecture. It is to men like these, as much as it is to the great architects of this period, that we owe our present heritage of fine houses.

Illustrated books and artists

The 1890s was a great period of the 'art book': for the first time leading artists found that they could specialize in the illustration of books as a profession. In the 1850s the softer and unhatched wood engravings had taken the place of steel engravings for book and magazine illustration and the next two decades were the heyday of the black-and-white illustrators. The magazine *Once a Week* became a great commercial success and between 1859 and 1865 used most of the major English artists of the period, from Holman Hunt to Whistler. In 1857 Moxon published *Poems by Alfred Tennyson* illustrated by a motley crowd of artists which included very original work by Millais, Holman Hunt and Rossetti. Although the woodcuts were of the highest quality, they were not engraved by the artists, who had no say in the production of the rest of the book. This was commonplace at this time; the artist often did not even design the engraved title page.

The dissatisfaction of the Pre-Raphaelites, and their most talented follower William Morris, with this state of affairs led to the creation of the private presses where the books were created in every aspect by the artist. He designed and cut the plates, chose the paper, often designed, cut and then set the type, and possibly even printed the book himself on a hand-press. Finally he designed the binding and bound the book. This was the art ideal, inspired by the Arts and Crafts Movement, and it led to the founding of the Kelmscott Press. Morris started to produce printed pages in 1874 and continued to print books until his death in October 1896. By the nature of the work done these books never in any remote way reached any but the smallest and richest of publics. Typically, this was something that Morris deplored but never did anything about; his popular books were as vilely printed as any.

One Sunday afternoon in 1891 the 19-year-old Beardsley brought his portfolio to show to Burne-Jones. As Beardsley afterwards told it, Burne-Jones after looking at the drawings said ' "I *seldom* or *never* advise anyone to take up art as a profession but in *your* case *I can do nothing else*" '.[10] He then asked Beardsley to stay to tea with the Wildes who happened to be there. Later it was Beardsley who was to become Oscar Wilde's finest interpreter, replacing Shannon. In 1892 attempts were made to make the art book more commercial. Dent's *Morte d'Arthur* was a conscious attempt to copy the products of the Kelmscott Press in a commercial manner. Dent even went to one of Morris's 'house artists' Burne-Jones for advice, and it was he who suggested the as yet unknown Aubrey Beardsley. It was only after this commission that Beardsley saw the Kelmscott books for the first time. But he proceeded, much to Morris's disgust, to try to create as close a copy as he could, though at the same time claiming that Morris's ' "work is mere imitation of old stuff, mine is fresh and original" '![11] He first came before an astonished public with these illustrations, and with them launched the popular interest in decadent, or possibly Art Nouveau, black-and-white book illustration. Ricketts and Shannon had already paved the way, and the work of the French decadents was much admired, but there was something in Beardsley's attenuated line which still contained just a recognizable hint of the Pre-Raphaelites and Burne-Jones. It was this hint that people who would have liked to have thought themselves advanced, could feel sympathy with. One of the most interesting things about Beardsley's almost instant success was that it would seem to have been the first time that an 'advanced' artist became a success in England just because he was 'advanced'. This was later to dog most artists with impossible demands requiring that they be 'forward-looking' at all times, and it led to the destruction of such diverse talents as Augustus John and C. R. Mackintosh. Beardsley himself, already dying of tuberculosis at the age of eighteen, soon relapsed into a pornography only slightly superior to the norm, bored with his success and without anything now to replace his over-exposed style.

Another figure who must be noticed in any discussion of the Decadence was F. Rolfe, self-styled Baron Corvo who, in 1891, was commissioned to paint the ill-fated murals at the Church of the Immaculate Conception in Christchurch, Hampshire. Rolfe's combination of real talent, extreme neurosis, Catholicism and homosexuality make him a typical figure of the Decadence. Like so many other minor artists of this period he soon burnt himself out, and his art is less well remembered than his rackety life which has been well documented in *The Quest for Corvo*.

There was considerably more to arts and crafts of the 1890s than the work of the again recently fashionable Art Nouveau. Most of the artists and architects that we are looking at here would have rejected Wilde and Rolfe as sophisticates dangerously affected by the new French malaise. In the work of Beardsley, like Mackintosh and Jessie M. King, they would have seen the traditions of Morris and the Pre-Raphaelites continued and developed. Aestheticism with its cult of Japan and languid indolence was harder to accept. In fact by the 1890s it would have already died if it had not been for Oscar Wilde. It is interesting that the three artists most involved in the second stage of Japanese Aestheticism—Whistler, Beardsley and Ricketts—should all have been closely connected with Wilde. To the average designer of the nineties there was a clear distinction between Aestheticism and its suggestion of free-thinking socialism, and the equally socialist but rather puritanical Arts and Crafts Movement. Anglo-Catholicism, which was an important factor in many artists' and architects' lives at this time, was able to straddle both camps.

In the 1890s Oscar Wilde seemed to be everywhere—he published three books in 1891 including his masterpiece of the Decadence *The Portrait of Dorian Grey* and also an over-clever group of fairy stories called *The House of Pomegranates*. Both books had covers designed by Charles Ricketts, in an angular Neo-Classical style which so often accompanied highly decadent work. One thinks of Herbert P. Horne, poet, architect and aesthete, and the earlier Godwin houses in Chelsea (one for Wilde himself) which purported to be in a Japanese style but whose architecture is much closer to Soane or the French Neo-Classicists, than anything that came from Japan. To people brought up with the austere ideals of the Gothic Revival, even this sophisticated simplicity seemed decadent.

To the advanced artistic world, 1894 was the year of the Yellow Decadence: the year which saw the publication of Beardsley's outrageous cartooning illustrations to Wilde's *Salome*, and the first publication of *The Yellow Book*. With *Salome* Beardsley openly allied himself to the flagrantly homosexual Wilde circle, and this was to do little for his reputation when Wilde's inevitable crash came in the next year, especially as the great poseur was arrested carrying a yellow-jacketed book, although it was not in fact *The Yellow Book*. Although the illustrations to *Salome* are both jokey and slightly obscene, they none the less carry a sort of decadent punch. This is the 'Japanese look' light years beyond the refinements of Walter Crane or even E. W. Godwin. For *The Times* the illustrations ' "would seem to represent the manners of Judaea as conceived by Mr. Oscar Wilde portrayed in the style of the Japanese grotesque as conceived by a French *décadent*.

The whole thing must be a joke, and it seems to us a very poor joke!" '12 *The Yellow Book* was a very different matter. In spite of the fact that the first number had a cover by Beardsley and a number of other illustrations, and articles by Richard Le Gallienne, Max Beerbohm's 'Defence of Cosmetics', and a poem with a Beardsley illustration by that arch-decadent Arthur Symons, it also had pieces by Henry James, Richard Garnett and its editor Henry Harland, all of whom within a very short space were to become members of the literary establishment of that time, which might be called proto-Georgian. Even Arthur Waugh, Evelyn Waugh's very literary establishment father, contributed to it.

Another, and in many ways finer, talent as book illustrator, Laurence Housman, brother of A. E. Housman and himself a writer, published his most important illustrated book in 1892—the relatively little known *Jump to Glory Jane*. Housman, unlike Beardsley, was interested in all aspects of book production and in this small book he created a perfect commercial example of the 'Book Beautiful'. The book illustrates a delightful poem by George Meredith of a Shaker girl dancing or rather jumping her way to heaven. Each page, except for the more pictorial frontispiece and title page, consists of a variation of the same, though subtly varied, jumping figure dressed in a long skirt and poke bonnet. Each opening is differently composed. Sometimes the figure is at the top of the page, sometimes the text meanders beside a group of the figures, sometimes the design runs diagonally across the page. Each page is completely different, and yet the book has complete unity. It is one of the most satisfying artistic books ever offered for sale commercially, and was a happy augury for commercial book design for the next decade or so. Housman went beyond Morris and Beardsley in the decorative use of the blank parts of each page. *Morte d'Arthur* is a book with heavy borders and solid set pieces deeply framed, each plate taking up the whole page. In *Jump to Glory Jane*, however, each page is treated as space into which the text and the pictures can be placed wherever the artist considers that they will be most satisfying to the eye. *Morte d'Arthur* looks back, through Morris, to early printing. *Jump to Glory Jane* acknowledges the early book techniques, the Japanese understanding of the value of undecorated space, and the intense black quality of the wood block; Housman also makes use of lithographic techniques, when they can serve his purpose. The book reminds one perhaps more of Newton and Lutyens in architecture—men happy to use new techniques, but wishing to retain the quality of the old work—than of Lethaby or Prior who delighted to use the Arts and Crafts Movement to create the crankiest of results.

1894 was the year of the opening by S. Bing of the shop La Maison de L'Art Nouveau in Paris. The shop gave the name to the style that Newton, Voysey and so many of the Arts and Crafts architects despised. But the opening represented an important breakthrough, since here for the first time modern English artefacts were on permanent show on the Continent. Within a few years it would be quite common to see British works featuring in Continental shows, the work of Ashbee, Baillie Scott and Mackintosh being particularly popular; but the real pacemaker in this matter was Frank Brangwyn. Indeed, the exterior of L'Art Nouveau had a mural by Brangwyn right across its facade, and inside were examples of his painting, his furniture and his rugs.

Brangwyn was a very remarkable artist, who like Alfred Gilbert has been largely ignored since his death, though it is difficult in his case to see why. The son of a not very successful architect and designer, his training could not have been more acceptable. He was trained in the South Kensington Schools (now the Royal College of Art) and came under the influence first of Mackmurdo and then William Morris. He worked for Morris between 1882 and 1884, when he left him for an adventurous life beside and on the sea. He used to beg voyages of captains as supercargo, paying for his fare with portraits of the ship. At that time his paintings were dark and rain-swept, appropriate for one brought up in the gloomy North, for he had been born in Bruges as were two other figures of the turn of the century, Fernand Knopff and Maurice Maeterlinck. His voyages soon took him to a brighter and sunnier world and his pictures brightened too. Soon he had developed his style: pictures made of large slabs of bright colour depicted men and women working or parading. He became essentially a mural artist, being able to fill great spaces with his colourful and dramatic paintings. As well as this, in the earlier part of his career, as might have been imagined of a pupil of Mackmurdo and Morris, he was an accomplished craftsman and furniture designer. He developed an interesting personal style for his interiors, which took Classical elements, in particular, Doric columns and tryglyphs, and treated them in an Arts and Crafts manner to create panelling which formalized the space into which he placed furniture treated in the same manner. Although all his woodwork was very controlled, the carpets and the walls themselves flowed with riotous patterns of flowers and fruit. This style must have presented a remarkable contrast when it was placed beside the already twisting forms being created by Bing's Continental artists.

Sculpture

If Continental Art Nouveau existed at all in England it was in the work of that surprisingly shadowy figure Alfred Gilbert. Although there were two books written about him in his lifetime and he designed the majority of the modern royal monuments that have any distinction—and in Eros he created a lasting symbol for London—yet his work is hardly known either in England or internationally. There is no other country in the world where this could have occurred—the reason must be that his sculpture, in spite of its Art Nouveauish quality, was never modish and that he continued to work in this style from the 1880s well before it was generally current, right up till his death in 1934. His Queen Alexandra Memorial Fountain of 1926–32 is probably one of the finest and subtlest Art Nouveau fountains anywhere; however, you will not find it in any book on Art Nouveau, since by 1932 the style had officially ceased to exist.

It was in 1892 that the Shaftesbury Memorial Fountain was commissioned, and it was unveiled in 1893. Like so much to do with Gilbert the history of this memorial is complex. Originally it had been offered to Queen Victoria's favourite sculptor Sir Edgar Boehm, who had earlier made a bust of Shaftesbury, and it was Boehm who had suggested his pupil Gilbert as he also the same year suggested Gilbert to Queen Victoria for the Clarence Memorial. However, Gilbert announced that he would rather build something that would symbolize Shaftesbury's life's work than a bust for the glorification of his tailor.[13] But the building committee insisted on a bust, and this Gilbert incorporated into a low wall which he designed to go round the edge of the fountain. However, when Eros went up ' "there followed a fearful howl against the parapet" ' and so Gilbert then decided to bow for the ' "first and last time to Public Opinion" '.[14] The parapet, and the bust, were taken down, thus leaving Eros as a slightly obscure monument to Shaftesbury but a splendid centrepoint for London; as appropriate for the time of Irving, Beerbohm Tree, Pinero and Henry Arthur Jones, who were at the unveiling, as it is now to the students who, perhaps more appropriately, cling around this base of a statue of the god of love. Unfortunately like all symbols Eros is rarely looked at as a work of art, and this is a pity since it is one of the most distinguished pieces of public sculpture in England.

We are told by Isabel McAllister that Gilbert made a loss of £4,000 on Eros.[15] But he, never a provident man when it came to his sculpture, was to be bankrupted twice over by his other commission of the year—the Duke of Clarence Memorial in Windsor. This was only completed in 1920 after the Royal Family had finally resorted to paying him piecemeal for each item cast. It is surprising that the bankrupt and extremely advanced Gilbert should have retained the approval of Queen Victoria, Edward VII and George V when very few other Englishmen considered him to be of any importance. However, Gilbert gave them in the Clarence Memorial the finest royal tomb since the Tomb of Henry VII and Elizabeth of York made by Pietro Torrigianni for Westminster Abbey in 1512–18. It is ironic that Gilbert's great tomb should have been built in memory of the one member of the Royal Family that it is unanimously agreed would have made a disastrous monarch. The tomb is placed in the centre of what has become the Albert Memorial Chapel and is surrounded by monuments to Victoria's family, but, as Pevsner says 'The room is now dominated by Gilbert's masterpiece, and it is impossible to overlook it'.[16]

On a stone base the bronze sarcophagus stands, and on it lies the sculptured body of the prince. Sweeping up over his head, and following the line of the mouldings of the sarcophagus, a great stone angel with outstretched wings holds out a laurel wreath. The mouldings of the base, the sweep of the angel's wings and the balance of the vertical and the horizontal elements create a design which is far from ordinary. Around the sarcophagus, and almost hiding it, Gilbert has built a tall and elaborate fence, a screen of highly wrought sculpture, built out not from the ground, but from the base of the tomb, thus making it clear that the two elements are one. The jumpy verticals of the screen contrast with the smooth sweeps of the mouldings of the sarcophagus and the white fluffy stone of the figures, which just projects above the bronze. Above it all hovers the angel. This screen is divided with upright columns which flow from the base to become for a short time traditional Doric columns, almost immediately to burst forth again into an elaboration of foliage intertwined with architecture. The foliage finally swings across to its neighbour in a thin band to form an aedicule for a statue, which in its turn rests on a column supported by a pair of angels, whose wings seem to form a great froth of foliage between the uprights. Each of the statues, or rather statuettes since they are no more than 9 inches high, is magnificently imaginative. Typical is the figure said to represent the Blessed Virgin Mary. Our Lady stands as it were entwined in a rose tree, presumably an early example of the influence of Burne-Jones's *Briar Rose*. In this case the figure looks tenderly down at the bush which grows up from her feet and spreads out in front of her; on her head she wears a crown of rose thorns, shaped like an Edwardian lady's hat. The statue is basically of bronze but it is coloured in elaborate enamel, which, Gilbert says, ' "is not paint, neither is it enamel. It is produced by a medium which by many experiments I thought would serve me well, as it has abundantly proved. . . . Some of the colours are vitreous, though not in the sense that they have been treated by heat. The sarcophagus is made of Mexican onyx, and is actually, in its construction, rather a piece of engineering work than of masonry." '[17]

The work took an immense time. The 9-inch high statue of St. George, Gilbert wrote, ' "occupied two years of steady work. The armour is absolutely an invention. Every detail is contrived as to be a working model of a suit of armour that could be worn. The shapes of its parts and the ornamentation of them are merely a résumé of the entire monument . . . which has the appearance of Gothic; and yet I maintain that there is not the slightest resemblance to anything we know of Gothic work, unless the use of shells and of other natural forms may be said to have influenced me, as they doubtless did the Gothic craftsman of mediaeval times. . . . The pedestal [of the statue] is a free use of the conventional form denoting a reptile, arranged geometrically so as to form a base for the figure of the Dragon and All Evil, which the Saint had overcome." '[18]

Here we have a clear statement of the attitude of the designers of the nineties, be they architects, interior decorators (as many architects were to become), sculptors (most of whom were in those days concerned with architecture in one way or another), or mural decorators (who as easily could double as book illustrators, and for that matter could well be architects also). Traditions were there to be used and developed from. At the same time new materials should be used, but that did not mean just because the materials were experimental that this should dominate every other factor. Eros is the first large piece of sculpture to be cast in aluminium and yet there is nothing particular in the design to suggest aluminium except for the fact that it would have been impossible to cast that particular piece in anything but aluminium.

Equally Gilbert, like so many other designers of this period did not change his style as fashion took him. When he went bankrupt in 1900 he had not cast all the statuettes for the Clarence monument. Rather than let the plaster casts fall into the hands of his creditors he very properly destroyed them. It was not until 1925 that he felt he could return from Bruges where he had exiled himself and where he had stayed throughout the German occupation of the 1914–18 war. George V then asked him to make the four statues again and gave him a grace and favour studio to work in. The four statuettes of 1926 hardly differ in style from the designs of thirty years earlier. To an English designer of the 1890s design was not a matter of fashion; it was a matter of doing what he did best supremely well.

Music

Although in the years leading up to the 1890s the Germans found much to admire in English art and architecture, they would not have considered that there was much of interest in English music. From Purcell to Elgar there was not an English composer who could in any way be compared with the great Austro-German masters, or even with the lesser Franco-Italian opera and operetta composers, with the possible exception of Sir Arthur Sullivan in the field of light opera. However, at the turn of the century, both Elgar and Delius were being given performances all over Germany. Although *The Dream of Gerontius* was a relative failure in its first performance in Birmingham in 1900, it was only recognized as a masterpiece after the Düsseldorf performance in 1901. The fact that English music was given rapturous receptions on the Continent meant that English composers were able to throw off their provincialism and join the mainstream of music for the first time for 300 years.

At the same time a different, and seemingly contradictory, movement was developing which led musicians back into provincialism and into their own past. The folk-song revival hit England, the outlying parts of the Austrian Empire and Scandinavia at about the same time. One of the main tenets of the Arts and Crafts Movement was that the artist–craftsman should go out into the countryside to learn from the village craftsman who had retained the old craftways since the Middle Ages. It would seem almost certain that the folk-song revival stemmed from this attitude and particularly from the genius of William Morris who, though not himself musical (although Burne-Jones was), inspired an interest in all things to do with the countryside. It cannot be just a coincidence that the old folk-song 'Brigg Fair', which Delius later used for his dance rhapsody, was collected by Percy Grainger in Lincolnshire, in the same year, 1900, that the Barnsley brothers and Gimson moved into the deep Cotswolds. This influence of English folk-song, with its deep underlying nostalgia (or that is how English composers tended to see it), seems to have been unacceptable on the Continent. Strangely Scottish folk-song had been a favourite of German composers right since the time of Haydn —it fitted into a clear ethnic mould. It is interesting that Elgar, whom Continental critics admired, would have little to do with folk-songs.

A third and related influence was the old choral tradition. The English choral festivals in the great industrial towns like Leeds and Birmingham had an insatiable need for new oratorios and, throughout the nineteenth century, English and Continental composers supplied these, though few are now played. The greatest of these festivals was no doubt the Three Choirs Festival, founded in the eighteenth century. It is the centre of musical life in the West Country moving each year between the three Western cathedrals nearest the Midland's industrial belt— Worcester, Hereford and Gloucester. Some of the most important composers involved both with the musical revival which started in the choral field and the folk-song revival, were intimately connected with this festival. Indeed a surprising number of composers were born, or brought up, within the sound of the bells of one or other of the cathedrals. These include: C. Hubert Parry (1848– 1918) born in Bournemouth but brought up in the family estate of Highnam, four miles from Gloucester; Sir Edward Elgar (1857–1934) born at Broadheath, eight miles from Worcester, and a resident of Worcester and Malvern for the early part of his life; Ralph Vaughan Williams (1872–1958) born at Downe Apney, Gloucestershire; Gustave Holst (1874–1934) born at Cheltenham, Gloucestershire; Ivor Gurney (1890–1937) born at Gloucester; and Herbert Howells born in 1892 at Lydney, fifteen miles from Gloucester.

The Arts and Crafts Movement had a bias towards the West of England, particularly the Cotswolds, and Cecil Sharpe and Percy Grainger found many of their finest tunes in the West Country, though perhaps further to the West than Gloucestershire. The Arts and Crafts men had a profound influence on the young musicians growing up in the 1890s—both Holst and Vaughan Williams came of age during that decade. Elgar was fifteen years older than Vaughan Williams and though not much affected by folk-songs and the Arts and Crafts Movement—to judge by his houses he did not have much architectural sense—he was profoundly influenced by the countryside around Worcester and Malvern. In his letters he constantly refers to the beauty of the Malvern Hills; he lived within sight of them until 1911, and it was during this period that most of his finest work was written.

Michael Kennedy in his *Portrait of Elgar* shows how out of touch the young Elgar was with the musical centres, and how difficult it was for him to hear any

live music except during the Three Choirs Festival. He quotes from an unpub-
lished article which describes how Elgar managed to hear an unknown piece of
music:

> I lived 120 miles from London. I rose at six, walked a mile to the railway
> station, the train left at seven; arrived at Paddington about 11, underground to
> Victoria, on to the [Crystal] Palace arriving in time for the last three-quarters
> of an hour of the rehearsal; if fortune smiled, this piece of rehearsal included the
> work desired to be heard but fortune rarely smiled and more often than not the
> principal item was over. Lunch. Concert at three. At five a rush to Victoria;
> then to Paddington, on to Worcester arriving at 10.30. A strenuous day indeed;
> but the new work had been heard and another treasure added to a life's experi-
> ence.[19]

1892 was the year in which Edward Elgar wrote the Serenade in E minor for
string orchestra. With its intensity and its deeply felt yet at the same time un-
demonstrative and indefinable English quality, something new had come to music.
It was a clear work of genius with an international quality that even Delius was
unable to match. Here at last in this provincial Roman Catholic music teacher from
Worcester, England had produced the musical genius that she had been waiting
for during all those interminable Victorian oratorios and cantatas, which were
listened to with the uneasy feeling that in this one activity Britain had no greatness.
Elgar, like so many British designers of this period, does not seem to have felt the
need for his style to develop, nor does he seem to have wished to follow the latest
Continental fashions. In the early days he was provincial and out of touch, but
when he became famous and moved in the most sophisticated musical circles he in
no way changed his style. Although his career spans the period of the post-
Wagnerian Second Viennese school, which included Mahler, Strauss and Schön-
berg, none of them seems to have had any effect on Elgar. He discovered his style
quite late in life, and never altered it. With its combination of an intense love of
the English countryside tinged, at least before 1914, with a belief in the British
Imperial destiny he displays a dichotomy that ran through so much English
artistic thought at that time.

One evening early in 1898, a discussion took place in the village of Colwall,
near Malvern, which is below Voysey's then just completed Perrycroft. Elgar
was visiting his 75-year-old mother. They stood at the door of her house and

looked along to the back of the Malvern Hills, with the Herefordshire Beacon, where Caracterus was said to have made his last stand against the invading Romans. Mrs Elgar, as she wrote to her daughter Pollie exclaimed: ' "Oh! Ed. look at the lovely old hill, can't we write some *tale* about it" . . . "Do it yourself, Mother" [said Elgar], he held my hand with a firm grip. "Do" he said. "No, I can't my day is gone by if I ever could" . . . in less than a month he told me *Caractacus* was all cut and dried and he had begun work at it'.[20] Thus Elgar's last, and best, dramatic cantata *Caractacus*, first performed at the Leeds Triennial Festival of 1898 before such musical celebrities as Hubert Parry and Gabriel Fauré, came to be written. Dedicated to Queen Victoria, it is a work shot through both with a passionate love of the English countryside, in particular the Malvern Hills, and a deep belief in the imperial destiny of England. This belief Elgar was seriously to question at the end of his life, but in the year after the patriotic excitement of Queen Victoria's Jubilee, for which he had written *The Banner of St. George*, there were few who doubted England's right to govern the whole uncivilized world, any more than the Romans at the time of Caractacus had doubted their imperial destiny.

All this may perhaps seem spurious to us, but as Elgar remarked to his friend Jaeger, ' "I knew you wd laugh at my librettist's patriotism (& mine) never mind: England for the English is all I say—hands off! there's nothing apologetic about me." '[21] This, to us, strange mixture of romantic delight in rural simplicity, and imperial ideals runs through the thinking of so many artists of this period that it must deserve serious consideration. However much the artist might chose to go and hide himself away from the coarseness of urban and Imperial England it was always with him, largely because everyone in the country, and not least the artist, lived on the wealth, if only at second and third hand, created by the factories and the Empire. Elgar and Lutyens accepted this in a way that perhaps some of the others did not, and it was because of this that their work has been denigrated by those of later generations who have been unable to see beyond politics when they discuss art. It was also Elgar and Lutyens who have left behind the most moving responses to the collapse of that world in the Great War, for it is only Elgar's Cello Concerto and Lutyens's war memorials such as the Cenotaph and the Thiepval Memorial Arch, that today seem in any way appropriate to that most ghastly of all wars.

Art Workers' Guild Masque

The same mixtures of ideals were displayed in the Art Workers' Guild Masque of 1898. In April 1897 Walter Crane first put forward to the Guild that they should put on a highly didactic and allegorical masque, which came to be called *Beauty's Awakening: A Masque of Winter and Spring*. The masque was to be a reinterpretation of beauty and the beast, in which Fayermonde, the spirit of beauty, surrounded by her attendant maids (named after Ruskin's seven lamps of architecture) is put under a spell by the wicked Malebodea and her attendant demons, named Philistinus, Bogus, Scampinus, Cupiditas, Ignoramus, Bumblebeadalus, Slumdum and Jerrybuiltus. These demons also attack the fair cities of the world, but each is defended by an artist—for instance, Venice is defended by Titian and Florence is defended by Dante, only London is defenceless. However, Trueheart wakes Fayremonde and puts the demons to flight which means that London is now safe and with the help of freedom, commerce, labour and invention is enthroned and can take her place with the fair cities of the world.

This somewhat naive allegory was taken up with delight by the Guildsmen in October 1898 and it was agreed to hold the masque in June 1899. Such important artists as C. R. Ashbee, J. D. Batten, John Belcher (the architect), J. Harold Cooper, Louis Davis, Nelson Dawson, Arnold Dolmetsch, Alexander Fisher, Henry Holiday, Selwyn Image, W. R. Lethaby, Mervyn Macartney, Joseph Pennell, Halsey Ricardo, Charles Harrison Townsend, Peter Waals, Harry Wilson and T. R. Wray all joined Walter Crane in this project; never before in England can so many important artists have come together in one theatrical event. It was suitably commemorated by a special summer number of *The Studio* for 1899, beautifully produced with a number of colour plates and typography by C. R. Ashbee.

The masque was finally held on 29 June 1899, and three days afterwards, in the heart of the City of London in the Guildhall, perhaps a surprising choice considering the plot. Without a doubt it created a great deal of interest—the Art Workers' Guild possesses two large books of newspaper cuttings on it. However, as H. J. L. Massé has commented:

As a theatrical presentation the Masque was beautiful beyond words [but it] . . . was hardly likely to commend itself to the City Fathers, who were to have a private performance to themselves. . . . It seems more than probable that if the libretto had been submitted to the Court of Common Council for approval, no performance, either public or private, would have been allowed in the Guild Hall.

From the beginning the Masque was doomed to be a financial failure. . . . There was no efficient control over the ordering of materials or properties. Expensive brocades were ordered where cheaper fabrics would have looked just as well for the few performances that the Guild was allowed to give. . . . The cost of tickets for such a new and uncertain venture was prohibitive.[22]

The very fact that there was no curb on expenses, much of which was in any case borne by the artists who created the designs, meant that the masque had a quality quite unlike any theatrical show. The costumes and the scenery were subject to the highest standards of craftsmanship—carving and decoration that could hardly be seen by the audience was exquisitely done. The throne designed and made by W. R. Lethaby was covered with minute symbols which would have been quite invisible off the stage if it had been used. As it was it was finished too late for the show. As Janet Ashbee, wife of C. R. Ashbee, wrote: 'Wilson's lamps, that looked so beautiful on paper, . . . turned out such dull shapeless masses of silk, their subtle symbolism quite lost in the half light'.[23] But this did not seem to matter too much to the Guildsmen, for the object was designed as much to give pleasure to the people using them on the stage as they were for the edification of the, largely philistine, audience. The masque was an extraordinary event for these artist Guildsmen, many of whom have been hailed as the precursors of modern design, honestly believed that by creating this exquisite revival of ancient masques they could change the attitude of capitalist businessmen who made up the City Vestries, that they could turn them from squalid money making, as they saw it, to a belief in beauty and, implicitly, to a belief in socialism. If that is not what they believed they could do, it is difficult to see why they should have decided to stage the masque in the centre of the City of London rather than in the West End where they might have found a more receptive audience.

Of course it could not be done. But the fact that the masque was put on at all, and put on in the very centre of capitalism, meant that at least some people began to take notice of the Art Workers' Guild's ideals. As Massé wrote in 1935: 'There is no doubt that our Guild Masque of 1899 was the seed from which Pageants . . . have sprung up since all over the country'.[24] That these pageants and all the related village events should have been so indissolubly linked with the Arts and Crafts Movement in the popular mind is a measure of the Guild's success, and also, when that movement came to seem intolerably precious, a measure of the Guild's failure during the 1930s when it, and it alone, set out to oppose the forces of Modernism sweeping in from the Continent.

Home arts and industry

The importance that people of the 1890s attached to an integration of all the arts, bringing up the applied arts to the same level as the so called 'fine' arts, and also the belief that the creation of that art could, and should, be made available to people at all walks of life, is probably best exemplified not in the work of the obvious intellectuals, who in a rather superior way went down to the country to teach the countryfolk to keep to their old traditions, but by the work of people such as Mrs G. F. Watts at Compton in Surrey.

The Wattses were not simply country folk; they were townee intellectuals as much as Ashbee or Gimson. Although the second Mrs Watts's artistic work cannot be said to have overtopped that of her husband, the great, if sometimes dull, portrait painter G. F. Watts, in her own field she is probably equally important. Mr and Mrs Watts moved to Compton, near Guildford, in 1890, when they commissioned Ernest George to build for them a large Tudor house which they called Limnerslease, a name which caused a certain amount of mirth amongst their fellow artists. Since it combines Limner and Easel, Burne-Jones took to calling it 'Painterspalette' or when he was feeling more waspish 'Daubersden'. The area around Compton was immensely popular with the rich middle classes who wished to live in the country but still be in ready touch with their office in town, for it contained stunning views from the ridge called the Hogs Back, which runs west-ward from Guildford. Here was Lutyens's and Jekyll's unspoilt Surrey within easy driving distance of a station for London.

In 1896 Voysey built one of his larger houses, Greyfriars, here, high up on the Hogs Back overlooking Compton and the triangle formed by Guildford, Milford and Farnham. There must be few other places, except possibly the neighbourhood of Vicenza, which can show in such a small area such a collection of houses of the same period designed by such a multitude of major architects. For in this area of eight square miles there are four houses by Lutyens, three by Voysey, and houses by Guy Dawber, Philip Webb, Baillie Scott, Arnold Mitchell, Forsyth and Maule and a number of houses by that great Farnham original, Harold Falkner. If one spread the net a little wider to include the area around Godalming then one could add at least four major masterpieces by Lutyens, two major works by Shaw, another fine house by Webb and also the delightfully sensitive work of Thakeray Turner.

Mary Watts was thirty-three years younger than her husband, who had been born in 1819 and only married him when he was sixty-nine. The first Mrs Watts was the teenage Ellen Terry. She soon left the elderly painter for the much more glamorous married architect E. W. Godwin, who after some years fathered her son Gordon Craig. Watts was a rather tiresome hypochondriac who had been looked after by doting women all of his life. Mary was but one of these, but it was she who had the staying power which in the end meant that it was she who succeeded in marrying him. She was moreover a lively artist, who early in their marriage in 1886 became interested in the Home Arts and Industries Association, an association in which artistic ladies taught labouring men how to use their hands to create works of art—yet another example of the Arts and Crafts Movement's concern that all should take pleasure in the creation of works or art or craft. At this time there were a great many women's craft societies and many of them produced works of the highest quality, though usually of the decorative sort. One thinks of Louisa, Marchioness of Waterford, who was also closely associated with Watts and Ruskin and painted murals in the village school, outside the gates of her castle, at Ford in Northumberland. Here the lady of the manor, again considerably more talented than merely amateur, taught the villagers country crafts that had died and art to those who wished to learn. In this way these ladies reflected the work of the more highly publicized people such as C. R. Ashbee.

The Compton Pottery works were entirely created and run by the second Mrs Watts. It was found that there was a fine bed of clay at Limnerslease and this seemed to indicate to Mary that pottery was the craft that should be introduced. I quote from *England's Michelangelo* by Wilfrid Blunt:

When in 1895 the Compton Parish Council, deciding that there was no space left in the churchyard for further burials, acquired a new plot—a piece of rising ground not far from the house—Mary saw her great opportunity; she would provide it with a mortuary chapel, designed by herself and carried out with terracotta decorations made under her direction by the villagers. In the following year a kiln of a pattern approved by William De Morgan was set up in the grounds of Limnerslease, and evening pottery classes started. 'The Squire, the Rector, and the Lady of the Manor', alleging that they were unable to attend of an evening, 'came during the day each to make their brick with its pattern on it'—and so escaped contamination.[25]

The building and all the outside terracotta work was ready for dedication in 1898, but the interior was not finished until 1906, two years after Watts's death. Wilfrid Blunt again:

The Watts Mortuary Chapel is a creation of genius, unique in England. . . . the exterior . . . colour comes as something of a shock, for though Mary optimistically hoped that it would 'tone down in time', in fact the Chapel, for all those black Irish yews planted to steady it, still strikes as discordant a note of scarlet on that green Surrey hillside . . . Symbolism pervades everything, from the ground plan, which combines the Circle of Eternity with the Cross of Faith, to every square inch of decorated surface. There are friezes representing the Spirit of Light, of Love, of Truth, and of Hope, and every buttress is a Tree of Life. The pillars of the doorway, 'rising from bases upon which there is a suggestion of a half crushed evil with closed eyes, bear the great name "I AM", and support a Garment of Praise'.[26]

Now to turn to Mrs Watts in her *The Word in the Pattern* which Blunt quotes above:

Interwoven with the initial letter 'I' is the hand in the nimbus of glory, the Celtic symbol of God the Creator. The 'I AM' stands guarding the man on his knees . . . reverently interpreting parables from the book of nature, that tell him of life after death. With the interlacing cord of Celtic art—which, whatever meaning may have been attached to it in those early times, is here used as a symbol of the unity of a divine life and law, running through all things—is inwoven the name of Christ, the Alpha and Omega.[27]

The interior of Compton Chapel, which was not in fact completed until 1906,

D.H.–C

is a riot of Celtic patterns in gesso, tinged it must be admitted perhaps with a little
Art Nouveau. As Wilfred Blunt says:

> The entire wall surface . . . is smothered with angels and cherubs' heads, with
> sprawling vines and pert little clusters of wild-flowers, with *art nouveau* strap
> patterns, text and medallions all carried out in gesso in low relief and gilded and
> painted in glowing colours . . . no one can fail to be amazed that so complex,
> so *professional* a building could have been produced by a woman with no
> architectural training, assisted (so far as we know) only by the local builder and
> blacksmith and a handful of enthusiastic but ignorant villagers. . . . indeed, one
> can pause to wonder whether the world might not have been the richer had she
> devoted the best years of her life to her art rather than to her aged, ailing hero.[28]

Part II

THE·HOVSES

Chapter one

BULLERS WOOD 1890

IN 1890 as far as houses were concerned R. Norman Shaw still dominated the field with his sudden turn to Neo-Georgian (or an approximation to what was later to be called Neo-Georgian) with his 170 Queen's Gate, Kensington, London, and Bryanston in Dorset. But a subtler precursor of the architecture that was to come in the next twenty years was Ernest Newton's first important house, Bullers Wood, Chislehurst. It is appropriate that we should first discuss a Newton house, since in many ways his work defines all that is best in house architecture of this period. There is no striving for effect, which so often mars the more obviously exciting work of his much admired master Norman Shaw. Although in his time Shaw's architecture seemed to belong to a more sophisticated world than had the architecture of his master Street (who for all his sensitivity remained a High Victorian throughout his career), they both seemed to feel a vulgar need to thrust both themselves and their buildings on to the landscape, which in the end makes their architecture seem slightly naive and even unsophisticated. In contrast as W. G. Newton says of his father's work: '. . . growing out of more commonplace origins [it] is less exciting and dramatic very often than is the work of Shaw or Lutyens. You will less often say on seeing one, "This is a Newton house"; but perhaps more often, "This is the house for this position".'[29]

This means that with the work of Newton and so many of his minor Edwardian contemporaries, there is at last no need to apologize. The houses are styleless but very stylish; the plans do not have the spatial elaboration of a Lutyens's house although every room is the right shape for the job. But at the same time Newton's houses are without the wilfulness of detail that you can find in the work of someone like Philip Webb. Most architects suffer from megalomania, forcing on to their clients their ideas, whether they be disguised as socialism or Classicism. However, it seems that Newton never gave his clients anything that they did not entirely want and need—for this reason his houses are difficult to write about, but they are clearly easy to live in. Newton's name is never mentioned by estate agents

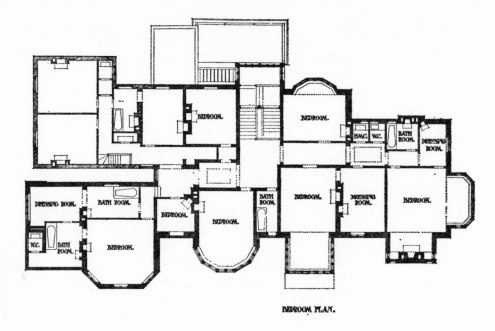

BEDROOM PLAN.

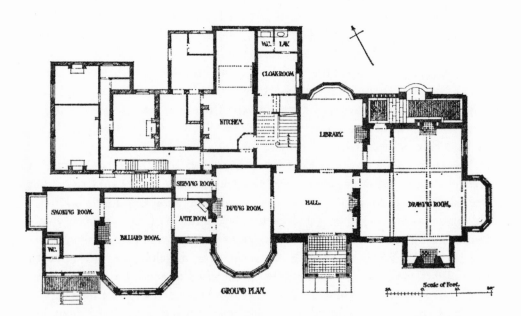

GROUND PLAN.

Bullers Wood, Chislehurst, Kent, Ernest Newton 1890. Ground and first floor plans

when one of his houses is up for sale, unlike Lutyens or Shaw whose names are often attached to the most unlikely buildings. It is possible though that a Newton house would be described as 'a genuine Tudor gem' or 'a gracious house from the time of Queen Anne', nobody realizing that it was in fact a fine example of late Victorian architecture. Newton, like Voysey, seemed to have little desire for stylistic progress within his own work; it is almost impossible to date by style alone a Newton house. Right from Bullers Wood in 1890 until his last building in 1921, there seems to be no obvious development. Newton's first houses in 'advanced' Neo-Georgian easily pre-date Lutyens, but his last work, in 1921— the hall for his old school, Uppingham in Leicestershire—is appropriately in the Jacobean Renaissance style of neighbouring Kirby Hall.

His practice was slow to develop. He was articled to Shaw in 1873, having originally intended to go into the office of one of the least inspired of the Gothic Revival church architects, Ewan Christian. He started practice on his own six years later, having become Shaw's chief assistant and clerk of works for one of his blander houses, the castellated Flete in Devonshire. As was usual Shaw gave the generous parting gift of a plum commission—in Newton's case this was the Convent of the Sisters of Bethany in Lloyd Square, London, WC1. However, it was not in institutes and churches that Newton was to make his name, but in the design of houses, and this part of his career had to wait another ten years before it was to flower. It was not until 1888 that Newton got his first important house commission from a Bromley family of successful merchants named Sanderson. This was the refacing with additions of Bullers Wood, a Victorian house at Bickley outside Bromley, turning it from, we are told, a nondescript stucco villa into a fine house of red brick and dressed stone. It was to become one of the few examples of an Arts and Crafts refacing. This is, of course, largely a contradiction in terms since Newton's splendid display of structural honesty using only the very best materials, still merely masks the true structure in just the way that the much despised stucco did to the original house.

The house was originally a straightforward, rather blocky villa to which Newton added an entrance hall and staircase and a large L-shaped drawing room, with a master bedroom over. On the main facade he designed a series of bays and an entrance porch (see plate I). He understood better than anyone the need for really deep bay windows, and at Bullers Wood all his bays are enormous—almost small rooms in their own right—with vast mullioned and leaded windows running right up to the ceiling. On the entrance front particularly he uses these bays to give a new rhythm to what originally was a very ordinary facade. The first bay on the left, that of the billiard room, projects from a short wing, which belonged to the original house; immediately next to it a completely different bay curves out, lighting the dining room. It is 20 feet wide of mullioned and leaded windows running up two storeys to the main cornice, which here sweeps out to take in the curve.

Bullers Wood – entrance elevation. The existing villa is on the left

Hardly has this bay died into the wall than another pushes out. This, the entrance porch, is one of Newton's most expressive works, which later he might have hoped to repudiate, for here there is still a touch of Shaw and High Victorian architecture. The porch, once again running up two storeys and lighting one of the main bedrooms above, is made entirely of broad mullions and leaded windows, and projects over 12 feet forward from the wall. There is a traditional very wide entrance door and immediately above it there is a flat wooden canopy which cantilevers another 5 feet, supported not on brackets but with wires tensioned off the upper porch. Above, lighting the entrance hall is a run of nine thin strips of leaded glass alternating with vaguely Jacobean pilasters. Above this are the six mullion windows of the upstairs bedroom. Capping it all is the great cornice over an egg-and-dart frieze. A little further down the facade, the deep ingle chimney of the drawing room fireplace projects with its powerful crow-stepped gable and large brick chimney over. This chimney ends the facade and carries it round the corner where the terrace suddenly drops down. From it there rises another deep bay, this time running up three storeys and looking out to the north to London, over a steeply falling bank.

Not one bay is similar in shape or size, even the gaps between the bays differ.

Bullers Wood – perspective of garden front and staircase by W. R. Lethaby

Yet there is always less plain wall surface than there is window. The facade is saved from disintegration by the strong cornice under the steeply pitched roof. This cornice is similar to Shaw's on his Neo-Georgian town house, 170 Queen's Gate, which as it happens was being built during the same years as Bullers Wood. Above the house there rise five fine tall, solid and completely plain brick chimneys. Shaw could never resist modelling his chimneys, any more than could Lutyens in the early days. Newton, however, knew when to leave well alone.

We enter the house through the wide porch with daylight streaming in through the strips of leaded windows between the wooden mullions. In front is the entrance door under a great leaded fanlight. Newton understood the subtleties that can be achieved by contrasting filigree leading and solid panels of wood. This was something that Frank Lloyd Wright was to bring to perfection some fifteen years later in his Prairie Houses. It is a great error to believe that leadwork in windows makes a room darker. The breaking up of the blank surfaces of large sheets of glass adds a delicate glitter, without noticeably excluding any necessary daylight, which cannot be achieved by any other technique. The entrance porch leads into a very formal Classical hall. To either side of a Kentian fireplace are doors under pediments, above is a deeply moulded Kentian ceiling. The purity of the Classicism is very surprising for 1889, particularly in a house whose general style is half Tudor and half Jacobean. It pre-dates anything similar that Lutyens did by at least ten years. It is something that we will find throughout this study; the styles of all periods are mixed but none the less in the final result all the styles have been melded together to form a cohesive whole. Ninian Comper was to call this 'beauty by inclusion' when he later came to design his splendid churches taking the same cavalier approach to stylistic accuracy.

Bullers Wood – perspective of entrance hall by Raffles Davison

Many of the old houses most admired by the late Victorians had grown over the years. In a new house this *mélange* of styles perhaps gives a sense of spurious history, but also, and more importantly, it suggests an undoctrinaire approach by the architect. It shows that the architect intends to give his client what he believes he needs instead of forcing him into a straitjacket of style, be it Classical or Modern. At Bullers Wood we can see Newton successfully continuing with this beauty by inclusion in the staircase. This rises from the corner not the centre of the hall; late Victorians did not like through vistas—they much preferred a slight sense of mystery in a house. From the hall the stairs rise through an arch, which is then reflected in a pair of pure Doric columns at the landing, and above there is an accurate frieze and cornice. All very Classical, but at the landing Newton forms a small room, shades of the later Lutyens! Lit by a deep mullioned and leaded window, here all is Tudor.

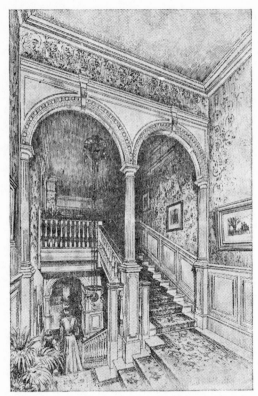

Bullers Wood – perspective of staircase by Raffles Davison

The showpiece is the drawing room, which was well known at the time, through illustrations, both on the Continent and in England. It was a white-painted

Bullers Wood – perspective of drawing room by Raffles Davison

panelled room, 30 by 30 feet, with fireplaces at either end, the walls divided with thin Jacobeany Ionic pilasters. Above there is a deep frieze and a heavily beamed ceiling. The frieze was painted in a flowing, curving leaf pattern by William Morris, much in the style of his *Acanthus* wallpaper. All the beams are stencilled, the larger with a similar pattern to the frieze and the smaller with a more formalized design. The colours throughout are subtle, light pinks and greens on a pale cream base. On the floor there was a Morris rug and most of the furniture, including a glass-fronted cabinet with ogee-shaped panels, was made by the Morris firm. The room is light and uncluttered almost to a point beyond comfort—there seem to have been few places to sit down. It would be impossible to say what period style it is in. The beams and leaded lights are a sort of Tudor, the furniture has both Gothic and Georgian overtones, and the fireplace surround is Classical.

In contrast to all this rather refined elegance is the billiard room. Here Newton saved a room from the old house, the refaced bay that we noticed at the entrance.

This room is in the coarsest High Victorian Jacobean. The 'plasterwork' strap-work and pendants are in fact a masterly display of the woodworker's craft, for they are all made of wood. One feels that Newton delighted in this contrast and insisted on keeping this room, as he did a small portion of the white stucco face of the original house, which he left untouched at the side.

Instead of altering an old house to give the impression that it had been built in a newly fashionable style, Newton here suggests that Bullers Wood was built and altered over many periods, with each generation making additions to it to express the style of their own time. This might imply a lack of intellectual purpose in Newton's vision. However, since he was an architect of crystal clear integrity with an adamantine vision the design has complete cohesion, so that it ends up by expressing the best of its own period. As W. G. Newton says: 'It has style, but it is not in a style. It has the broad touch which particularly marked his work . . . It stands on its hill with dignity, and essentially looks a piece of building.'[30] No client could ask more of his architect. It was this empirical approach, which is almost unknown to architecture anywhere in the world, before or after this date, that made English architecture so outstanding, and so admired.

Chapter two

STANDEN AND AVON TYRELL 1891

PHILIP WEBB was a puritan who had a profound effect on architecture, a great deal of it negative. Where Webb retained the humourless harshness of the Gothic Revival in his architecture his influence was almost always bad; however, he had a profound understanding of nature and of natural materials, and this love, again and again, saved his buildings from the dour serious-mindedness of Lethaby, or the distorted neurosis of Voysey's liberalism. When Philip Webb designed patterns, his designs, like those of his friend William Morris, always took their subjects direct from nature, with only the distortion that nature herself might make, and so he cared deeply for the landscape into which his few houses went.

In 1891 Philip Webb started on what was to be his last major house, Standen near East Grinstead in Sussex. In the same year Lethaby built his only great country house, Avon Tyrell, near Ringwood in Hampshire. They make an interesting comparison. Webb's career was in 1891 drawing to a close, although he was only sixty. Never prolific, he was to do only two other buildings before his retirement in 1900; he then lived on for another fifteen years, doing nothing. His career seems to encapsulate the problem of the Arts and Crafts architect of the 1890s. Refinement made them wish to create something closer to natural life, but in the end they found it necessary to reject even the whole building process as being too close to the professional world that they had spurned. Add to this a strong sense of puritanical guilt, which Webb passed on to his young admirer Lethaby, who then passed it on to the rest of the world, and one arrives at a stultifying position. The pity was that Webb, unlike his early friend Morris, or his later friend the craftsman–architect Ernest Gimson, did not recognize this problem early enough. He never turned to the making of things with his hands. None the less at its best Webb's architecture is very fine.

His first job was William Morris's first married home, the Red House, Bexley Heath, of 1860 which, with all its Gothic trim, is not in any way typical of Webb, who was not very 'advanced'. Many of his houses are straightforward enough, without any unnecessary decoration, though a lot of them suffer, like Shaw's houses, from a coarseness when moved through which is not obvious from photographs. Webb always had a few devoted clients, often very rich, and like the rich, then and now, often liberal free-thinkers. For these people he built grandiose houses, of which Clouds at East Knowle in Wiltshire is probably the most famous. It was commissioned in 1876, but was not completed until 1886. It burnt down two years later and was rebuilt and finally finished in 1892, by which time the harsh angularity and the Gothic puritanism of its exterior must have seemed thoroughly out of date.

However, the interiors, except for the vast and unattractive central hall, have an elegance and sophistication not usually to be found in large country houses of the 1870s. The library has white-painted book shelves, projecting into the room; one is coved at the top and brought forward to form an ingle at the fireplace. The panelled dining room with only the frieze carved, has great arches opening to the tall sash windows and a ceiling with the minimum of moulded plasterwork. On the wall there are shelves, with a few plates propped casually on them, suggesting a cottage sideboard rather than the serving table of a Victorian mansion. This is not a room that would have appealed to Peel or Palmerston, but it entirely suited the Balfours and the Wyndhams and their like who were now so disastrously ruling England. It is appropriate that they affected to believe that the house had been built by magic.

Standen, which Webb built between 1891 and 1894, was a very different matter. Here his client was not a great Whig proprietor but a solicitor, J. S. Beale, with a good practice who none the less knew a number of people who had commissioned houses from either Webb or other 'art architects' such as Halsey Ricardo. It has been fashionable to suggest that Webb created a styleless architecture which led in some tortuous way to modern architecture. This is nonsense. None of the architects that we will be discussing, except possibly Lethaby, was concerned with the search for modern architecture. This was something that had occupied the minds of Gothic Revivalists in the 1840s and commercial architects in 1850s, but it was not something that concerned anyone in the forefront of their field in the 1890s. Their concern was to create a house suitable for its surroundings and which could be happily lived in by their clients; style came into consideration, of course, but only as one of the many factors which affected the design. For this reason someone like Philip Webb was as willing to design a house in the Georgian style—for instance Smeaton Manor of 1878—as in the Gothic at the Red House.

Neither style was better nor more honest than the other. In Standen we see him willingly mixing both the styles together. It has recently been discussed very fully by Mark Girouard.[31] In this and in one other important respect it is unlike the other houses that we will be looking at. Although it was built for a member of the middle classes, it is considerably bigger than most of the houses that people such as Voysey and Lutyens were to build. It is nearer in size to a Victorian mansion, with its seven reception rooms, its long service wing and its multitude of bedrooms, than say, to Lutyens's Orchards or Voysey's Broadleys. In this it compares more with Lethaby's over-large Avon Tyrell.

The first thing that one notices about Standen is a surprising divorce between the cottagey style of the architecture used and the monumental bulk of the house. When Webb came to the site he found, tucked into the hillside, a delightful tile-hung small farmhouse. He immediately recognized that this cottage had to be

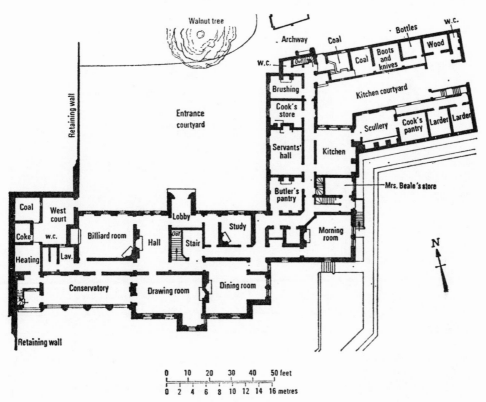

Standen, East Grinstead, Sussex, Philip Webb 1891. Ground floor plan

preserved, and to be integrated into the main building. This meant, of course, that he was presented with a number of problems both in architectural scale and in planning. The planning problems he got over brilliantly; in his scale perhaps he was not so successful.

One approaches Standen from above, an approach that we will discover in numerous houses. The drive seems almost to be a farm-track winding beside farm cottages. Finally it comes down beside the old farm building, retained in its integrity. This building is extended by a slightly lower long roof; at its end a low service wing juts out. Beyond it gables and chimney pile up, indicating the main body of the house. At this point the wall under the roof is cut back and without any other indication it opens into the entrance courtyard. This is an entrance as fine as any that we shall see. Lutyens could not have done it better. In fact Lutyens learned from it, using a similar trick at both the entrance to Orchards, in 1898,

Standen – perspective of entrance forecourt

and the entrance to the Salutation at Sandwich of 1912. The Sandwich entrance even makes use of an old cottage in its composition.

The north-facing entrance court is really rather surprising. It is cut into a steep bank, quite close, so that it is not easy to look at it as a whole. Webb realized that this would become a gloomy space if he were to provide his clients with a formal frontispiece, not that they would want such a thing. Instead he throws in a whole series of diffuse elements making little effort to bring them together. One enters the court through the arch close to the steep bank, an element that one had not expected since the bank has been masked by the cottage on the other side of the arch. To the left, the low roof of the entrance wing runs up to the main block of the house, where it is stopped by the square bulk of the sand-rendered water tower. In the roof of this wing there are large dormer windows whose gables are clapboarded in unpainted oak which has weathered to a light grey. The roof is brought down to the ground floor windows, which are Georgian sashes set in red brickwork. As this wing comes to the tower there projects a stumpy two-storey-high octagonal turret. This strikes the first discordant note for it is faced in a Tudor chequerboard of stone and brick.

From here the main entrance facade runs across in a straight line, until it is stopped by the retaining wall at the end of the court. This is a long and seemingly diffuse facade, which is handled with a splendid understanding of architectural balance. The materials also are various. There are two types of red brick and a red tiled roof, but the porch is of local yellow limestone. There is also a grey stone contrasting with the render of the water tower and the grey weatherboarding. The rhythm of the fenestration is complex, mixing Georgian sashes, stone mullions and blank brickwork. Taking a unit as one of the sash windows, the rhythm on the first floor runs thus: brick, sash, sash, brick, sash, brick, stone, stone, stone, sash, sash, brick, brick, sash, brick, sash, brick, sash, brick. Below, this rhythm is repeated but with variations to take in the doorway and the stone-mullioned bay, and for good measure here Webb also adds a wood-mullioned leaded window in amongst the Georgian sashes. Above all this the roof sweeps serenely through just above the first floor windows, there are a few dormers and above ride three simple tall chimneys.

The two garden fronts are much calmer (see plate III), but even here they lack the repose of some of the later small houses by the next generation. Webb is constantly trying to suggest that his great house is really little more than a cottage. The result of this inverted snobbery is that the elevations lack the assurance of, say,

Newton's work. Newton would never have tried to falsify the nature of his buildings. If he built a large house it looked like a large house, and a cottage looked like
a cottage. Take Webb's garden front. This is an extraordinary affair, only saved
from disaster by his complete sureness with architectural form and his deep understanding of the use of natural materials. From the right the facade starts with a
hipped roof, under which there is a red-brick wall. The roof is soon stopped by the
tall, rendered water tower which we saw at the entrance. On its flat top there is a
little square box with a little pointed roof, and beside this there rises a tall chimney.
Beyond the tower the crest of the roof continues through in a straight line, covering the main body of the house. In front of this roof, and taking up most of the
facade, five weatherboarded gables project forward over walls clapboarded on the
first floor but of stone below. Although this use of material suggests that this
block is a later addition it is in fact this part which contains most of the principal
rooms. The use of regular sash windows, and what at first sight looks like an
entrance-porch in the centre of the facade, might equally suggest that this is an
existing building which has had an addition wrapped around it. The fact that it is
not, and that the seeming entrance-porch turns out to be a bay by the drawing
room fireplace gives precisely that suggestion of play-acting that one might
imagine that Webb of all people would have carefully avoided.

The interiors are elegant, with a great deal of white-painted panelling set off
against some of the lighter Morris papers. It is interesting to see Webb using wallpapers in the main reception rooms here. It was at about this time that wallpaper-
ing began to become unfashionable—Voysey used his own designs in only one or
two of his houses. At this time people felt that mass-produced wallpaper had the
taint of commercial exploitation and so they turned to stencilling for their interiors.
Both Baillie Scott and Mackintosh used stencils and so were able to bring their own
patterns into the house. Had they used wallpapers it would have meant that they
would have had to introduce an alien pattern into their rather precious schemes.
If Voysey had not designed wallpapers himself he also, no doubt, would have
used more stencils. Although we have seen Newton using Morris and Co. at
Bullers Wood, this is the last time that he did so, for from then onwards he seems
to have used only plain paint. Lutyens seems never to have used wallpapers, and
his clients clearly believed wallpaper to be vulgar. Lutyens, however, did at times
use surprising colour schemes, with violent contrasts, setting flat slabs of wall
painted in black or scarlet against the sparkling white of his, sometimes, over-
scaled architectural features. Webb eschewed such extravagances, for even his use

of wallpaper here might well be a form of inverted snobbery, suggesting a simple cottage interior.

The most interesting and most successful thing about these interiors is the complete casualness with which the styles are handled. Classic fireplaces are built on to Tudor panelling, and sash windows contrast with tudory Gothic arches. Dr Girouard finds that some of the fireplace surrounds are 'unlovely . . . and would have been better away'.[32] This seems a little unfair, particularly as he rightly points out that Webb's puritanism was constantly trying to tone everything down. He quotes George Jack's remark: 'Webb's . . . "very inventive imagination at all times struggling with an austere restraint which feared unnecessary expression".'[33] But no one, for instance, could call the fireplace in the hall puritanical. It is a delightfully extravagant affair, which was to have a profound effect on Lutyens and other architects of the next generation. A moulding curves in a full semicircle over a flattened Tudor arch. Through this is smashed a large sharply angled keystone which pushes up to support an ordinary moulded mantelpiece, and part of a fire surround, which Webb seems to suggest had existed upon the wall before the newer work was added. This would seem to be an early example of the exaggerated playing around with Classical features which became common practice in the next twenty years. Lutyens certainly saw this fireplace; there is record of his having visited Standen very early on, and his 'farmhouse' fireplaces in Munstead Wood and Fulbrook may derive from it. His fondness for playing tricks with voussoirs may also have its source here. Webb was to be a profound influence on Lutyens's architecture in other ways. Lutyens's tall plain chimneys with their little hipped roofs of tiles are direct copies of Webb's as is Lutyens's habit, in his early houses, of breaking up long facades by, as it were, throwing together two or three quite different blocks, designed as separate units. Girouard rightly suggests that Webb would have been a greater architect had he been able to rid himself of his niggling puritanism. Webb was lucky enough to have in Lutyens a follower who rejected the puritanism, but distilled the best into an infinitely lighter and more elegant architecture; though having removed the puritanism Lutyens removed a great deal of the intensity of this architect, who after all was a pupil of that greatest and most intense of the High Victorian architects, Street.

W. R. Lethaby was never able to rid himself of this Webbian puritanism, and it was this puritanism that so appealed to Prussians such as Gropius when they set about founding the Modern Movement. Unfortunately, it is this quality, allied to intellectual self-indulgence, that makes Lethaby's architecture so unattractive. In

1891, having left Norman Shaw's office in 1889, he was given by Shaw his first big house, Avon Tyrell in Hampshire built for Lord Manners, a relation of the Wyndhams, for whom Webb had built Clouds. Artistic, sensitive members of a ruling class, such families cared less and less for ruling and more and more for living an ideal life, half Gothic and entirely Classic, which bore little resemblance to that of their rumbustious fox-hunting ancestors.

Avon Tyrell, like Clouds, is an aristocrat's mansion. However, it is worth considering here, if only to see how an architect who had been chief assistant to Shaw for ten years approached the problem that seemed to cause so much trouble for Webb at Standen, for Lethaby also tried to carry the cottage style into the field of the great house. Shaw, like his earlier chief assistant Newton would have seen no problem. He would have thought it neither sensible nor politic to attempt such a thing when building for a magnate. What Shaw would have done we can see at Bryanston in Dorset, which he had started in 1889 for the second Lord Portman. Bryanston does not pretend to be anything but a viscount's mansion. Classical, symmetrical, and, as Andrew Saint points out,[34] rather French in its formality and details.

Avon Tyrell is not as vast as Bryanston, but it is not small and Lethaby emphasized its size by planning it in one straight line, with just the slightest of projecting wings. Then he piled three floors one on top of the other, running the wall up flat, without any break through three storeys. It gave the house the blocky look that he had been developing in Shaw's office. 42 Netherhall Gardens, Hampstead, was one of the last jobs that Lethaby did for Shaw and its vertical blocky

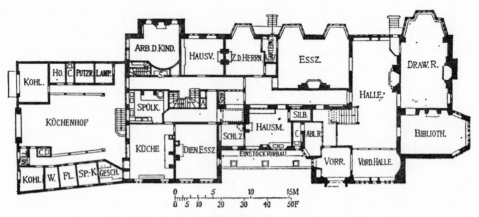

Avon Tyrell, Hampshire, W. R. Lethaby 1891. Ground floor plan

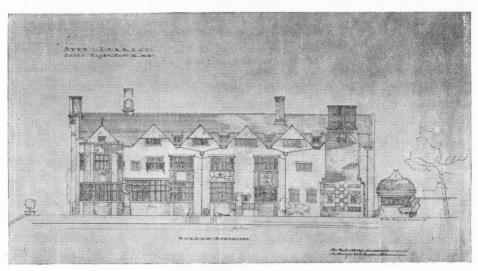

Avon Tyrell – garden elevation

quality is said by Kornwolf[35] to have influenced Voysey in his Bedford Park
house. Certainly it and Avon Tyrell seem to have influenced J. J. Stevenson
and E. R. Robson in their contemporary board schools. Or could it have been the
other way around? It would have amused Lethaby, as it would have amused
Morris, secretly to suggest in an aristocrat's country house a London board school.

While Shaw liked to allow even his Classical buildings to spread out and to hug
the ground, particularly in the country, Lethaby is much more tight-lipped. The
whole garden front of Avon Tyrell (see plate II) suffers from al ack of 'give',
strange in an architect trained by Shaw, most extrovert of architects. To the left of
the facade projects a very short wing; this, and the large window beside it, light the
grand drawing room. After this there are three small bay windows, not at all deep
with angled faces, looking as though they have strayed from a group of 'semis'.
Above there is a line of mean-spirited gables, of oddly flat pitch with windows
pushed up under the tile-hanging. A large tudory chimney at the right stops the
facade. This chimney starts well enough with alternating brick and stone panels,
rising in a flat plane till it reaches to just about the level of the eaves. Here the flues
start. But hardly have they done so than they are ungenerously chopped off.
Having presented us with quantities of unadorned brickwork, Lethaby, with a
sudden access of Arts and Crafts honesty, proceeds to drape the facade with
gutters and downpipes. Lead pipes, beautifully made no doubt, run together from

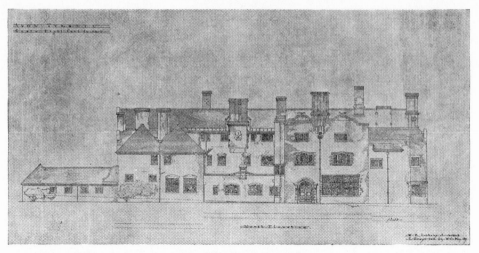

Avon Tyrell – entrance elevation

each pair of gables to meet at a rain-water head, vaguely placed just below the height of the roof of the two-storey bays, so that a pipe can take the water from the roofs of these also. The effect of all this is merely chaotic, having none of the contrived wit that so many of the Arts and Crafts architects used when they were handling downpipes. It is displays like this that make one realize how sensible Lutyens was in his later refusal to show downpipes at all.

The entrance front is equally unappetizing, since here Lethaby has carried the expression of different functions to an exaggerated degree. Each room is shown almost as a different block, with a different roof and a differing position on the ground. The drive brings us past this huddle of different sized kitchen buildings and leads up to the front door which is in a much taller, separately projecting wing right at the end of the building. This wing runs high and is oddly assymmetrical. To the left is the front door under an elegant semicircular hood; to the right is an enormous transomed and leaded window, which lights the great hall that runs right through the house. Above this there are two depressingly squat gables of different sizes, topped by tiny stone peacocks and divided by another of Lethaby's stumpy chimneys. To the left of this gawky and unwelcoming entrance the service wing tails off, stopped by a wing which comes forward under a pair of pleasant hipped roofs—giving perhaps the impression that this is a well proportioned small house that has been swamped by an Elizabethan palace (in much the way that Webb at Standen forced his Queen Anne house into the front of his group of

Tudor buildings). But while Webb very successfully handles his diffuse elements so that one almost believes that Standen took many centuries a'building, Lethaby's harshness overlays everything at Avon Tyrell so that it is quite obvious that this house was all built at one time.

The interiors are big and rather barren; even in old photographs where one can see them as they were furnished for Lord Manners, they have an institutional character, more appropriate for the school which Avon Tyrell now is. One feels here, as one never feels in that greatest of Lutyens's palaces, Viceroy's House, New Delhi, that this would not be a happy house to live in. There are no ingles, no delight, no corner to write in, nowhere to have a private conversation—all things that Norman Shaw loved. Here all the walls are straight and all the ceilings of the main rooms run through at the same height. The institutional character is increased by such a thing as the glazed glass draught screen which runs across the great window by the front door, looking for all the world like an addition put in to form a porter's lodge.

It is only by the excellent craftwork that the interiors are enlivened—particularly the woodwork, with its simple dowelled panelling to the walls and the doors, and the wonderful plasterwork to the ceilings and the friezes by Ernest Gimson. Here there are wit and delight in natural things that are so lacking in the rest of the house. But even Gimson seems to have been overcome by the grandeur of the commission, or the puritanism of the architect, and his delightful flower and bird motifs derived, as Pevsner cleverly points out, not from Elizabethan plasterwork but from embroidery patterns of that period, are kept within very rigid panels. The Lethaby chimneypieces, praised by Pevsner as having 'no historic connotation any longer',[36] seem hard and ungiving against Gimson's work. There is no doubt, however, that the smooth chequer of grey and black Derbyshire marbles in flat planes relieved only by the simplest of mouldings were admired and copied by such designers as Adolf Loos, and through them penetrated into the main stream of German modern design.

All in all Avon Tyrell stands out as something very different from the other dream houses. There is a gawky doctrinaire quality about it. One feels that here the architect is making a statement about his beliefs, and that these beliefs are more important to him than are the needs of his client. This is something that a Newton or a Lutyens would never have dreamed of. Even Voysey, doctrinaire though some of his beliefs were, certainly gave his clients what they wanted. There is a story that when he tried to offer a client something other than his white walls and sweeping roofs she burst into tears and exclaimed: 'But I have always wanted a Voysey house!' One cannot, on this showing, imagine anyone begging for a 'Lethaby house', although his later house at Four Oaks in Birmingham is pleasantly unpretentious and undoctrinaire enough. Perhaps it was that Lethaby had little sympathy for his aristocratic client and what, no doubt, he considered to be his antisocial way of life. But that once again is something that would not have worried Shaw, Newton, Lutyens or Baker. To them every client was a human being and every client deserved to be housed in the best possible way. The great pity is that the Lethaby's doctrinaire approach is the one that has dominated so many architects in the twentieth century.

Chapter three

PERRYCROFT 1893

BOTH today and at the turn of the century a house by C. F. A. Voysey is instantly recognizable. One recognizes Goodhart-Rendel's caricature, though perhaps he was for once being less than fair, when he wrote in 1957:

> When I was a child I was excited by fairy-tale houses having enormous roofs and practically no windows, by doorways to Wonderland having arches so low that an ordinary person would need to eat one of Alice's reducing cakes in order to pass under them, by tables whose legs not only went down to the floor but sprouted upwards towards the ceiling, by patterns made of cockyolly birds inspecting with surprise square trees slightly smaller than themselves; but when these phenomena pranced out of picture books into reality my excitement gave way to distaste.[37]

Perhaps though it was this fairy quality in Voysey, as in Lutyens, which so appealed to his clients and still appeals to us today. It was this quality that the generation that came after the 'truth of the trenches' of the Great War, not unreasonably, rejected. How Voysey arrived at his style is not at all clear. His father was a 'free thinking' vicar who was forced out of the church, after a sensational trial for heresy when his son was fourteen, because he would not subscribe to accepted dogma. No doubt it was from him that Voysey got his uncompromising puritanism. Voysey's father went on to found the Theistic church, and Voysey drew some of his most important clients from this church. Voysey's education was dogged by his inability to spell; his father educated him and he was sent for a short time to Dulwich College. In 1874, at the age of seventeen, he decided to become an architect, since in those days this did not require any qualifications whatsoever. If qualifications had been required it is doubtful also if Lutyens, who was very largely uneducated, would have become an architect. It is hardly surprising that these architects later came to reject the RIBA's attempts to create architects' registration exams. Voysey first went into the office of J. P. Seddon, one of the lesser-known Gothic Revivalists though he was a close friend of William Morris and designed some of the early furniture for Morris's firm.

In 1880 Voysey joined the office of George Devey. For many years Devey has enjoyed a somewhat inflated reputation largely because, although he was a brilliant water-colourist, he never allowed his work to be published, since he had an aristo-cratic clientele who did not take kindly to pictures of their houses being splashed across the pages of architectural magazines or the walls of the Royal Academy. However, recently architectural historians have been to look at his houses and they have found to their dismay that although they are full of the kind of romantic tricks that one would expect of a successful water-colourist, the houses themselves are often harsh and ungiving. Most of Devey's houses are in some variation of the Tudor style, most of them being in stone and red brick combined in as haphazard a fashion as could be expected if a house were built over a long period by singu-larly incompetent or impoverished builders. Where this elaborate wall surface does not occur, there will almost certainly be half-timbering and a plethora of gables. Against all this Voysey clearly reacted. He used only one material, and that the 'dishonest' stucco, few gables, only the minimum of half-timbering and that progressively getting less, and everything forced if possible under one simple roof.

In 1885 Voysey married and set up house in Bedford Park. In this house he started to design his ravishing wallpapers and fabrics and to make a number of architectural designs which he sent for publication to the various architectural magazines. Since unlike his master he rarely had aristocratic clients, which in Mr Brandon-Jones's opinion he would have dearly loved, he never had to worry about publishing his work, and indeed throughout his life he assiduously publicized every design that came off the drawing board, thus assuring himself continued interest from architectural historians. He left Bedford Park in 1886 and went to Wandsworth where he continued to design wallpapers. They were such a success that in 1893 they were exhibited at the Columbian exhibition in Chicago amongst all the Neo-Classicism, where they must have seemed to have come from another world. The architectural designs that he was producing at this time were frankly not of much interest and some of the planning was embarrassingly amateurish. The earlier designs display the usual wealth of tile-hanging, half-timbering and turrets, but these were slowly pared away. In 1890, he was commissioned to design Walnut Tree Farm, Castlemorton near Malvern, and his mature style was almost

Walnut Tree Farm, Castlemorton, Worcestershire, C. F. A. Voysey 1890. Perspective of garden front by Raffles Davison

born. Voysey is an example of an artist who early discovers the limits of his talent and then keeps well within those limits. The style progression within Voysey's work is even less than that of Newton, and Walnut Tree Farm has most of the attributes of a matured Voysey house. Here are the stucco walls, the slate roof, the low eaves with dormers poking through, the canted bay and the tall white chimneys capped by slates and tall chimneypots. Perhaps there is a little more half-timbering—the hangover from his master Devey—than we might expect to see later, but otherwise everything is the same as in his last houses in 1919.

By 1891 his practice was in full swing and in this year he built two of his most idiosyncratic houses, both of them as it happens in or near London—The Studio in West Kensington and the house in South Parade, Bedford Park. The Bedford Park house so clearly displays Voysey's tiresome bloody-mindedness, that it deserves notice. Bedford Park was the first artistic suburb, with strong leanings to Aestheticism. Although the earliest houses were designed by the arch-aesthete Godwin, most were built by Norman Shaw. They were built between 1876 and about 1886, in a much publicized red brick, with tall pitched roofs, tall chimneys and much white wood trim. When he lived there Voysey had watched the slightly absurd antics of the first aesthetic residents, no doubt with the somewhat superior

House in South Parade, Bedford Park, London, C. F. A. Voysey 1893. Perspective of entrance
front by Raffles Davidson

attitude of a young puritan artist who had yet to make his way in the world. His
opportunity came when he was commissioned to build a studio house on the
suburb's grandest road, South Parade. His first design was a rather romantic little
cottage, using red brick and a certain amount of render. However, the second
design rejected all that for something much more offensive. He designed a tall
three-storey slab, rendered in white, topped by a low-pitched slate roof. The
windows are small narrow strips of leaded glass punched into the wall without
much in the way of coursings. Everything is designed to suggest that this house
is different from its neighbours. It is in white stucco instead of red brick, the roof
is low-pitch grey slate instead of high-pitched red tiles, the chimney is in stucco,

unmoulded without caps compared with Shaw's highly moulded red brick, and finally the windows are small, and use leaded lights in a way that was distressing to the Bedford Park residents who believed in large, white-painted wooden sash windows—so that God's good light and air could be let into the house. Although to us this un-neighbourliness of Voysey and his client seems modern in its unpleasant destructiveness of its surroundings, to the people of Bedford Park the house seemed reactionary and dishonest. Instead of an honest display of building materials which had been advocated since Pugin and the Gothic Revival, Voysey reverted to the old and bad Georgian practice of stucco, instead of large open windows he created small windows which let in hardly any light. Later in life Voysey rejected any suggestion that he had had anything to do with the origins of the Modern Movement, but 14 South Parade, Bedford Park shows that he had a lot to do with the start of the movement at its most puritanical.

Of course we must accept Voysey as one of the key figures in English architecture of this period, but his position is none the less extraordinarily anomalous. Hailed as a precursor of the Modern Movement by Continental critics, he is seen as a creator of the semi-detached style by others. Disliked for his over-conscious Art Nouveau designs, he himself attacked the extreme Glasgow designers as 'the spook school'. Revered Master of the Art Workers' Guild, he seemed to care little for the crafts and nothing for the indigenous architecture of the countryside. When he was praised by avant-garde journalists as a pioneer of modern architecture,[33] he repudiated this in the *Architects' Journal* saying that 'I am sure that those who express such views have no intention of libelling me. I make no claim to anything new'.[39] It was Voysey's insensitivity to the landscape that most appealed to the moderns: 'fling down a white house anywhere and show them'. On the only occasion that he used stone—once in a scent shop in Bond Street and the other time above Bath, in of all things a bungalow—he reverted to a castellated Gothic, both, one would have thought, singularly inappropriate buildings on which to essay such a style. And yet at their best the simple Voysey houses and cottages have a delightful ease and an elegant welcome that most clients would wish their architects to give them.

1893 was the year of the first important Voysey house, Perrycroft, Colwall, just outside Malvern, over the border in Herefordshire. It is his first house of any size and every characteristic Voysey detail is already in use. Perrycroft is set, only a few miles from Walnut Tree Farm, in a northern fold of the Malvern Hills with magnificent views across to Wales. It was designed for J. W. Wilson, and is a

normal-sized country house of its period. All Voysey plans are of the simplest—
rectangular rooms of various sizes strung together between parallel lines. Perrycroft is uncommon in that it has a U-shaped plan, but otherwise the planning is
much the same.

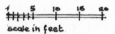

scale in feet

Perrycroft, Colwall, Herefordshire, C.F.A. Voysey 1893. Ground floor plan

Perrycroft – perspective of entrance court by Raffles Davison

The entrance, from the main road high up along the hillside, is past a lodge in a sweeping drive, which looks down on to the roofs and chimneys of the house, and beyond them across the valley to the hills of Wales. On the right we first come to the stables which, with their tudory oak framing, still have a touch of the early designs about them. The upper parts above pebbledash walls are half-timbered, though in a very simple pattern—just vertical stripes which break up the plain wall surfaces. To each side there are tall battered and entasised chimneys and in the centre, under an arch, there is a cupola.

The drive continues on and makes a sharp turn between trees down to the house, and suddenly, and rather typically of Voysey, one seems to have arrived in the backyard. In fact the front door is perfectly clearly demarcated to the right of the U-shaped entrance court, but right in front of one is the servants' entrance under a tower. This is something that a really clever planner such as Lutyens or Newton would never have tolerated. It cannot be explained by Voysey's inexperience at this time in his career, because he makes a similar 'error' in a number of later houses, including both Greyfriars, Puttenham and Broadleys, Windermere. Perhaps Voysey thought that his high-thinking clients should not mind such things particularly as this front door position means that every living room in the house makes full use of the wonderful views. The front entrance itself comprises of a splendidly broad pair of doors made of three, wide oak planks bolted together, and with decorative hinges designed with a flat pattern of flowers at their ends. In the

DH–D

Perrycroft – elevations; entrance front (top), garden front (bottom)

far corner of the court there is, untypically for Voysey, a small tower, which bursts out at the top with curved voluxes between vertical strips of glass, not dissimilar to Newton's porch at Bullers Wood. The tower is roofed in lead in a reverse curve on which stands a tall weather vane. Beside the tower, which contains the back stairs, running along the first floor of the main house is an unbroken strip of windows which lights the upstairs passage. The whole court is handled with care, the vertical and horizontal emphases balancing one another, like the entrance to Standen, but tucked into the hillside the general effect is slightly gloomy.

Perrycroft – perspective of garden front by Raffles Davison

On the other hand the outward-facing elevations are splendid. There are bay windows to most rooms which come just where they are required, with little attempt at balance or symmetry. None the less the walls are carefully articulated. At the lower level the wall kicks backwards and forwards, forming the bays, whereas the upper floor carries through on one plane, jettying out to support the heavily overhanging roof eaves. At the same time the walls are broken vertically by buttresses and by great battered chimneys which stick out at right angles from the wall and run up above the eaves (see plate V). It is these great chimneys that one remembers most about the outside of Perrycroft; these five slabs of white, with at the top just slots for the smoke, holding down the great hipped roof with the whole house under it, as it lies tucked into its hillside—a strange exotic, but only in the way it exaggerates all the elements that go to make up a sense of home-liness in a house. The front door with wide welcome combines with an over-powering sense of enclosure against the weather. The small windows are divided into even smaller leaded panes and are then cosily tucked under the great deep eaves. Even the vast chimneys suggest a great ingle or house place with fires burn-ing and oxen roasting. Everything is exaggerated against its true functional needs; everything in the end is almost a caricature of a house. Or, as Goodhart-Rendel said, a house out of a fairy book. But at this time most of the children's book illustrators were drawing castles or the simple Georgian farmhouses that Randolph Caldicott liked to show as a background to his pictures. It was only many years after Perrycroft was completed that such people as H. Willebeek Le Mair began to use the Voysey house in the backgrounds of her illustrations.

It is one of the characteristics of design of this period that it took elements from buildings of all periods and then gave them a slight exaggeration. Newton and Lutyens knew how to do this subtly, but Voysey and Mackintosh emphasized these traditional elements to such a degree that they began to look like a new architecture. It was just these elements that so appealed to the Europeans who studied the works of Muthesius, and it was from these exaggerated and in many ways un-English elements that Adolf Loos developed his architecture. One can see this exaggeration even more inside the house. The plan itself is simple enough, but it is the detailing that is so odd. The fireplaces in the downstairs rooms are almost as tall as the ceiling. Slender columns rising to 6 or 7 feet support a mantel-piece that it is almost impossible to reach on tip-toe, certainly it would be impossible to rest an elbow on the shelf (see plate VI). The white columns are contrasted by plain green slabs of marble, sometimes offset by a circular mirror. These built-in mirrors in a living room are rather surprising for this date. In the early part of the nineteenth century, the use of mirrors in grand houses was very common; Baroque tricks were often played by Barry and his contemporaries. Then mirrors were taken up by publicans, and so their use became vulgarized. After about 1880 it was very rare to see a fitted mirror in a gentleman's house. Lutyens would certainly never have used one. But Voysey, who tended to work for a slightly less pretentious client, often used mirrors in his overmantles; indeed they often give the only glitter in an otherwise simplistic interior.

As often as not Voysey's clients allowed him to furnish their houses throughout in his style. He would set his simple though once again somewhat exaggerated oak furniture against his plain, painted walls. The final result, though elegant and quite sophisticated, was far from 'homely'. It is difficult to see how his rooms could be lived in by a normal family for, as in Frank Lloyd Wright's houses, any item introduced into it not designed by the master, instantly seems out of place. It says something for the ordinary Edwardian family that they were willing to put up with such restraints on their daily life, in order to have an 'artistic' home. Both Frank Lloyd Wright and Voysey included a large number of straightforward though artistic clients in their large house practices. Inevitably over the years all the Voysey houses have been refurnished and since even Georgian furniture can seem coarse and out of place in these refined interiors, the houses now present a mere shell of their original elegance. In Perrycroft the present institutional furnishings and light fittings are particularly disastrous.

Chapter four

REDCOURT 1894

NEWTON had lived since 1884 in the Bickley Park Estate, near Bullers Wood, in a house that he had built himself when he was twenty-seven. The house was, as one might imagine, given its date and provenance, in the Norman Shaw style; half-timbered, tile-hung and red brick, though as John Newman has pointed out, even here Newton is more symmetrical than Shaw would have been and 'the house is noticeably crisp and spare'.[40] Newton built a large number of other houses round Chislehurst and also near Hampstead between 1885 and 1906, for William Willett, who commissioned other architects to build for him on his superior estates. As the years were to go by these included C. H. B. Quennell, E. J. May and the young Curtis Green. Newton designed his houses sometimes in the Shavian Surrey style but more often in his version of the Georgian vernacular, using the bay windows and cornices that we have seen at Bullers Wood. In 1898 he built a delightful group of buildings in the neighbouring market town of Bromley—a coaching inn and related shops, which with their perfect good manners and reticence were to have a salutary effect on the design of pubs and shops for many years to come. Recently they, like so much else in our high streets, have been altered so that now at ground level little remains of Newton's sensitive designs.

For a short time his career turned to churches, no doubt through his connection with the Sisters of Bethany at Lloyd Square. He built them a chapel in 1891 in a smoother style than the Shaw-like High Victorian of the main building, and in 1892, with the help of Lethaby, he built the elegant St. Swithun's Hither Green, Lewisham, London—a church with excellent proportions which none the less has that extraordinary coldness that seemed at that time to be affecting many advanced church architects. After St. Swithun's Newton turned back to houses and from now onwards this was to be the major part of his work. In 1894 he built the first completely new true Newton house, Redcourt, Haslemere in Surrey. He had now thrown off all the remaining Shaw tricks and was already using those elements which he continued with for the rest of his career. At Redcourt the most obvious

Shops and pubs, High Street, Bromley, Kent, Ernest Newton 1898. Perspective by Raffles Davison

of these details are the tall shuttered sash windows, and the two sorts of bay window: one, half of a hexagon on plan; the other, a very flat semicircle, usually with leadwork, and sometimes cantilevering from an upper floor. The entrance porch is a deep bay, though this is often exchanged for a full circle of columns, half into the house and half projecting with half of a lead-covered dome over. There are usually at least three different window forms on the facade and often leaded windows are mixed with straightforward Georgian sashes. Often these leaded windows are designed in a form of fenestration that is entirely Newton's own, comprising a triplet of windows, the centre being arched to create a kind of flattened Venetian window—a true Venetian window having a full semicircular head. All Newton houses have large and excellent chimneys often decorated in in flat diaper patterns, but rarely elaborately moulded. The roofs are always simple and often project from a plain parapet or a heavily dentilled cornice of the type that we have seen at Bullers Wood. The detailing is exquisite and Newton, if possible, always used decorative leadwork for his gutters and downpipes, at the positions of maximum impact.

The overall effect of most of Newton's houses is Georgian although he is always extremely careful to keep within the character of the countryside in which he is

Chapel of Sisters of Bethany, Lloyd Square, London, WC1, Ernest Newton 1891. Perspective of interior by Raffles Davison

building. So we find that Overbury village, which lies just beneath the Cotswolds, is in Cotswold stone, but when he is extending a yeoman's farmhouse in Sussex, as he did at Oldcastle in 1910, he builds a perfect Sussex vernacular addition, with tile-hanging and tall chimneys outdoing Shaw in his romanticism but still retaining the character of the original house, something that Shaw could never have done. As Newton himself said:

The planning is without doubt the most important thing in the designing of a house. 'To be happy at home is the ultimate result of all ambition.' No one can be quite happy in an ill-planned house any more than in ill-fitting clothes, and although the 'cut' and 'style' are much, they count for nothing in a garment which pinches and annoys the wearer in a hundred ways. . . . although house building is very much a practical art, the practical requirements may be met gracefully and pleasantly; there is scope for dignity, humour and even romance.

Our housebuilding ought to develop naturally. In the animal world abnormal variations are considered as apart from the general scheme of progress, and are popularly called 'freaks', and the conscious breaking away from normal lines of development so conspicuous in much of the building of the last few years, especially on the continent, may perhaps be not unkindly called 'Freak architecture'. A natural architecture is a rational healthy builder's art expressing itself soberly through the medium of masonry and carpentry.

Newton then continues in a passage which explains why his architecture is so little appreciated today:

This 'New Art' was no doubt originally the outcome of a genuine if somewhat perfervid enthusiasm, and of a desire to shake off all unnecessary restrictions, but it has mistaken liberty for licence, has abandoned all reserve, and threatens to retard, if not destroy, the growth of a sane and reasonable architecture.[41]

Redcourt is set high on the hills above Haslemere and is approached through lodge gates and a drive which curves to a formal entrance forecourt. The front door is contained in a square bay, the door itself has a simple curved head, reflected by the curved head of straightforward canopy which stretches out over it. To either side, the facade at first glance seems to be symmetrical, formally arranged with Georgian windows. But the right-hand side has a bay window in the centre and on the left the middle windows are omitted, leaving just the brick wall. On looking at the plan all this asymmetry is seen to be perfectly logical, the ground floor dining room needing to be lit by the bay and two other windows, whereas the drawing room on the other side is lit with a large bay so does not need the additional side light. The first-floor plan works with equal logic, the bedroom over the drawing room has its bay, the next bedroom has a delightful alcove formed by the porch and the three windows to the right open on to a dressing room and a smaller bedroom. All is perfectly logical, nothing is forced. Newton's plans are always a delight to read, in particular for his mastery of balanced asymmetry, which is possibly the most difficult of all forms for the architect to handle without forcing. Very few architects, and this includes even such masters as Shaw and Lutyens, are averse at times to fudging a window, forcing a point. Newton seems never to put a foot wrong.

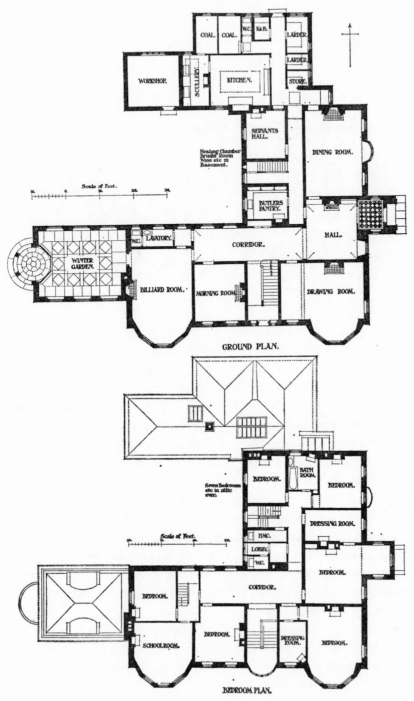

GROUND PLAN.

BEDROOM PLAN.

Redcourt, Haslemere, Surrey, Ernest Newton 1894. Ground and first floor plans

Redcourt – perspective of entrance and garden fronts by Raffles Davison

If this is doubted it is only necessary to consider the garden front (see plate XX). Here Newton presents us with a strictly formal elevation, except in one very important aspect. To either side of the facade there are bay windows, each with three sash windows and decorated over with the Newtonian lozenge. In the centre, the facade runs through flat but here it is capped by a pair of gables with his Venetian windows. Below one might expect the fenestration to be a line of four sash windows, and at the ground floor a door in the centre. But this would be too bland a solution for any architect brought up in the traditions of romantic asymmetry of Shaw's office and would in any case not suit Newton's ground plan. So the second of the four sash windows is converted to a flat lead-covered cantilevered bay, which projects over a garden door. Around the top of this bay there is a decorated lead gutter which continues along the tops of all the windows. The downpipe from this gutter is carried down between the two leftward windows, thus reflecting the projecting bay to the right, forming with its thin horizontal and vertical line a perfect balance to the asymmetrical bay. On the inside the functional reason for this asymmetry becomes clear.

We enter through the entrance hall and once again, as at Bullers Wood, we are moved diagonally across the hall. Although a certain amount of this had to do with draughts, architects always preferred a degree of complexity at the entrance; in

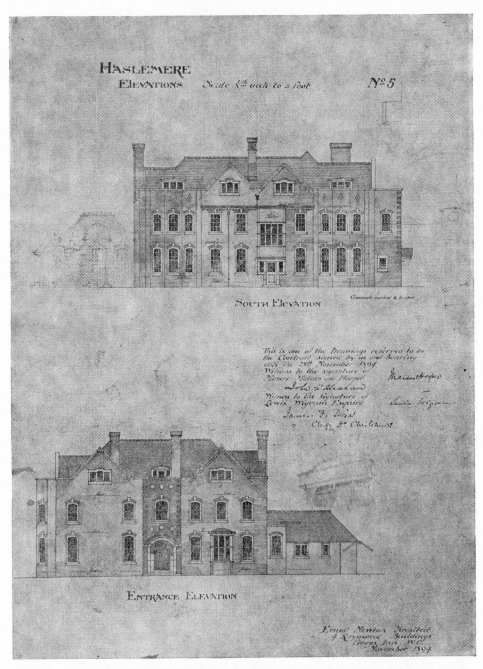

Redcourt – contract drawings elevations of garden front (top) and entrance front (bottom)

Redcourt – perspective of dining room by Raffles Davison

this Lutyens was an expert, as he was at all convoluted planning matters. In the hall on the right by the fireplace is the dining room and to the left through an arch is the door to the drawing room. If we walk through the arch we enter a short vaulted corridor which, just beyond the drawing room door, opens out to form a T-shape. From it the staircase rises, lit at landing level by the bay that we have seen outside. This window faces south and of course floods the corridor with light. Below the staircase a door leads out into the garden. The corridor then carries on past the morning room to the billiard room. If one continues through this one comes to the winter garden, a delightful formal room, with arched windows in the roof and at the end the first of Newton's rotunda entrances. We have been led through the house passing through a series of different spaces each lit differently, yet the whole thing has been completely simple; there have been no complex nooks, no tortured turns that we might have expected from, say, Ernest George or Norman Shaw. At the same time Newton has made use of these architects' High Romanticism; he has kept the essential picturesque interest of complex space relationship and lighting, and somehow simplified it until it all looks as if it could be done just by throwing rooms together where they were needed and only then seeing what facade would result. Newton's is the supreme example in architecture of the art that conceals art. The very fact that there are no complexities, and no dark corners or unusable spaces means that Newton houses can be lived in in the way that they were always intended to be lived in—without alterations—and so Redcourt has lasted for over eighty years without any major alteration. Although the rooms at Redcourt are beautifully proportioned, they have a styleless quality which means that they can take whatever furniture there is about: there is no need to furnish a Newton house in any particular style, unlike so many architect-designed houses right from the time of Adam, through Voysey and Mackintosh to the present day. This is something that Newton shares with Lutyens and all the truly great house architects. When an architect forces his style on to someone's home, later generations will find it difficult to live in, with the result they will want to alter or destroy the building. While the works of such eccentric architects as Soane and Webb have not survived, many of the less imaginative buildings of their contemporaries are still with us.

Redcourt – perspectives of fireplaces by Raffles Davison; drawing room (left) and morning room (right)

The ceilings of the main rooms at Redcourt have fine plasterwork, largely comprising groups of flowers running in ropes in a vaguely Carolingian manner, and the fireplaces are Classical. The craftsmanship throughout the house is excellent in all the simple things like doors and skirtings, carefully designed and beautifully made. This was probably the greatest period of English craftsmanship; certainly taken as a whole it was far superior to that of Georgian times. It is one of the ironies of the period that at the very time when architects were going into the countryside and often building for themselves in an attempt to create living craftsmanship, architects such as Lutyens and Newton with a proper sense of good building were able to get very much finer workmanship than those who had dedicated themselves to its revival. This, however, did not occur in furniture work, where such artist-craftsmen as Gimson and Waals created a far superior product than anything that could be produced by a commercial firm.

Before we leave Redcourt we must just notice the gardens, which reflect the move to formality taking place at this time. The main drive arrives at a formal forecourt, a rectangle surrounded by surprisingly urban railings, made into a square by the addition of flower beds in each corner. Turning left down a path in the centre of the fence we come upon a terrace which runs across the front of the house, and some 30 feet from it. From here there is a crescent of hedges forming a court and, in the centre, steps lead down to a square lawn surrounded by hedges and herbaceous borders. In the centre there is a sundial and from here inevitably there are splendid views over the landscaped meadows. The terrace continues on until it reaches the tennis court, which is precisely centred on the rotunda of the winter garden, though this is neither on the centre line of the main body of the house, nor at the centre of the court. The designer of this carefully planned layout was T. H. Mawson, garden designer, town planner and architect, who lived on Windermere in the Lake District, which ever since Wordsworth had been the romantic's favourite place of resort. However, he seems to have been unable to accept Gertrude Jekyll's romantic woodland garden and to have been strongly influenced by the Classicism now coming into garden design. In his *The Art and Craft of Garden Making* of 1900 Gertrude Jekyll is not mentioned, although Reginald Blomfield's *The Formal Garden in England* and J. D. Sedding's *Garden Craft*, both of 1892, are praised on the first page, as later is Edward Kemp's very formalizing *How to Lay Out a Garden*. Here is the other side to Jekyll's romanticism. One of the results of the aesthetes' interest in the Queen

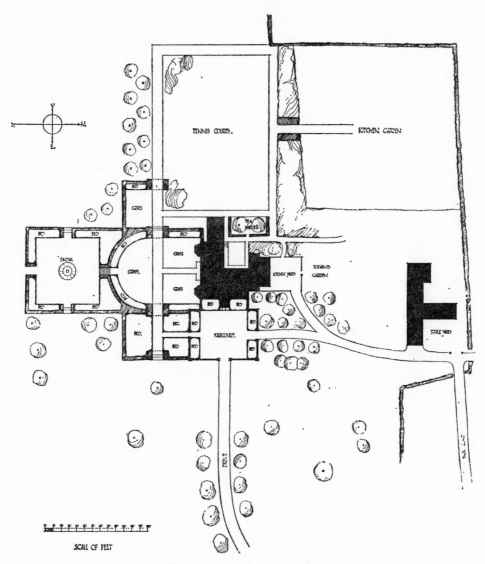

Redcourt – garden layout plan

Anne style was a reawakening of an interest in the formal garden. To us it seems surprising that well before they were able to accept formality in their homes people were willing to accept formality in the garden. In fact Jekyll's woodland garden was a reaction against this almost contemporary reaction against the High

Victorian combination of Romanticism with Formalism. Mawson nicely encapsulates this when he complains that:

> The modern garden, made up of serpentine walks and drives leading to nowhere, lakes in all sorts of apparently unnatural and impossible situations, cast iron fountains and even grandfather's clocks of the same material, unlovely girder bridges, little mountains and miniature alps, an assortment of rockery stones, arranged like so many grave stones, weak and sickly conifers sadly proclaiming their alienship; all the outcome of exactly the same set of ideas, the whole being subject for ridicule and an exhibition of misdirected energy.[42]

In the place of this somewhat depressing view of the end of the Romantic Movement Mawson suggested, as in 1892 did Reginald Blomfield, a more formal and architectural approach. The lines of battle were drawn when William Robinson took violent exception to the return to the formal garden. In 1883 he had edited *The English Flower Garden*, which included a contribution by Gertrude Jekyll. He 'invented' the herbaceous border, and was the leader of the 'natural' approach to gardening. It was the architects who tried to make a move to the more formal and architectural styles. Blomfield with his strong leaning to French architecture was in the van of this movement. In the end the battle was resolved by Lutyens who, although he himself had a strong leaning to Classicism, was none the less Gertrude Jekyll's closest collaborator. Between them they were able to combine the two strands and to produce a compromise which became acceptable to both parties. However, before that came about the battle was intense, particularly as Robinson was an intemperate contestant. As Betty Massingham says: 'He quarrelled with H. J. Elwes, traveller and gardener, with George Maw, authority on the genus crocus before Mr Bowles, and with Sir Reginald Blomfield, the architect. He kept up a persistent battle with the gentle director of Kew, Sir Joseph Hooker, on account of Latin plant-labelling, and he angered the villagers when he bought his manor house, Gravetye, in a needless fuss over a right of way. . . '.[43] He even managed to annoy Lutyens when discussing the possibility that Lutyens might work at Gravetye and Lutyens was not one to be annoyed by future clients: ' "Been for a long walk with W R. I left him—he bores so . . .",'[44] Lutyens wrote.

The garden at Redcourt is interesting in that it was laid out only two years after these garden books had been written, but it reflects this move to formality only in the layout of the courts exactly next to the house; the rest is landscaped garden.

Nothing here is particularly extreme, all follows the traditions set by Bridgeman and Kent in the middle of the eighteenth century. There are formal courts around the house, but these slowly change to more informal landscaping as the garden moves away from the house. Indeed the only difference between this and Jekyll's woodland garden is that she tended to bring her trees nearer to the house; Lutyens insisted on more architecture around his houses than ever Newton did. Some later Newton houses were grander, and at his 1906 Ardenrun he set off his large and largely symmetrical house with a grandiose 'French' garden of terraces and lawns leading to radiating paths between shrubs. But even here this is not allowed to continue more than 160 feet from the house; after that all becomes natural as the garden sweeps down to a landscaped lake.

Chapter five

STUDIO, OAK PARK 1895

1893 was the year of the Chicago Columbian Exposition. This has always been considered a watershed in the history of American architecture. From this date, for a short though important period, Classicism triumphed over the commercial style of the Chicago skyscraper. As William H. Jordy put it: 'The juxtaposition of the domed, lagooned, and colonnaded White City of the Columbian Exposition of 1893 and the harsh reality of the tall commercial buildings of the Loop is among the familiar and dramatic confrontations in American cultural history. Why, when Chicagoans and many visitors to the city admired the severe commercial buildings, did this approach fade so speedily in the nineties?'[45]

To Louis Sullivan it seemed the end of everything; from then on life seemed to ebb out of his architecture. To Frank Lloyd Wright, just starting practice, it seemed the destruction of an American architecture which was just beginning to flourish. It seemed to him that the rich east coast sophisticates, many of whom had been trained in that most sinful of cities, Paris, had triumphed over the sons of simple farmers who had built their farmsteads with their own hands. To Lloyd Wright an English type of Arts and Crafts Movement was unnecessary—had not his own uncles broken the ground and themselves built their own homesteads? However, Chicago had come a long way from those simple rustic days (though only forty years in actual time) and it was now one of the richest cities in America. And these newly rich men, who probably hadn't read Ruskin, believed that Classicism was the highest level of man's architectural endeavour. Here was the problem: a homespun architecture on the one hand, which as Lloyd Wright saw it would be consciously simple and developed low for the open spaces (in spite of the fact that most of his buildings were built on suburban plots laid out on a grid-iron pattern); on the other hand others believed that in a relatively rough place you should supply a smoothly Classical architecture. Some like McKim, Mead and White, whose brilliant Boston Public Library was completed in 1893, were able to produce seductive masterpieces in this style. It is interesting to see here

FRONT (EAST) ELEVATION

Boston Public Library, Copley Square, Boston, Mass. McKim, Mead and White 1888–95.
Elevation to Copley Square (above) and details (right)

the same situation which was to be tackled a few years later by Baker and Lutyens
in the even newer cities of South Africa, and to see that they also turned to
Classicism.

To an Englishman, used to seeing the clumsy attempts at Classicism by even
the most learned mid-nineteenth century architect, the Boston Public Library
comes as a surprise. Here is a Classical building designed in 1888 for which there
is no need to make any form of apology. It has all the intellectual clarity of the
Beaux-Arts schools, with the lightness of the best of the Italian Renaissance. One
only has to compare, as Jordy does,[46] the Brattle Square elevation with that of
Labrouste's Bibliothèque Sainte-Geneviève of 1844–50, on which it is closely
modelled, to see this. The Paris facade is much too long—nineteen bays as compared with Boston's thirteen—and it runs through with very little emphasis,
whereas at Boston there are three full arches at the entrance. Beside these arches
there are triplets of delicate bracketed lamps, which sweep out from the wall
with a spiky Venetian elegance contrasting perfectly with the rather solemn
rusticated base. As far as we are concerned the interiors are possibly of more
interest since they in many ways represent much better the ideals of rich and
sophisticated America than does the Frank Lloyd Wright prairie house. One
enters through a simple vaulted hall with Adamesque decorations. To either side
are the newspaper rooms, also vaulted on simple Doric columns in a French
Beaux-Arts manner, with the vaulting bricks showing. Immediately to the front,

ROOF CRESTING 'A'
$\frac{3}{8}"=1'-0"$

COPPER CRESTING

TOP OF POLE 15'-0" ABOVE RIDGE

Ⓐ

STONE CORNICE COPPER CHENEAU

CORNICE 'B'
$\frac{3}{8}"=1'-0"$

ELEVATION

PROFILE

COPPER CHENEAU AND GUTTER

WROUGHT IRON GRILLE 'C'
$\frac{3}{8}"=1'-0"$

Ⓑ

THE PUBL.T BY THE PEOPLE AND DEDIC

Ⓔ

Ⓑ

Ⓔ

FREE-TO-ALL

Ⓒ

CENTERLINE OF FACADE

Ⓓ

WROUGHT IRON GRILLE

IMPOST 'D'
$\frac{3}{8}"=1'-0"$

ELEVATION & SECTION OF MAIN FACADE
SCALE $\frac{1}{8}"=1'-0"$

IMPOST 'E'
$\frac{3}{8}"=1'-0"$

EXTERIOR DETAILS
THE BOSTON PUBLIC LIBRARY, BOSTON, MASSACHUSETTS, McKIM, MEAD AND WHITE, ARCHITECTS

Boston Public Library – perspectives; entrance hall (top left), main staircase (top right), reading room (bottom left) and delivery room (bottom right)

is the grand staircase in a golden marble, defended half way up by great lions facing inwards. At the upper level there are panels painted by Puvis de Chavannes whose pale blues contrast better with the golden marble here than they do in the Hôtel de Ville in Paris which has a similarly painted staircase built in a cold blue stone. In front is the great vaulted reading room, lit up high by tall arched windows, though down below the book stacks are lit at eye height by small windows which read as slots on the outside, a trick taken straight from Labrouste. The catalogue room (originally the delivery room) is in a contrasting red and dark brown; here all the architecture is Italian Renaissance with magnificent Corinthian doorcases and a great Albertiesque fireplace. In contrast to this Classicism are the murals by Edward Abbey of the Legend of the Holy Grail, dark glowing colours with red predominating, against the multitude of golden haloes which glitter through the dark haze. This is a magnificently complete room, which even with its present card indexes and other library paraphernalia still maintains its magic. To the centre of the building there is an enchanting courtyard—a contrast to all this Gothic gloom and Classical grandeur. There is a Doric arcade at the ground floor and above three storeys on all sides giving a perfectly proportioned serene enclosure. This is a small court, somewhere where you can browse through a book taken from the shelves. Obviously based on so many Italian courts it none the less has a softer more remote quality, since here the arcades are not the main central circulation space but rather a cloister, as in a college.

Before this McKim, Mead and White had been known as house architects, most of their finest work, including what in England would be called their Neo-Georgian houses having already been built before the 1890s. The 1890s seem to have been a fallow period in American architecture. McKim, Mead and White turned more and more to large commercial buildings, and Frank Lloyd Wright was yet to make his mark, most of the houses by which he is remembered being built after the turn of the century. That great master of house building, H. H. Richardson, had died in 1886, and the Shingle School, whose work he had largely inspired, had had its greatest flowering in the late 1880s. The school of Richardson particularly understood the need for careful detailing. The wood details in Richardson's small library buildings, which he built in the suburbs of Boston in the late 1870s and early 1880s, are some of the finest ever produced. His use of turned balusters contrasted with solids has an elegant delicacy only seen in the finest furniture-makers of the period, such as Collinson and Lock in England. The ceiling beams to the staircase of the Glessner House in Chicago (1885–7), which so tellingly contrast with the elegant balusters, are of a solidity not to be found in any of the work of Shaw. Indeed whenever a Richardson house is compared with a Shaw house on the ground, the American's work always seems preferable, through the quality of its detailing and craftsmanship. This is a situation which is reversed when the buildings of Frank Lloyd Wright are compared with those of Lutyens. Lutyens's detailing and workmanship always seems to be sounder than those of the American, in spite of Wright's much vaunted craft background.

The career of Frank Lloyd Wright started in the early 1890s. Two years older than Lutyens, like Mackintosh he had started by training in the offices of successful commerical architects, Adler and Sullivan of Chicago. Sullivan was one of the great designers of his generation, an unrivalled pattern designer in a period of great pattern designs. Although his partner was a successful commercial architect, Sullivan was never really happy in designing office blocks in the fastest growing and most corrupt city in the world. He passed on to Wright, who called him his 'Lieber Meister', the belief that the 'art architect' should in some way keep himself superior from the day-to-day business of building commercially. All Wright's admiration for Sullivan did not stop him taking on a number of private commissions, when he should have been working full time for his 'Meister'. Between 1890 and 1893, when he set up on his own, he built a number of houses both under Sullivan's name and his own, in the artistic suburb of Oak Park, where he was living. These were often traditional clapboarded houses, with steep pitched roofs and tall chimneys. In 1892 he built a house for George Blossom which is a straightforward Colonial Revival house, with Venetian windows and a circular columned porch. This would seem to have been his only attempt at the Neo-Colonial style. The buildings he did under Sullivan's name, sometimes for members of the Sullivan family, are more daring. The Albert Sullivan house of 1892 was a delightful small town house with a first-floor bay window and a deep cornice to the flat roof incised with formalized Sullivanesque decoration.

It was in 1895 that Frank Lloyd Wright can be said to have arrived, with the completion of his own house and studio which he built at Oak Park. Like so many architects' own houses, this is not an entirely satisfactory building. Wright seems to have thrown into it every idea that his clients had rejected. Architects so often feel, particularly when they are at the beginning of their careers, that none of their best ideas will ever get beyond the drawing board and so they leap at the possibility of building them into their own homes. This can, of course, be a good thing since they will then be forced to recognize that ideas that are bad must be rejected; good ideas on the other hand may be seen by clients and taken up. This is particularly true of Wright's Oak Park Studio, set in the very centre of what was to be his most important collection of clients. In the first nineteen years of his career he built up a successful practice from this studio. However, this, like everything else in Wright's turbulent life was not to last. In 1909 he left his wife, children and practice and went to Europe with the wife of Edwin H. Cheney, one of his neighbours and clients, thus abruptly terminating his connection with Oak Park. His staff, and in particular the very talented draughtsman Marion Mahoney and Walter Burley Griffin, carried on his practice, though the scandal, and also a change in taste, had put an end to his suburban work by the outbreak of the Great War.

The Studio had been started as long ago as 1889, when Wright first joined Sullivan as an assistant, but its real importance began when he started to build up his own practice and to employ staff in 1893, when he was commissioned to build the Winslow House. H. Allen Brooks says in *The Prairie School*:

The Studio was the center of Frank Lloyd Wright's creative activity, and it was there that numerous architects received their training. . . . Yet it was not a school, but rather an unconventional office where employees came in response to Wright's work, and assisted according to their skill.

The environment was congenial—it was an informal, pleasant place to work. There were four rooms: a reception hall, small octagonal library, Wright's office, and a two-storey drafting room accommodating a half-dozen desks. The furnishings were of Wright's design—Japanese prints and miniature casts of classical sculpture, numerous vases and bowls, and a profusion of foliage and wild flowers . . . In this home-like setting, a close rapport existed among the members; much was shared in common—their work, their admiration of Wright (whose unusual attire some adopted), and even their political views . . .

Beside the Studio, and connected to it, was Wright's home. . . . Wright, as announced on his stationery, was at the Studio from 8 to 11, at his Chicago office from 12 to 2, and at the Studio again evenings after 7. Thus it was his principal place of work, his drafting room at home.[47]

The Studio was also the place where the Wright style is properly seen for the first time.

The Winslow House of 1893, built a short distance away in River Forest, which is the neighbouring suburb to Oak Park, cannot really be said to have the full Wright character. To the front it is a simple block topped by a great hipped roof with heavily overhanging eaves. The ground floor walls are of roman brick with stone trim to the windows and in the centre. To the left there is a *porte-cochère* and to the right a bay window. On the front elevation of the ground floor there are four sash windows, with a lower door in the middle, the central three elements being brought slightly forward. On the first floor a terracotta decorated frieze runs to the full depth of the three sash windows. It is a surprisingly staid affair, almost Neo-Georgian, with its sash windows and its rather forced symmetry. It seems more to have been designed by a Classical architect who late in life has decided to eschew Classical ornament while keeping to Classical forms. There are definite similarities between this house and the houses that Giles Gilbert Scott built in St. Marylebone and Hampstead in London in the 1930s. There are the same symmetrical shapes under a hipped roof, the use of planes brought forward one in front of the other, and the same habit of emphasizing the sash windows. Whether Scott was influenced directly by the Wright design is another matter, though he was an architect who looked at other people's work. Although Wright never used these forms again in a house, they became the commonplace for commercial architects who had been grounded in Classicism, and were used with considerable success on the Art Deco skyscrapers in the 1920s. From there they penetrated to England and into Scott's work, for instance the Battersea Power Station bears a distinct relationship to Wright's early commercial buildings like the Larkin Building at Buffalo of 1903, which is in its turn clearly Classical in all but the specific use of the orders.

In his own house on the other hand Wright took another, and for him probably more satisfactory, line. The houseplace is emphasized with great roofs. Throughout his career, a great outspreading roof was always to dominate Wright's houses. The flat-roofed factory style of his other buildings was only acceptable for houses on the dry warm west coast of California, everywhere else the roofs dominated. Even in 1950 when Wright came to review the *Lutyens Memorial Volumes* for *The Builder*, it was Lutyens's use of roofs and chimneys that he particularly picked upon to praise. Lutyens no doubt would have reciprocated the compliments. The original house has a pitched roof built straight on top of the ground floor windows, at first glance giving the impression that the house is nothing but roof-supported on an open base, the ground floor windows being well behind the plane of the wall over. To the rear of this Wright added a large, single-storey playroom for

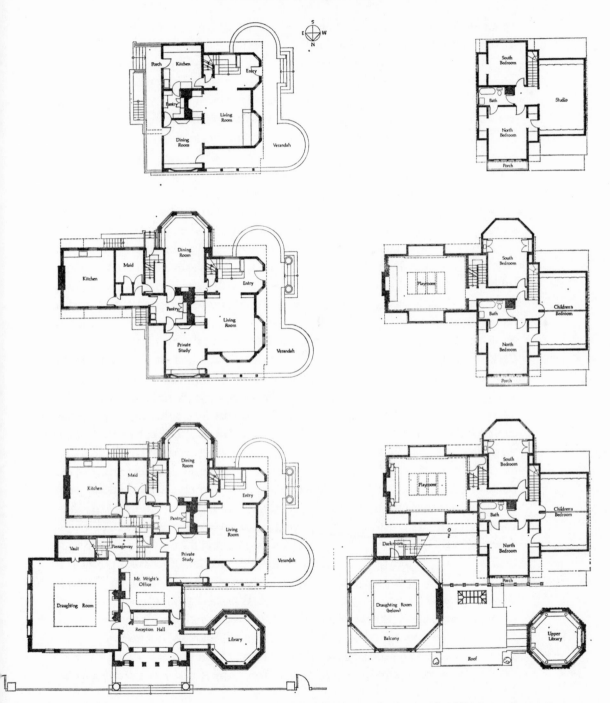

Studio, Oak Park, Frank Lloyd Wright. Ground and first floor plans. 1889 (top), 1895 (middle), 1898 (bottom)

his children. This room is dominated by a shelf which runs round at door and window head height acting as a lintel and capping to all the openings and also as a high shelf to the fireplace, a trick not dissimilar to Voysey's contemporary designs in England. Even the light fittings—cubes supporting hanging brackets—project from this cornice. Above this the ceiling curves up to a roof-light with leadwork in Wright's typically geometric yet naturalistic style. As Wright says in his autobiography, rather typically speaking highly of his own work: '. . . the playroom was a beautiful playroom and did its work well. The allegory at the end' —over the fireplace—'the Fisherman and the Genii from the Arabian Nights: the Genii, first design, done in straight-line pattern. A lesson was to be drawn from the subject matter by the children. I forget what it was. Perhaps never to be too sentimental, or curious, or meddlesome, or there would be consequences.'[48]

Behind the house and attached to it by a staircase, Wright built his Studio in 1895. The six-year difference in the two buildings show, for this is a much more sophisticated affair. The entrance is by a terrace, with steps to both sides between flat, flower-filled urns supported on the brick balustrade. These flat urns were a favourite motif of early Wright buildings and he used them with tremendous effect on his terraces and also at corners of flat roofs in the Heurtley House, Oak Park of 1902, the Coonley House, Riverside of 1909 and the Imperial Hotel, Tokyo 1915–16. Lutyens was also fond of these urns in his gardens but in his Viceroy's House, New Delhi he too places flat urns on the cornice of the building. The terrace leads to the entrance portice. Four squared-up columns, with capitals carved in the form of angels, support a heavy entablature of brick; to either side of these are large sculpted Michelangelesque figures—a surprisingly Classical and pretentious entrance for the studio of an architect who preached democracy to the point of mania. In a typically Edwardian manner, one enters the building, not straight ahead, but by turning to left or right, through small lobbies into the ante-room. A top-lit room with a heavy wood cornice ties together the doors and the windows, as in the playroom. By the windows overlooking the portico there is a wide desk which was used to display Wright's splendid collection of Japanese prints. It is rather a poky room and is clearly not designed in any way for relaxing in. The two-storey studio also is somewhat over-designed. Wooden pylons support horizontal strips of wood, which themselves demarcate strips of windows, or flat surfaces for drawings. The drafting tables themselves are simple enough, but there seems nowhere to put pens and the general clutter of tracings and sketches which make up the normal working atmosphere of an architect's office, however neat he may be.

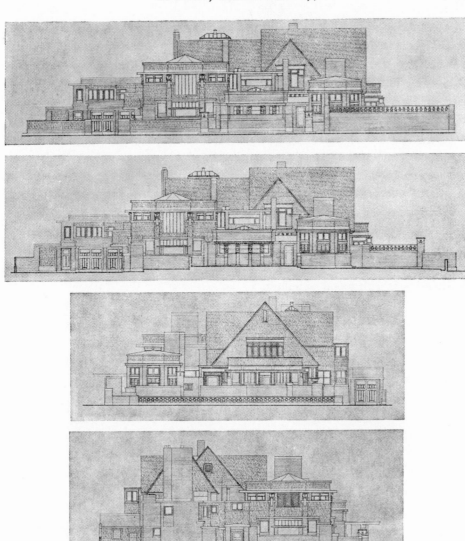

Studio, Oak Park, north elevation at side walk (top), north elevation at building (middle top), west elevation (middle lower), east elevation (bottom)

The gallery front was painted with edifying texts and carefully posed flower arrangements in pots balanced on columns. Games of cricket, or rather baseball, played with T-square and rubbers, like those played in Lutyens's office could never have occurred here. It was not for nothing that during this period Wright's work was being praised by the magazine *The House Beautiful*, whereas Lutyens was publicized by *Country Life*. Although it all may seem rather too precious, none the less there is in these early Wright houses an understanding of the true nature of house design which could be as easily appreciated in brash Chicago as in rural Surrey. Although Wright clearly saw little need to be tied down by any particular style, building as he was on virgin land on square suburban blocks, he none the less did not find it necessary to ignore the recognized requirements of the house, enclosure, warmth and welcome. At least in these early days his approach to each problem was completely open-minded; the client's requirements dictated the plan and the materials to be used. The demands of a one-family house do not require the use of new materials of startling constructions and so Wright did not use them. At the same time when it was necessary for him to use steel, and his great cantilevered balconies and slots of windows could not have been achieved without modern engineering, then he was perfectly willing to use it, and to disguise it by facing it with wood panelling.

1   Buller's Wood, Chislehurst, Kent, Ernest Newton

II   Avon Tyrell, New Forest, Hampshire, W. R. Lethaby

Standen, East Grinstead, Sussex, Philip Webb

IV   tead W d, near   Ialming, Surrey, Edwin Lutyens

v   Perrycroft, Colwall, Herefordshire, C. F. A. Voysey

VI Perrycroft, fireplace

Munstead Wood, gallery

Berrydowne, Ashe, Hampshire, Edwin Lutyens

Fulbrook, Elstead, Surrey, Edwin Lutyens

X

The Barn, Exmouth, Devon, E. S. Prior

The Pleasaunce, Overstrand, Norfolk, Edwin Lutyens

Long Copse, Ewhurst, Surrey, Alfred Powell

II   Lea Cottage, Charnwood Forest, Leicestershire, E. Gimson
(the wing on the left is a modern extension)

Moor Crag, Windermere, Cumbria, C. F. A. Voysey

Broadleys, Windermere, Cumbria, C. F. A. Voysey

XVI   Les Bois des Moutiers, Varengeville, Seine-Inférieure, France, Edwin Lutyens

Blackwell, Windermere, Cumbria, drawing room, M. H. Baillie Scott

XVIII   Les Bois des Moutiers, garden front

IX   Orchards, near Godalming, Surrey, Edwin Lutyens

XX   Redcourt, Haslemere, Surrey, Ernest Newton

Chapter six

MUNSTEAD WOOD 1896

EDWIN LANDSEER LUTYENS was born at Thursley in a still very rural Surrey on 29 March 1869, the son of a scientific army officer who had turned to painting hunting pictures. Although Captain Lutyens was a friend of Sir Edwin Landseer, and indeed named his eleventh child after him, he was a scientist and inventor of some importance—his range-finder was used by the British Army in the Crimean War. The combination of art and science is one that ideally all architects should have. Two other architects of this period were also related to practical scientists; Ninian Comper's brother designed aeroplanes and H. V. Lanchester (of Lanchester and Rickards) was the brother of E. V. Lanchester, the manufacturer and designer of one of the finest vintage marques of motor cars.

Since Edwin, or Ned as he always preferred to be called, was a sickly child he was not allowed to go to a boarding school and so was allowed much more freedom than most of his contemporaries. Instead of the school room or playing fields, he would wander by himself round his father's studio or the builder's yard in Thursley, where all the traditional crafts were still practised. In this way he naturally learned the craft tradition of building right from the beginning. He never had to unlearn, as so many of his more sophisticated contemporaries had to, the things that they taught, and still teach, in the schools. To him the act of building and buildings seen in three dimensions were always more important than mere exercises on the drawing board, be they ever so clever. Later in life he was to turn to elaborate proportioning systems, but he never lost his facility for seeing a building as a whole.

When he was sixteen he went, for just over a year, to the South Kensington Schools where he read architecture and where he is thought to have first met Detmar Blow. At the age of eighteen, already full of excitement and knowledge for his art, he joined Ernest George's office which at this time was, as we have seen, brim full of talent. He came under the romantic influence of that fine architect, and also got to know Norman Shaw at about this time. Christopher Hussey

D.H.–E

in his monumental life of Edwin Lutyens[49] says that Baker and Blow used to go with him to meetings of the Art Workers' Guild, though they did not become members for another thirty years. This was largely because the Guild has always required that applicants show their own completed work, which means that architects must wait many years until they are established in their own practices before they can join; most architects do not set up on their own much before their mid-thirties.

However, this long delay before working for himself was not to be Lutyens's way. In 1889, when he had just turned twenty, he was commissioned to build his first house, a small house, by the standards of the 1880s, at Crooksbury just outside Farnham in Surrey. He immediately left George and from then on there was no turning back. Next year he met Gertrude Jekyll at the house of the rhododendron expert Harry Mangles, Littleworth Cross, just a few miles away from Crooksbury which he was still building at that time. She immediately gave him advice on the garden and their collaboration was to continue until 1923 when, she at the age of eighty, they collaborated at Gledstone Hall, the last great country house that Lutyens built on a virgin site. Miss Jekyll lived for another ten years after this, dying in 1932.

Though she was born in London her family home had been at Bramley, near Guildford, from the time that she was five, so she, like Lutyens, could claim the rights of countrymen in their own countryside when the rich Londoners moved in and started building their houses on the brows of the Surrey hills. The houses then were right in the country, an unspoilt and completely rural country in the 1890s, but none the less only a few miles from a railway station with fast trains to the city. For the Surrey house was essentially suburban, designed only for living in, and not in any sense a working house, as a great house or a manor house always is—a centre point of the community, often having farmland attached with barns and orchards, stables and cowsheds. The few outbuildings to a Surrey house would contain just the equipment needed to run a large garden, and the stables needed for the family horses (seldom more than three or four) were mostly used for carriages, before the days of the motor car which came early to this rich man's land. Horses were no doubt used for hacking, but rarely for hunting; it is difficult to imagine setting off to the meet from an early Lutyens or a Voysey house. In the Cotswolds things were different. Although the rather 'artistic' Gimson and Ashbee kept away from this side of rural life, most of Dawber's houses were designed either as small manor houses or as hunting boxes, and they are still used for this purpose today.

It is an irony that Munstead Wood, in many ways the beau idéal for so many
of the suburban Surrey houses, should have been built as a working house for a
native of the country. For Gertrude Jekyll was very much a working gardener,
and she designed her house to be an efficient machine just as her garden, to which
it so perfectly belonged, was designed to display a form of gardening which was
to transform the English garden. The history of garden design, like the history of
architecture, to which of course it is related but does not slavishly follow, is the
swing between Romantic and the Classical. Often in periods of High Classicism,
such as the late eighteenth century, it was the garden that first turned more
Romantic, if a very unnaturalistic Romanticism; in the nineteenth century the
reverse was true. It was quite common to see Romantic villas set in formal gardens,
this move to formality being something that was reacted against first by William
Robinson and then by his friend Gertrude Jekyll. It is not easy at first sight to
understand precisely what is the difference between a Jekyll garden and, shall we
say, a Repton garden. One of the reasons for this is the existence of nature itself
which leads to the almost continuous cry of all garden designers that they are
returning to nature in a manner which their predecessors could not comprehend.
The result is so often nothing more than an attempt not so much to copy nature
in its natural state, which in any case a garden by its very character cannot do,
since the purpose of a garden is to offer nature tamed, but to offer a reinterpretation
of nature as seen through the eyes of the approved painters. There is nothing
necessarily wrong in this approach, since it is to artists that we look to give us
new visions of the landscape. Gertrude Jekyll had originally been a painter, and
a very sound nature painter at that. She was a friend of Ruskin and was much
influenced by Brabazon Brabazon but also by the Morris post Pre-Raphaelite
world. This was a world that combined a love of nature with a puritanical belief
that in all the arts things should be left as nearly as possible in their natural state,
and that evidently must go for gardening as it does for furniture-making and
building. Harold Falkner, whom Betty Massingham quotes in her *Miss Jekyll*,
says of Jekyll's garden at Munstead Wood:

It is to be noted that G.J.'s favouring of this colour scheme [at Munstead
Wood garden] was almost exactly William Morris's; purples and brick reds
shading into white on a green and white patterned ground. And so . . . into the
spring garden and here the scheme varies from year to year, but generally begins
with blueish white arabis, scillas and muscari (heavenly blue and the darker

ones) to creams of double arabis ... white and yellow. The flaming reds were
used further on where, on favourable occasions, a setting sun shone and burned
like the reds in old glass.[50]

All this intense colour, which Morris had himself taken from the Pre-Raphaelites,
was set against the cool woodland greens, just as in a Pre-Raphaelite picture.

There then is the Jekyll garden, but what of the house? Here too her influences
are entirely pictorial, from paintings of this period, and indeed from children's
book illustration also (Hussey is surely right to point out the immense importance
of Randolph Caldicott on the development of Lutyens's style). In these illustrations the houses are never seen as a whole, there are just delectable glimpses, a
gable here and a chimney there, perhaps a peep through the undergrowth, and
this is something that Gertrude Jekyll sought to achieve at Munstead Wood. But
only here be it noted, where she was Lutyens's client; elsewhere when he had the
upper hand her bosky woods were always kept well away from his architecture.
In fact the ideal of the house romantically growing from the accompanying foliage
was by the 1890s rather old-fashioned. Since the first importations of rhododen-
drons in the 1830s these plants had tended to get nearer and nearer to the house,
so that it was quite common to find the drives to houses overgrown in such a way
that it was only possible to catch just a few glimpses of the house as one travelled
down the twisting drive, until it was upon one, and even then it is never possible
to take in the whole facade at one time. As we have seen, Gertrude Jekyll knew
Harry Mangles well and his house at Littleworth Cross is still surrounded by great
rhododendron bushes. What Gertrude Jekyll really did was to change from this
type of exotic planting round the house to more indigenous English woodland.
But it is important to remember that it is only one side of Munstead Wood that
was planted up in this fashion. At the rear there is a formal little courtyard, and it
was in fact this formality that was to be more typical of the future Lutyens–Jekyll
gardens. Gertrude Jekyll wrote *Wood and Garden* in 1899 and *Home and Garden*
in 1900, and both these books became immensely popular with the suburban
gardener. Since Munstead Wood is used in both of them as a model, the woodland
garden ideal caught on. Anyone visiting the Chelsea Flower Show knows it is still
very much a living style of gardening.

At Munstead Wood, as is only appropriate, the garden came before the house.
Indeed the land close to the family home was bought in the early 1880s. When
Gertrude Jekyll's father died in 1875 the Jekyll family bought land a few miles

from Bromley, at Munstead Heath near Godalming, and built themselves a house there. The artistic Gertrude lived with her autocratic mother between trips abroad where she studied architecture and painted, under the tutelage of such friends as John Ruskin, and the immensely talented but now little remembered water-colourist Hercules Brabazon Brabazon. In 1883 she took up photography while it was still in its early, and in many ways best, phase, and became an excellent photographer—most of the photographs in her *Country Life* articles were by her. She had always been interested in gardening. As early as 1881 she was judging the precursor of the Chelsea Flower Show, and in 1882 she bought fifteen acres of land next door to the family garden, so that she could create a garden of her own, at the same time getting away from her mother who was by then well over seventy and as domineering as ever. After making the garden she hoped to build a house for herself. Eight years later, when the garden had matured, she met Lutyens at tea at Harry Mangle's and she had found her architect.

But she had had a long time to think about her house and she asked advice of all her friends, Brabazon Brabazon, James McNeil Whistler and of course Ruskin, the great expert on architecture. Once when she asked him about suitable English marbles for a house he replied, sounding rather like Morris, that: ' "good white-washed walls and tapestry"—are best for—"walls of rooms in cold climates" '.[51] So many of the best Edwardian houses have just this wall decoration. Over the years Gertrude Jekyll continued to live with her mother, and to go on with her garden. In 1894, Lutyens designed for her a small cottage, which they called The Hut, but it was a larger house that she had been thinking of for all those years, and her ideas were imbued with all the Webb ideals one would expect from some-one closely connected with Burne-Jones and his set. As early as the late 1870s she had made an embroidered quilt for Burne-Jones and Leighton. It was this valuable high art connection that she was able to contribute to the young Lutyens's education. If anyone can be said to have educated Lutyens in architecture it is Gertrude Jekyll. It would be interesting to know how much of Munstead is Jekyll and how much Lutyens; Jekyll gives much of the credit to Lutyens but certainly he had not designed anything to compare with its sophisticated simplicity before, and was only once or twice to reach such quality in this style again. However, Lutyens clearly had a highly receptive imagination and he was constantly turn-ing to new design ideals. If it had not been Gertrude Jekyll who introduced him to Webb, he would have found Webb for himself—the Webb of Standen, and some of the smaller houses, but not the Webb of Clouds, which was both too grand and too Gothic for Lutyens. It is ironical that Lutyens, who loved a lord like the best of us, usually built middle-class houses for second generation *nouveau riche* and never built palaces for magnates until he came to build the greatest palace of them all, the Viceroy's House, whereas Webb and Morris, both socialists, should have spent most of their lives 'pandering to' the aristocracy and 'the filthy rich'.

It is rare for a house to be built on a virgin site which is none the less in a fully matured garden. It has advantages, particularly for conceiving picturesque effects, and Munstead Wood was, in spite of Jekyll's practicality, conceived in picturesque terms. However, it has its disadvantages also since the client usually will have developed firm ideas on its siting. There was a certain amount of argument about this here; Gertrude Jekyll's position for the house was altered and finally it was sited south of the prepared garden and brought up close to an existing chestnut copse that bordered the south of the site. Thus surprisingly the main front of the house faced south 45 feet from the nearest trees. The result is that there is a splendid sense that the house was set in a clearing in a forest. It was in fact impossible to take a complete photograph of this elevation. Unfortunately recently insensitive hands have been at work here, and the trees have now been cut back with the result that a lot of the magic of the main facade has been lost, and at the same time the mullions to the windows have been altered so as to destroy its proportions.

The building of Munstead Wood was obviously a wonderful experience for the fifty-year-old gardener of genius as it was for her young architect, and since this is in many ways the key house in our parade and since in Gertrude Jekyll it has had a magnificent chronicle in the first chapter of her *Home and Garden* entitled 'How the House was Built', I make no apology for quoting the chapter almost entire. It is only when it is read in its entirety that the full flavour and delight of the best of turn of the century building can be caught. What also comes over is that rare thing, the client's total admiration for her architect. It is one of the very few honest testimonials that an architect has ever received in public print. What pleasure it must have given the still young Lutyens when he first read it in 1900, but how surprising too to find that in spite of all the praise his name is not mentioned once.

Does it often happen to people who have been in a new house only a year and a

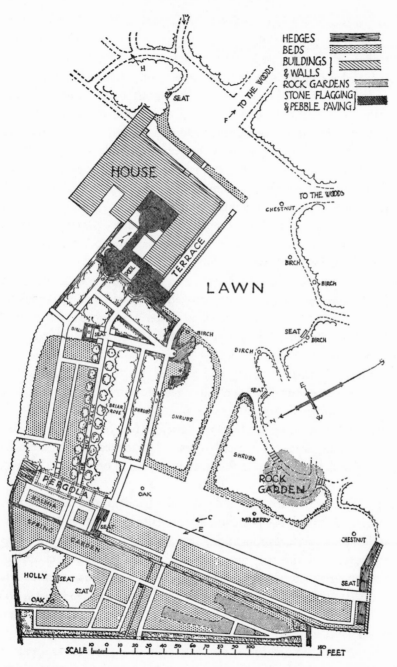

Munstead Wood, near Godalming, Surrey, E. L. Lutyens 1896. Garden plan

half, to feel as if they had never lived anywhere else? How it may be with others I know not, but my own little new-built house is so restful, so satisfying, so kindly sympathetic, that so it seems to me.

In some ways it is not exactly a new house, although no building ever before stood upon its site. But I had been thinking about it for so many years, and the main block of it and the whole sentiment of it were so familiar to my mind's eye, that when it came to be a reality I felt as if I had already been living in it a good long time. And then, from the way it is built it does not stare with newness; it is not new in any way that is disquieting to the eye; it is neither raw nor callow. On the contrary, it almost gives the impression of a comfortable maturity of something like a couple of hundred years. And yet there is nothing sham-old about it; it is not trumped-up with any specious or fashionable devices of spurious antiquity; there is no pretending to be anything that it is not—no affectation whatever.

But it is designed and built in the thorough and honest spirit of the good work of old days, and the body of it, so fashioned and feared, has, as it were taken to itself the soul of a more ancient dwelling-place. The house is not in any way a copy of any old building, though it embodies the general characteristics of the older structures of its own district.

Everything about it is strong and serviceable, and looks and feels as if it would wear and endure for ever. All the lesser permanent fittings are so well thought out and so thoroughly made that there is hardly anything that can possibly get out of order; the house is therefore free from the petty worry and dislocation of comfort so commonly caused by the weakness or inefficiency of its lesser parts, and from the frequent disturbance occasioned by workmen coming to do repairs.

Internal fittings that are constantly seen and handled, such as window-fastenings, hinges, bolts and door-latches, are specially designed and specially made, so that they are in perfect proportion, for size, weight, and strength, to the wood and iron-work to which they are related. There are no random choosings from the ironmonger's pattern-book; no clashing of styles, no meretricious ornamentation, no impudence of cast-iron substitute for honest hand-work, no moral slothfulness in the providing of all these lesser finishings. It takes more time, more trouble; it may even take a good deal of time and trouble, but then it is just right, and to see and know that it is right is a daily reward and a never-ending source of satisfaction.[52]

Now in a passage that reminds one of the most extreme and sophisticated of the Arts and Crafts architects, one feels the passionate belief in the doing of natural things the proper way that was all around at that time. Even as close to London as Godalming there were still country builders able to continue in the traditions of their forefathers, provided they were prompted rightly.

Some heavy oak timber-work forms a structural part of the inner main framing of the house. Posts, beams, braces, as well as doors and their frames, window-frames and mullions, stairs and some floors, are of good English oak, grown in the neighbourhood. I suppose a great London builder could not produce such work. He does not go into the woods and buy the standing timber, and season it slowly in a roomy yard for so many years, and then go round with the archi-tect's drawing and choose the piece that exactly suits the purpose. The old country builder, when he has to get out a cambered beam or a curved brace, goes round his yard and looks out the log that grew in the actual shape, and taking off two outer slabs by handwork in the sawpit, chops it roughly to shape with his side-axe and works it to the finished face with the adze, so that the completed work shall for ever bear the evidence of his skill in the use of these grand old tools, and show a treatment absolutely in sympathy with the nature and quality of the material.

Though the work of the London builder is more technically perfect, it has none of the vigorous vitality and individual interest of that of the old country-man, and all ways of working according to local tradition are necessarily lost. The Londoner has to take the great baulks of foreign timber as they come from the merchants' stacks, and shape them with the pitiless steam-saw; the timber then passes through several hands, each working a different machine at every stage of its conversion. The very atmosphere of the crowded London yard, with its fussy puffings of steam, its rumble, roar, and scream of machinery, the many subdivisions of processes of manipulation, all seem calculated to destroy any sentiment of life and character in the thing made. And what have we in the end? A piece of work that, though it has the merit of mechanical precision, has lost all human interest; it follows the architect's drawing with absolute fidelity, but is lifeless and inert and totally unsympathetic.

I am far from wishing to disparage accuracy or technical perfection of work-manship, but in the case of structural timber that forms part of a house of the large cottage class such as mine, and in a district that still possesses the precious heritage of a traditional way of using and working it, such mechanical perfection is obviously out of place.

Then there is the actual living interest of knowing where the trees one's house is built of really grew. The three great beams, ten inches square, that stretch across the ceiling of the sitting-room, and do other work besides, and bear up a good part of the bedroom space above (they are twenty-eight feet long), were growing fifteen years ago a mile and a half away, on the outer edge of a fir wood just above a hazel-fringed hollow lane, whose steep sandy sides, here and there level enough to bear a patch of vegetation, grew tall Bracken and great Foxgloves, and the finest wild Canterbury Bells I ever saw. At the top of the western bank, their bases hidden in cool beds of tall Fern in summer, and clothed in its half-fallen warmth of rusty comfort in winter, and in spring-time standing on their carpet of blue wild Hyacinth, were these tall oaks; one or two of their fellows still remain. Often driving up the lane from early childhood I used to see these great grey trees, in twilight looking almost ghostly against the darkly-mysterious background of the sombre firs. And I remember always thinking how straight and tall they looked, for these sandy hills do not readily grow such great oaks as are found in the clay weald a few miles to the south and at the foot of our warm-soiled hills. But I am glad to know that my beams are these same old friends, and that the pleasure that I had in watching them green and growing is not destroyed but only changed as I see them stretching above me as grand beams of solid English oak.[53]

After that she tells a marvellous ghost story that has nothing to do with Munstead Wood, and then continues with a tour round the house; but before we continue with her, a brief discussion of Lutyens's design might be worth while. Up till now Lutyens had tended to use brick and a plethora of tile-hanging, as indeed he was to on many other later houses, but at Munstead all is very much more chaste. Here the house is built of local Bargate stone and is roofed in local red tiles. The only thing that reminds us of the older Norman Shaw tradition is the small amount of half-timbering to the upstairs passage to the northern courtyard, though this is used structurally and has a definite purpose since, as the passage is cantilevered out from the downstairs wall, it must be light. The plan is basically a U-shape, and Lutyens as usual cannot resist playing tricks with it; but on the outside everything is serene. The splendid south front consists of two large gables which sweep down to the top of the ground floor windows, and are balanced, asymmetri-

Munstead Wood – perspective of garden front by Raffles Davison

cally to either side by low wings, one on the same plane as the main facade, the other projecting into the garden (see plate IV). The left-hand gable supports a tall chimney at right angles to the facade which is in turn echoed by another chimney above the gable on the roof line. As Gertrude Jekyll says the entrance is low and extremely unpretentious. Falkner knew it when Gertrude Jekyll lived there; he wrote: ' "The entrance was through an arched opening in a wall in a stone-lined corridor . . . Everything was always dead quite. The bell may have made some sort of tinkle or buzz at its other end, but the result at the operating end was nil until the door opened, and one was ushered in through a stone and oak hall and corridor with glints of bright brasswork, old oak and blue china." '[54]

This entrance porch is in fact the low wing that sticks out from the house and through a loggia opening gives one a glimpse of part of the garden as one waits to be let in. At the rear of the house, where the half-timbering cantilevers over between the arms of the wings, there is a little formal garden, with stone steps, the steps dropping down to two square pools. It is the first example of the Lutyens–Jekyll passion for playing architectural tricks with water, which was to find its final flowering in the splendid sub-Mughal gardens at Delhi. All the details are of the simplest: rectangular leaded panes are set in unchamfered oak frames set flush to

Munstead Wood – perspective of rear courtyard by Raffles Davison

the wall with the dowels prominent; only at the doorway is there the slightest suggestion of a Tudor arch.

The plan is complex yet simple. Having come through the porch with its views of the garden we enter a dark little vestibule—reminiscent of so many unpretentious cottage entrances—and then down a corridor, past the dining room—a small rather formal room—into the hall, the main living room of the house. From this large room, the staircase rises beside a great stone fireplace. To the right of this is the entrance to the workshop. Gertrude Jekyll always liked to make things, and in this room she had a carpenter's bench and a whole collection of tools, some used and others on display. In this room Lutyens built a quite absurdly grandiose fireplace which he was to repeat at Fulbrook in a much more formal setting. From the keystone in a flat brick arch there swings a curving vault, spreading about 5 feet out into the room and to either side of the fireplace, at its end supported on oak brackets. It is an early example of Lutyens's fascination with form, which was never to leave him even if it in the end developed into grotesqueries, which this fireplace only just avoids. One feels that had it not been for the stabilizing hand of Gertrude Jekyll, one would have seen something even more extreme.

The staircase rises five steps until it reaches the bookroom that Gertrude Jekyll mentions. It is interesting to see the mastery with which Lutyens handles its windows on the south elevation; since it is a half storey up it shows a break on the facade. This is carried off by allowing the eaves of this part of the roof to come

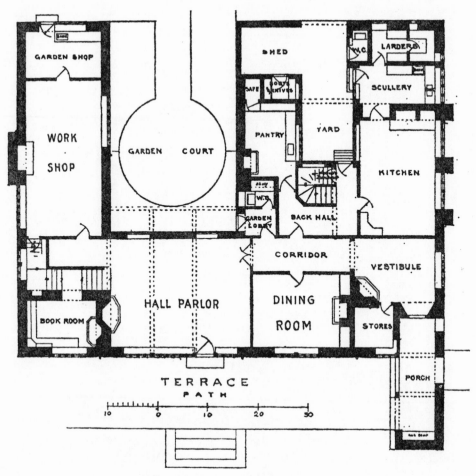

Munstead Wood – ground floor plans

higher, in fact lining up with the end of the gable's eaves. The fact that the whole elevation could not be seen at one time helped him to get away with this sleight of hand. Under the bookroom, steps go down to a small cellar. The staircase then continues up a further four steps to a generous landing, and from here it continues up to a corridor 10 feet wide, almost the width of the room (see plate VII). These wide first floor corridors are one of Lutyens's great contributions to house planning. Later he would use almost half of his available upstairs space for circulation, until in the second half of Folly Farm in 1912 practically all the upstairs is corridor of various sorts, the bedrooms being tucked in where they will. However, Munstead

Vestibule Fireplace

Hall Parlour
Munstead Wood
E L Lutyens Arch.

Munstead Wood – perspectives by Raffles **Davison;** entrance vestibule (top) and hall parlour (bottom)

was many years before such insanity, and the great corridor here with its horizontal leaded windows running between the great oak posts, all of course completely structural, reflected in the glazing to the cupboards on the other side, is
entirely usable—both as a corridor and a pleasant place in which to potter, for
Gertrude Jekyll kept many treasures in her cupboards. The planning of the kitchen
quarters is somewhat casual. Later in a house like Homewood at Knebworth,
Lutyens was able to sort out the complex problems of arranging for the front door
to be relatively close to the staff areas, while keeping the kitchen well away from
the rest of the house. Here there is a devious route from the kitchen to the front
door, as indeed there is for food service to the dining room. Another criticism of the
plan, which in these minor details shows it to be still the work of an inexperienced
planner, is the way in which the formal garden cannot be approached, or even seen,
from the house.

Let us now let Miss Jekyll take us round her house:

My house is approached by a footpath from a quiet, shady lane, entering by a
close-paled hand-gate. There is no driving road to the front door. I like
the approach to a house to be as quiet and modest as possible, and in this case
I wanted it to tell its own story as the way in to a small dwelling standing in
wooded ground. The path runs to an arch in the eastern wall of the house,
leading into a kind of long porch, or rather a covered projection of lean-to
shape. This serves as a dry approach to the main door, and also as a comfortable
full-stop to the southern face of the house, returning forward square with that
face. Its lower western side shows flat arches of heavy timber work which are
tied and braced across to the higher eastern wall by more of the same. Any one
entering looks through to the garden picture of lawn and trees and low broad
steps, and dwarf dry wall crowned with the hedge of Scotch Briers. As the
house is on ground that falls gently to the north, the lawn on this, the southern
side, is on a higher level and standing in front of the house and looking towards
the porch, the illustration shows how it looks from the garden side in late
summer when the tubs of Hydrangea are in full flower. The main door leads
into a roomy entrance and then to a short passage, passing the small dining-
room on the left, to the sitting-room.

The sitting-room is low and fairly large, measuring twenty-seven by twenty-
one feet, and eight feet from floor to ceiling. A long low range of window lights
it from the south, and in the afternoon a flood of western light streams in down

the stairs from another long window on the middle landing. The stairs come straight into the room, and with the wide, hooded, stone-built fireplace take up the greater part of its western end. The windows, after the manner of the best old buildings of the country, are set with their oak mullions flush with the outer face of the wall, so that as the wall is of a good thickness, every window has a broad oak window-board, eighteen inches wide. The walls are twenty-two inches thick, and as the local stone is pervious to water for some years after being freshly used, they are built hollow, with an outer stone wall nearly fifteen inches thick, then a three-inch air-space, and an inner wall of brick firmly bound to the outer with iron ties.

The steps of the stairs are low and broad. There are four short flights and three square landings; the first landing giving access to a small book-room, which has no door, but is entered by a curtained arch. It is a pleasant little room; a room good to work and read in. It always makes me think of St. Jerome's Study in the National Gallery; not that it has the least likeness in appearance, but because it has that precious feeling of repose that disposes the mind to study. The south wall is mostly window, the west wall is all books; northward is the entrance arch and an oak bureau, and on the fourth side is another bookcase and the fireplace.

The stairs feel pleasantly firm and solid; the main posts at the angles go right down and rest on brick masonry. The longest measures thirteen feet, and it was a puzzle to the builder how to turn the finial out of the solid, for no such work in this house is stuck on, and no lathe that he had could turn so great a length; but as there is no problem in woodwork that a clever carpenter cannot solve, he just had it worked out by hand.

The oak gallery to which the stairs lead is sixty feet long and ten feet wide. One feels some hesitation about praising one's own possessions, but it is a part of the house that gives me so much pleasure, and it meets with so much approval from those whose knowledge and taste I most respect, that I venture to describe it in terms of admiration. Thanks to my good architect, who conceived the place in exactly such a form as I had desired, but could not have described, and to the fine old carpenter who worked to his drawings in an entirely sympathetic manner, I may say that it is a good example of how English oak should be used in an honest building, whose only pretension is to be of sound work done with the right intention, of material used according to the capability of its nature and the purpose designed, with due regard to beauty of proportion and simplicity of effect. And because the work has been planned and executed in this spirit, this gallery, and indeed the whole house, has that quality—the most valuable to my thinking that a house or any part of it can possess—of conducing to repose and serenity of mind. In some mysterious way it is imbued with an expression of cheerful, kindly welcome, of restfulness to mind and body, of abounding satisfaction to eye and brain.

It is just these desirable qualities that are most rarely to be found in a modern building, and that one so much appreciates in those examples that remain to us of the domestic architecture of our Tudor and Jacobean reigns, and still more frequently in foreign lands in the monastic buildings. Indeed, one of the wishes I expressed to the architect was that I should like a little of the feeling of a convent, and, how I know not, unless it be by virtue of solid structure and honest simplicity, he has certainly given it me.

The gallery is amply lighted from the left by a long range of north window looking to the garden court. On the right are deep cupboards with panelled oak doors, only broken by panelled recesses giving access to the doors of three bedrooms.[55]

The space of the gallery is not encumbered with furniture, but has one long oak table of a fine simple type, oak linen chests (locally 'hutches'), and a chair or two. The large table is where needlework is cut out and arranged. I chose a room for my own bedroom near the further end of the gallery in order that I might the oftener enjoy a walk down its length, and every morning as I come out of my room, hungry for breakfast and ready for the day's work, I feel thankful that my home has on its upper floor so roomy and pleasant a highway.[56]

The final part is both a description of the actual building of the house and praise of the British workmen of the day, still country craftsmen who were using techniques that had little changed since medieval times. It is one of the most fortunate things that there were at this time architects who were able to make use of these men who within a generation were to be both physically and mentally destroyed by the Great War and to become virtually extinct. The irony is that had it not been for that war there is every chance that the next generation of architects would have carried on from where their elders left off and would have insisted on using the highest craftsmanship even in non-country conditions. However, this was not to be and now it is virtually impossible to find anyone capable of even the simplest techniques that Gertrude Jekyll here describes.

The building of the house was done in the happiest way possible, a perfect understanding existing between the architect, the builder, and the proprietor. Such a concourse of salutary conditions is, I fear, rare in house-building. It often happens that conflicting interests are at war with one another; indeed it seems to be usually supposed that the builder and the architect are in some degree antagonistic. Hence it arises that in buildings of any importance the architect has to post an expensive clerk of the works on the job, to see that the builder does not cheat the proprietor.

But where all three are reasonable and honest folk, at one in their desire of doing a piece of good work, this extra source of expense is not needed, and the whole thing, instead of being a cause of waste and worry and anxiety during its making, and possibly a disappointment when completed, is like an interesting game of serious and absorbing interest, every move having some distinct bearing on the one to follow; every operation being performed in its due sequence to the gradual building up of the completed structure.

From beginning to end there was no contract. The usual specifications were made out and were priced by a London firm, and as the total came out not greatly in excess of what the house might cost, the builder was set to work with the understanding that certain reductions should be made where we could as the work went on, and it was arranged that he should send in all accounts for payment at the end of every month, and that he should receive in addition a sum of ten per cent, on the whole amount of the cost.

The architect has a thorough knowledge of the local ways of using the sandstone that grows in our hills and that for many centuries has been the building material of the district, and of all the lesser incidental methods of adapting means to ends that mark the well-defined way of building of the country so that what he builds seems to grow naturally out of the ground. I always think it a pity to use in any one place the distinctive methods of another. Every part of the country has its own traditional ways, and if these have in the course of many centuries become 'crystallised' into any particular form we may be sure that there is some good reason for it, and it follows that the attempt to use the ways and methods of some distant place is sure to give an impression as of something uncomfortably exotic, of geographical confusion, of the perhaps right thing in the wrong place.

For I hold as a convincing canon in architecture that every building should look like what it is. How well that fine old architect George Dance understood this when he designed the prison of Newgate! On the other hand, does not every educated person feel the shock of incongruity when a building presents a huge front as of a Greek temple, and when, instead of the leisurely advance of classically-draped worshipper and of flower-garlanded procession of white-robed priest and sacrificial beast, such as he has some right to expect, he has to put up with a stream of hurrying four-wheelers with piles of railway-passenger's luggage and bicycles chained to their tops.

O! for a little simple truth and honesty in building, as in all else that is present to the eye and touches daily life!

Many of my friends, knowing that I dabble in construction and various handicrafts, have asked whether I did not design my house myself. To which question, though I know it is meant to be kind and flattering, I have to give an emphatically negative answer. An amateur who has some constructive perceptions may plan and build a house after a fashion; and to him and his it may be, and quite rightly and honestly, a source of supreme satisfaction. But it will always lack the qualities that belong to the higher knowledge, and to the firm grasp of the wider expression. There will be bungles and awkward places, and above all a want of reposeful simplicity both in and out. If an addition is made it will look like a shame-faced patch boggled on to a garment; a patch that is always conscious of its intrusive presence. Whereas an addition planned by a good architect will be like one of those noble patches such as were worked by some Italian genius in needlework two hundred years ago. The garment needed a patch, and a patch was put in, but instead of a clumsy attempt being made to conceal it, it was glorified and ornamented and turned into some graceful arabesque of leaf and flower and tendril, enriched by cunning needlework of thread of cord or delicate golden purfling, so that what began by being an unsightly rent, grew under the skilful fingers, quickened by the ready wit of the fertile brain, into a thing of enduring beauty and delight.

When it came to the actual planning of the house I was to live in—I had made one false start a year or two before—I agreed with the architect how and where the house should stand, and more or less how the rooms should lie together. And I said that I wanted a small house with plenty of room in it—there are seven bedrooms in all—and that I disliked small narrow passages, and would have nothing poky or screwy or ill-lighted.

So he drew a plan, and we soon came to an understanding, first about the main block and then about the details. Every portion was carefully talked over, and I feel bound to confess that in most cases out of the few in which I put pressure on him to waive his judgment in favour of my wishes, I should have done better to have left matters alone. My greatest error in this way was in altering the placing of the casements (hinged lights that open). In every long range of lights he had marked as a casement not the end lights but the ones next to them. I thought the end lights would be more easily accessible, especially in bedrooms, on account of the rather unusually large and long dressing-tables, that I like; and the casements were placed accordingly. Afterwards I found this arrangement so inconvenient, on account of rain wetting curtains, and of the flying in and out of the thin linen ones that act as blinds, that within a year I had them altered so as to be as originally designed.

Naturally in the course of our discussions we had many an amicable fight, but I can only remember one when one might say that any 'fur flew'. I do not now remember the details of the point in question, only that it was about something that would have added a good bit to the expense for the sake of external appearance; and I wound up my objections by saying with some warmth: 'My house is to be built for me to live in and to love; it is not to be built as an exposition of architectonic inutility!' I am not in the habit of using long words, and as these poured forth like a rushing torrent under the pressure of fear of overdoing the cost, I learnt, from the architect's crushed and somewhat frightened demeanour, that long words certainly have their use, if only as engines of warfare of the nature of the battering-ram.

How I enjoyed seeing the whole operation of the building from its very beginning! I could watch any clever workman for hours. Even the shovelling and shaping of ground is pleasant to see, but when it comes to a craftsman of long experience using the tool that seems to have become a part of himself, the attraction is so great that I can hardly tear myself away. What a treat it was to see the foreman building a bit of wall! He was the head man on the job, a bricklayer by trade, but apparently the master of all tools. How good it was to see him at work, to observe the absolute precision, the perfect command of the tool and material; to see the ease of it, the smiling face, the rapid, almost dancing movements, the exuberant though wholly unaffected manifestation of ready activity; the little graceful ornaments of action in half-unconscious flourishes of the trowel, delicate *fioriture* of consummate dexterity, and all looking so pleasantly easy that the movements seemed less like those of a man plying his trade than such as one sees in a strong young creature frisking for very pleasure of glad life.

I was living in a tiny cottage on the same ground, only eighty yards away from the work. How well I got to know all the sounds! The chop and rush of the trowel taking up its load of mortar from the board, the dull slither as the moist mass was laid as a bed for the next brick in the course; the ringing music of the soft-tempered blade cutting a well-burnt brick, the muted tap of its shoulder settling it into its place, aided by the down-bearing pressure of the finger-tips of the left hand; the sliding scrape of the tool taking up the overmuch mortar that squeezed out of the joint, and the neat slapping of it into the cross-joint. The sharp double tap on the mortar board, a signal that more stuff was wanted. Then at the mortar-mixing place the fat popping of the slaking lime throwing off its clouds of steam; the working of the mixing tool in the white sea enclosed by banks of sand—a pleasant sound, strangely like the flopping of a small boat on short harbour wavelets; the rhythmical sound of the shovel in the sloppy mortar as it is turned over and over to incorporate the lime and sand.

The sounds of the carpenter's work are equally familiar though less musical. The noises of saw and hammer are not pleasant in themselves, though satisfactory evidences that work is in progress, and a saw being filed is no less than a torture to any tender ear that may be near. On the other hand, I like to hear the small melodious scream of the well-sharpened plane as it shoots along the edge of the board and gives out its long, fragrant ribbon of a shaving, and the chop of the axe, and the blows of the mallet on the chisel that is making the mortises; for the sound of these blows, though of a dull quality, yet has a muffled music that is pleasant to hear. And another sound that is not displeasing is the beating of the cow-hair that is mixed with the wall plaster, the better to make it hold together; for exactly the same reason that in Egypt of old they made bricks with straw. The hair, when shaken out of the bags, is in thick lumps. A man sits before a board, and with two lissome sticks beats the hair till it separates. The air is thick with dust and particles of short hair; and probably the work, though light, is none of the pleasantest; but it always looks, particularly if two are at work near together, as if they were playing some amusing game.

One picks up many varied scraps of useful knowledge on a building; indeed the whole thing is a capital lesson for any reasonably observant person. As one example out of many, one learns why bricks should be used wet. A soft cutting-brick has a dry, sandy surface; mortar laid on this scarcely takes hold, it is inclined to fall off, carrying on its face the loose red sand that prevented it from adhering, just as the hod deposits its load of mortar surfaced with the dry sand that the labourer has sprinkled over it in order that the wet stuff should not cling to the wooden tool. But when a brick is wet, the moisture of the mortar at once fraternises with that of the brick, and the mortar is actually sucked into the pores. Dozens of such examples might be noted in illustration of the natures of building materials. And then one learns curious local terms, and from the older men many odds and ends of lore and wisdom, and one hears familiar words twisted in workmen's mouths into unusual forms; thus I learn that 'temporary' is the antithesis of 'permanent'. I also learn by inference that the maker of one useful material is deficient in the sense of smell, for when I came on a newly-unloaded stack of large rolls of something with an overpowering odour of creosote, and asked: 'What is this very nasty-smelling stuff?' I was told it was the Patent Inodorous Felt!

So I would linger about the works not exactly idle because always learning something new in the way of cause and effect, till the church clock of the distant town struck twelve and the foreman looked at his watch. Then came his cheery Yeo-ho, and at the welcome call the sounds on the building ceased and the men knocked off for dinner and the midday rest.[57]

Chapter seven

GROOTE SCHUUR 1896

ALTHOUGH Lutyens had built the first part of Crooksbury as early as 1889, it was not until 1896 that he began the series of houses that were to make his name. Indeed, it could be suggested that it was not until he had met Gertrude Jekyll in 1890 that his architecture became anything more than run of the mill. In the next few years though it matured at a remarkable rate and by 1896, when he built Munstead Wood for her, his first and best style is already fully developed. On the other side of the world his friend and senior in Ernest George's office, Herbert Baker, was also to start his real career, after very shaky beginnings, by meeting the person who was to be his great teacher and client. In Baker's case this was not to be an artistic lady, but one of the greatest of the Empire builders at the height of his career, Cecil Rhodes. Both these clients had one important thing in common—a very clear sense of what they wanted and a deep love of the simple products of the country people who had gone before. Just as Jekyll opened Lutyens's eyes to the traditional buildings, gardens and furniture of Surrey, so Cecil Rhodes showed Baker the Cape Dutch buildings, furniture and silver, which in those days were scorned by the average English settler as being boorish and provincial. In Groote Schuur, Rhodes attempted to create a house that would bring all white South Africans to a realization of their early heritage, and in this he succeeded beyond his expectations. Indeed it might be suggested without too much exaggeration that Rhodes's revival of the interest in Cape Dutch Arts and Crafts led to a stronger sense of community in the original Dutch settlers, which has resulted in recent years in the virtual exclusion of South Africa from the rest of the civilized world. If this is so then it would be most ironical since Rhodes tried desperately to bring South Africa closer to the rest of what he saw as European civilization. In Baker he found one of his finest instruments for this purpose.

Baker has described their early meetings:

My first meeting with Cecil Rhodes was shortly after my arrival in South Africa

in March 1892. . . . It was at a dinner at the house of Mr. Vincent. . . . I sat
. . . opposite the great man . . . I sat entranced at their talk on South Africa and
world affairs, but I said little or nothing, and went away much discomforted at
having proved myself so unable to make the most of this golden opportunity.
Yet I was consoled the next day when I was told by Mrs. Merriman that Rhodes
had asked her to tell him more about 'that silent young man'. Shortly afterwards, during an early walk below the mountain, I met him and Sauer . . .
returning from their morning ride on the Flats. . . . He stopped and asked me
to go to his house the next morning, as he wanted 'to restore it'.[58]

Baker has got his dates slightly wrong as Rhodes did not buy Groote Schuur, or
the Grange, as it was then called, until 1893. However by the end of 1893 Baker
was certainly at work on the 'restoration'. The inverted commas are intentional
since Baker and Rhodes between them created a Cape Dutch house on the flimsi-
est of evidence, in much the same way and for much the same reasons, as the
creators of 'Colonial Williamsburg' were later to design large and imposing
buildings on no more evidence than a small design on a medal. The house was
certainly an old one. It started as a large barn (which its name implies) in 1657,
and was sold in 1791 when it was converted into a house, which was burnt down
in the beginning of the nineteenth century. When it was rebuilt it had a flat roof
with a colonnade running along its front; in 1832, a steeply pitched roof and
gables were added, but by 1893 it had been taken over by the public works
department and converted into a typical British colonial house, with a flat hipped
roof, a central pediment and a colonnade running between two short wings with
rather charming oval windows at the upper storey. All in all a pleasant but not
particularly distinguished colonial house.

There was, however, a single watercolour sketch of the earlier, 1832, house,
and it was on this flimsy evidence that Baker produced the house that today most
people believe to be the most typical example of the 'Cape Dutch' style. Drawings
of the earlier 1830 house have now come to light, and had Rhodes and Baker
known them it is possible that Groote Schuur would have been restored in quite
a different way, since these drawings show a simple flat-roofed house with a
Classical colonnade running between two projecting wings. But of course we
must remember that Baker had come hot from Ernest George's office and that
George had for the last ten years been building in London, both in Chelsea and
Earls Court, red-brick houses with elaborate Dutch gables. And George's designs

are very persuasive, the best like that for W. S. Gilbert in Collingham Gardens, equalling if not overtopping the architecture of Amsterdam or Delft. In these buildings Ernest George combined Shaw's post-Gothic Revival sense of form with a post-Shavian attention to details and structural honesty. In his interiors George seems not so much to have turned to the simple neat interiors of Dutch houses but rather to the more lavish aristocratic interiors of medieval France, or Tudor England. This is particularly true of such things as the elaborate ingle in the Collingham Gardens house, with its heavy Tudor carving. Batsford Park, Gloucestershire, which was building while Baker was chief assistant, is in the Tudor-Elizabethan style. On the face of it Batsford is not dissimilar to Victorian houses in this style that had been erected since the 1830s, though the interior detailing is of a much higher quality. The panelling is more carefully detailed using, for instance, peg dowels and the door locks are all individually designed and craftsman-made. However, George never moved towards the simpler Tudor detailing that was to be the hallmark of his pupils, for to him panelling would only be one of many elements in the wall covering; above there would be stamped leather and above that again, elaborate plasterwork on the ceilings. This approach is reflected in a considerable degree in Baker's detailing at Groote Schuur.

Even after Rhodes bought the house the building history of Groote Schuur continued to be complex. Originally Rhodes had intended the house to be his home rather than official residence, but soon decided to make it what it has since remained, the residence of the Prime Minister of South Africa. It would seem that much of what we see of the house is what Rhodes wanted; Baker strictly followed Rhodes's numerous suggestions. Work on it started late in 1893. Rhodes was by then an extremely rich man and he said to Baker, make it ' "big and simple, barbaric if you like"; and "I like teak and whitewash". He abhorred the small and the mean and any commercial thing made with the machine and not with hands and brain.'[59] This first house seems to have retained more of the original features than the house that we see today; the colonnade would seem to have been still Doric, and the wing windows have their old straightforward pediments. While Rhodes was away fighting the Matabele War, and before he had moved in after three years' work, this thatched house was burnt down in December 1896. Rhodes and Baker immediately set to work to rebuild it again, this time consciously approaching the house as a monument to the traditions of the Cape Dutch. Thus this second house is contemporary with Munstead Wood, although there is nothing of Munstead in the house (though there is a lot of Munstead in

Rust en Vrede in Muizenberg, which Baker was building for Rhodes at his death in 1902).

The 1838 drawing[60] shows a house with two gabled wings of curious design joined by a colonnade. The gable elevation of the wings comprises, running upwards, first a pair of pedimented windows then at the top of the colonnade a large half-round window, capped by a circular window in the gable, which has straight sides. In the centre of the facade there is another similar, though slightly higher, and this time, pedimented gable, with the same motifs of a half-round window capped by a circular window. The roof is thatched and quite plain. There is another drawing which Baker knew which shows this central gable as being crowstepped. This odd, almost Italian style, is said to be unique in Cape Dutch, and Baker made very little effort to reproduce it. He retained the colonnade, but changed the order for some reason to Ionic from the simple Doric, which is shown in the earlier drawings and appears in a photograph[61] of Cecil Rhodes sitting on the stoep of the original house. He seems also to have retained the

Groote Schuur, Cape Town, Herbert Baker 1893–96. Perspective of entrance front by R. Gradidge

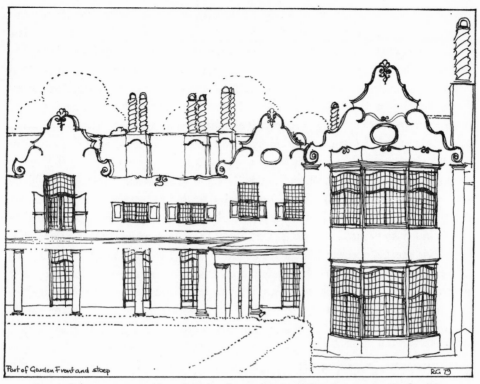

Groote Schuur – perspective of garden front, showing billiard room, by R. Gradidge

ground floor window openings but that is about all; the remainder is entirely his own invention. Instead of the simple pediments over the downstairs windows, he creates a frilly Baroque pediment, he rebuilds the arched windows and the circular windows but the proportions are quite different. In the centre he ignores them entirely, and places there a badly out of proportion bas-relief by John Tweed, his favourite sculptor. On the top of this fantasy, he designed wonderfully scrolled gables, capped with barley sugar chimneys, the whole a fantasy but a very persuasive fantasy, like George's Pont Street buildings in London.

The house nowadays seems to be oddly placed, on the lower slopes of Table Mountain, with the suburbs of Cape Town spreading all around it. It can be clearly seen from the main motorway to Cape Point. After the fire there was talk of moving it but it was decided to keep it in its original position. The result of this is that the house is approached from the west, from the slopes of Table Mountain from above, and since it faces due east looking towards False Bay, the roofs of

the back of the house are what are first seen. In this rear elevation Baker seems to
have paid little attention to what was there. From a flat colonnaded facade he
added a wing facing outwards, which contained the billiards room with Rhodes's
bedroom above, approached by its own grand staircase. This elevation is more
fantastical than the front, and bears even less of the true Cape Dutch tradition.
Along the whole of this long and slightly complex facade, there are no less than
seven curly gables, and above there are nine barley sugar chimneys. It is difficult to
know where Baker got these chimneys from; there is nothing like them on any
real Cape Dutch house and they seem more to be an interpretation of English
Tudor chimneys, seen through Dutch Baroque eyes. Much the same could be
said of the gables. The true Cape Dutch gable tended to be used only once, as the
centrepiece, and would then almost inevitably start with a vertical portion before
it developed its voluted curves. Baker's habit of ending ordinary end gables with
this device seems entirely his own, no doubt taken from the practice of English
Elizabethan house builders. In many places Baker more or less copies accurately
the traditional Cape Dutch windows, with their semi-sash windows fixed flush to
the surface of the wall and with their shutters covering only the lower panes.
On other occasions, as in a tudory oak bay with leaded lights, he reverts back

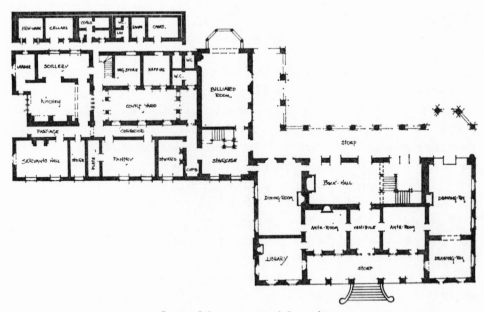

Groote Schuur – ground floor plan

to a more English tradition. The garden also echoes this English Tudor tradition, particularly in the parterre that runs behind the house up the slopes of Table Mountain.

In the interior this combination of English Tudor, as seen through the eyes of Ernest George, and Cape Dutch is even more apparent. The plan was originally simple and straightforward: a porch, then an entrance hall, with to either side two small rooms; beside these the main reception rooms in the wings joined at the rear by a long room running across the house facing west up the slope. To this room Baker added outside a long colonnaded stoep which turned west to follow the line of the large new service block. One enters through a fine and elaborate front door which is the copy of the original door destroyed in the fire and which Rhodes had taken from an old farmhouse; it is a much simpler design than Baker's doors. Immediately in front of this, one is presented with a typical piece of Baker invention—the arch that leads through to the main hall. This is made in teak as in much of the house; two pairs of Ionic columns support a cornice which suddenly arches up at the centre to form a broken arch, a conceit normally seen on the top of cabinets. No doubt this is derived from the break top to doors and windows of the Cape style.

The two drawing rooms on the north are delightfully and well proportioned. They belong to the earlier house, having survived the fire, and seem to belong to an earlier era than the rest of the house. Panelling runs up to about 8 feet and

Groote Schuur – view to front door from hall by R. Gradidge

then above this there is a frieze of Spanish leather, rising to a deeply moulded wooden ceiling. The chimneybreast, which juts into the room, is supported on volutes which in turn are supported by tudory columns. These are High Victorian rooms which in England would seem gloomy, but in the glittering sunshine of South Africa are cool and elegant. Baker has obviously moved a long way from this by 1896, the remaining rooms being very much lighter, though still much heavier than the Lutyens rooms of this period. Everywhere one looks, there are reminiscences of Ernest George's detailing—Tudor scroll moulds in fireplaces that purport to be Classical, deep beaming to all the rooms, fussy mouldings and panellings. But on the other hand the rooms are magnificently proportioned, light and airy, and much of the detailing and finish is exquisite. Baker consciously made an effort to bring local craftsmen of a high standard to work on the house; we know the names of many of the craftsmen in his team. Pride of place must certainly go to the great ironworker George Ness, a Scotsman whose workmanship is of the highest quality; his steel hinges to the shutters in the drawing room are delightful. The woodwork too throughout the house is excellent, using the local woods like stinkwood, and imported woods like teak, with a panache that might not have been expected in a country whose crafts traditions had to be revived from almost complete collapse before work could be started on the house.

It was not in the revival of local craftsmanship alone that Baker and Rhodes collaborated. Rhodes wished to see in Groote Schuur the whole Dutch tradition revived. And with this in mind he and Baker commissioned agents to buy important collections of tiles, china, furniture and hangings from all over Europe but with a particular bias towards the Dutch. The only country that was ignored in this search was England. So today, with the careful restoration and cataloguing by the last Prime Minister's wife, Mrs Vorster, Groote Schuur has one of the finest collections of Dutch artefacts outside Holland. It is a remarkable fact that Rhodes, at that time engaged in a violent struggle with the Afrikaner settlers, should have made this collection, which is comparable to the care with which the present Afrikaner rulers of South Africa are so carefully preserving Rhodes's gift to their nation.

After his success with Rhodes's house Baker went on to become South Africa's 'Architect Laureate'. Rhodes died before Groote Schuur was finished, and in 1906–8 Baker designed the splendid Grecian colonnade that looks down from Table Mountain to Groote Schuur as a memorial to Cecil Rhodes, a potent precursor of Lutyens's colonnaded war memorials of the 1920s. His practice expanded

and he soon had offices in all the major towns in the Union. He built elegant
Italianate Classical houses for the new diamond millionaires, such as Villa Arcadia,
Parktown, Johannesburg of 1909 for Lionel Phillips. He also built Gothic Revival
Arts and Crafts influenced churches for the Anglicans, such as Cape Town
Cathedral, designed 1899, and all the railway stations and government buildings
that a new country needs.

It was Baker who was to be the first to show how a great building could be
designed in the Classical Romantic style, and his Union Buildings at Pretoria are
in many ways the purest example of this style. In 1910 South Africa, after the
traumas of the Boer War, was officially declared a Union—a union of two equal
partners, the British and the Boers. This union was a rather precarious affair—
a joining of two peoples who had recently been such bitter enemies. In celebration
Baker designed a building which seemed to symbolize this partnership of equals.
The two vast blocks, each as big as one of the Whitehall ministries, are joined by a
great backward-curved colonnade. The absence of emphasis at the centre creates
for anyone trained in Classical architecture a shocking weakness—a duality.
Where one might expect a centrepiece there is nothing; where one would expect

Union Buildings, Pretoria, Herbert Baker 1910. Perspective of central gardens by R. Gradidge

the building to come forwards it drops back. No doubt Baker would have said that his great office blocks symbolized the two peoples linked together by the lightest of chains. This type of symbolic architecture seldom works and here on a general view it seems to be disastrous. However, it is in fact almost impossible to see the building as a whole except from a great distance and in this lies its very real strength, for any one part of the building, and the relationship between the disparate parts, is excellent.

The office blocks are in a splendid Roman Renaissance style, with pantiled roofs and balconies that project out, supported on a multitude of columns, over terraced gardens, reminiscent of the gardens of the Villa D'Este, though on a much larger scale. Pompous sculpture is piled over minor doorways, every feature leads to the centre of each block. At the end of these blocks, at the beginning of the colonnade, stand tall cupolared towers, reminiscent of the towers in much the same relative position at the Royal Hospital, Greenwich. From the towers the colonnades fall back in a curve of paired Ionic columns which sweep round past the centre to the tower on the opposite side. Each form is designed to reflect another: the tall cupolas in one view are tucked under the colonnades; in another the colonnade hangs between them. Tall pantile-topped chimneys thrust out of the pantiled roof and balance the horizontals of the great office blocks. Along the whole facade of both of the main blocks, the columned porticoes project over the main terrace forming an enfilade of a multitude of columns at different distances from the eye. The whole series of highly complex forms revolve around two highly symbolic centre points: one is a small temple intended for outdoor political addresses in the centre of a garden of stone benches, streams and bridges; the other is the memorial to the Great War placed at the very centre of the enormous crescent, but looking away from the buildings over the valley to the Voortrekker Monument which rises on the opposite hill. All heavily didactic no doubt, but none the less powerful popular architecture for all that. This is Classical architecture seen through the eyes of the Gothic Revival, becoming a truly three-dimensional architecture—an affair of balancing verticals and horizontals, controlled by Classical orders and overall symmetry, a fusion of the two great styles of architecture, the final and only proper end to the 'Battle of the Styles'.

Chapter eight

FULBROOK HOUSE, BERRYDOWNE COURT, THE PLEASAUNCE 1897

1897 was the year that Scottish Art Nouveau became commercially acceptable, so it is perhaps not surprising that it was now that Lutyens built his most eccentric houses: Fulbrook in the heart of 'Lutyens country' in Surrey, Berrydowne in rural Hampshire and the strangest house of all, The Pleasaunce at Overstrand on the north Norfolk seaside near Cromer. It is interesting that all these houses are virtually ignored by Butler and Hussey in the *Lutyens Memorial Volumes*,[62] which always try to suggest that Lutyens's genius was confined to a single path which moved swiftly from the Surrey vernacular exemplified so wonderfully in Munstead Wood to the Classical splendours of New Delhi. This is simply not so. Lutyens assayed many styles and around 1897 it looked not so much as though he was going to carry on the Webb vernacular tradition but as if he were going to join the camp of the eccentric Arts and Crafts designers such as Prior.

Fulbrook is the least eccentric of this group. Indeed on three of its facades it exemplifies the Surrey tile-hung vernacular to perfection, in many ways outdoing Norman Shaw himself. It was built for the daughter of Richard Henry Combe for whom Shaw built Pierrepoint. Lutyens possibly felt the need to show his older friend and adviser that he also could design with long ranges of tile-hung gables, set off with tall, brick chimneys, and perhaps show him also what he could do using structural timber honestly, not resorting to the faking that mars so much of Shaw's vernacular work.

One enters Fulbrook from low down, past a cottage and a small stable block and coming up to the rear of the house before turning into the entrance front. Beyond the forecourt a hill rises in formal terraces, while beyond the edge of the house, with a turret silhouetted against the sky, there runs a wide, brick path and then there is glimpsed in a sudden breathtaking moment the distant blue hills of the Devil's Punch Bowl. For Fulbrook, like so many of these Surrey houses, is built on the top of a south-facing ridge and takes full advantage of an area which has a surprising number of splendid sites with spectacular views. On

D.H.–F

each of these sites rests a house of this period and often designed by an architect of quality: Voysey's Greyfriars is placed two miles north of Fulbrook on the Hogs Back with its wonderful views south; Crooksbury is about a mile and a half to the north-west on the hills above Farnham and a mile or so south of this is Shaw's Pierrepoint; four miles to the east of Fulbrook is Godalming; and near it is Orchards with its views over Hascombe and Thakeray Turner's Westbrook which looks across the valley to Charterhouse, though here it is the entrance that has the view to the north—the garden looks south to the sun.

Fulbrook House, Elstead, Surrey, E. L. Lutyens 1897. Perspective of entrance front by R. Gradidge

The entrance court at Fulbrook is particularly splendid. To the left a gable sweeps down almost to the ground; in the centre there is a gabled porch and to the right a further gable pushes forward enclosing the court, with a great oak-framed leaded window which is wrapped round the corner and lights the stair-case. This wing, however, dies into another sweeping roof which follows the form of the roof to the left. Cut into it is a delectable little tile-hung octagonal turret, which is pushed half into the roof and projects half over a garden door, in a way reminiscent of Newton's garden door at Redcourt. It is said that this turret was added as an afterthought when a second lavatory was needed, a delightful example of Lutyens's brilliant ability to 'improvise', for the turret now seems vital to the elevation, both holding it together and at the same time giving it an interest that otherwise it would lack. To the right of this turret the facade suddenly makes a surprising lurch. The eaves here are raised higher than any-where else on the facade and a pair of bay windows, running up two storeys, forces a different scale into what until now had been a lovable, but perhaps a little bland, entrance front. Suddenly, as it were, the gawky youth (for this is a young man's architecture) shows beneath the carefully tailored clothes.

These gawky bay windows should give us warning of what to expect round the corner for here we enter suddenly into another and slightly nightmarish world. The hipped roof turns the corner displaying a gable with another bay window under it, thus considerably overlighting the two corner rooms. From here the walls make a number of lurches back and forwards, offering three immensely deep bays, with solid oak mullions and leaded lights, joined at the first floor with oak balustrades, all the bays of course looking south (see plate IX). Across all this, supported on rather flimsy-looking oak brackets, runs the flat underside of the roof. This roof, which is of a simple pitch, seems to have nothing to do with the structure underneath. There are precedents for this in Kentish Wealden houses, but there the trusses seem to hold up the roof whereas in the Lutyens house they seem to be much too flimsy to be any more than decoration, to such a degree that Lawrence Weaver suggests[63] that there must be steels imbedded in the roof, something that we might expect of Norman Shaw but not of Lutyens. In point of fact there are no steels but the result gives an impression of distinct structural instability. The reason for this is not so much the thin supports, which are in fact 12 by 9 inch oak beams, but rather the way that the roof is placed over the bay windows. This sense of instability comes about because the back part of the main roof springs from a position forward of the rearmost windows, thus suggesting that the roof is entirely balanced on a wall of glass. Should the roof in fact have been supported on the rear wall of the building it would have risen to twice the height of all the other roofs, and this would never have been acceptable to Lutyens. Since Lutyens understood architectural form better than any of his contemporaries, one has to accept that this sense of unease was not a solecism but was what he intended. In fact it would seem to be an early example of Lutyens's favourite habit when dealing with complex forms—a throwing together of diverse elements and, as it were, with a deft twitch of the hand arranging that they fall together as a coherent whole. Sometimes of course the trick doesn't quite come off, and the facade at Fulbrook seems to be one of these occasions, largely because he has not been honest in his expression of the structure. Later he became more adept in hiding his (structural) dishonesties. If, however, Lutyens made a mistake he always recog-

Fulbrook House – perspective of garden front by R. Gradidge

nized it and never repeated his errors. It must be remembered that when he was designing Fulbrook in 1896 he was still only twenty-seven years old, the age that architects now are normally just leaving their schools of architecture and looking for their first job in a firm so that they can learn how to go about the business of building.

The result of all these complexities is an interior of great interest. The deep bay windows of the drawing room, under the overhanging roof, look out through shadow over the hill to Haslemere. To either side of it rooms jut forward with windows which look both south and also across the house, through the oak and leaded windows of the bays, making the interior and exterior spaces balance and complement each other. There is one other feature in Fulbrook which everyone has noticed, for here, amongst all the oak and the leaded lights, Lutyens built his first full-scale Classical interior, with painted wood Ionic columns holding up corniced beams. Like Newton some years earlier Lutyens sees no problem in using Classical architecture within a Tudor exterior, but here, unlike Newton, Lutyens has allowed the essentially horizontal proportions of vernacular architecture to dominate with the result that the ceilings are rather too low to accommodate such Classical grandeur, which in any case he does not carry through with a

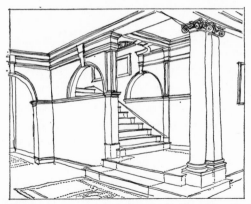

Fulbrook House – perspective of Classical staircase by R. Gradidge

proper singlemindedness. After Fulbrook whenever he built a Classical room, in whatever style of architecture the exterior was, he always saw to it that the exterior proportions were tall enough to accommodate his orders. Sometimes as at Papillon Hall in Leicestershire (1903) this resulted in gawky proportions on the exterior.

Although Fulbrook is such an early example of Lutyens's Classicism, in the staircase we already find him playing games with the orders. The L-shaped staircase passes up between arches each with a keystone in the middle. At the floor level above he cuts back the bulkhead with a curve which exactly mirrors the arches but lies horizontally. The spring, as it were, of this arch grows from the keystone of the vertical arches. An entirely original trick worthy of one of the great Mannerist architects of the Renaissance is being played by someone who has never before seriously designed in the Classical style! It is this incredible facility and wit that endears Lutyens to anyone who has an architectural eye, and it was this brilliance that some thirty years later was to lead to the miraculous solid geometry of the war memorials.

Berrydowne was Lutyens's second experimental house of 1897. Here the entrance is through an arch in a long wall that runs beside the main road, the opening being indicated by bulges in the wall with a cupola over. It leads into a formal rectangular courtyard with a perfectly traditional house at the far end. There is nothing to prepare one for the high jinks of the garden front. The garden front today is even more eccentric than it originally was, since Lutyens here, as in so many houses, made a later addition (see plate VIII). However the front as originally built seems eccentric enough, and gives the impression that it has been built in at least three different periods. In the centre of the facade there is a pair of tile-hung gables of great size, reaching from two ridges above the second-storey windows and sweeping down both sides to the top of the ground floor windows, here to be supported on one side by a pair of wooden corbels, with the flat bolection curve so loved by Art Nouveau architects. To the right of this symmetrical design is but one arch, and in the centre there is a large, oak bay leaded window, tucked under the gable, but asymmetrically placed. So far we have an early example of the M-gable which, in later years, was to become the standard design for semi-detached houses. However, at Berrydowne, Lutyens has only just begun. At the rear of this M-gable, there peers an extraordinary chaos of roofs. To the right, beyond a tall slab of chimney, is a hipped roof, which then develops into a gable, and to the left another roof, seemingly not on the same plane as the right-hand roof, and which runs at right angles to the main 'M' of the gable, parallel to the front. This is cut off sharp to the left just beyond the gable. Suddenly a completely new element appears, a seemingly separate small house, with to the left a hipped roof supported by a tall chimney, but hardly has this roof begun than it is stopped off abruptly, to present a tile-hung gable, considerably in front of the end of the main block of the house, but in line with the M-gables. To crown it this block has corner windows running round both sides, another early use of a motif that was to become popular, both with the International Modern Movement and the suburban house. The whole facade presents the most extraordinary jumble, and it is difficult to see what Lutyens was striving for, particularly as the plan is perfectly straightforward. The downstairs comprises from left to right a study, drawing room with loggia and a dining room. Upstairs each block jutting forward represents bedrooms, whilst the windows on the rear plane light passages.

A few years later Lutyens (or another architect working in his style) made an addition to the house and even then made no effort to resolve the facade. This time he added to the right and here he built a straightforward gabled extension. The gable faces forward, contrasting with and making little effort to relate to the two monster tile-hung gables beside it. Lutyens always much enjoyed adding to his own early architecture, and often when he had to add to one of his Romantic houses, he would give it a Georgian wing, though sometimes he would reverse the process. When he had to make a large addition to the simple Georgian box that he first designed at Folly Farm, he added in 1912, at the height of his Neo-Georgian period, a wildly romantic addition, with roofs sweeping down to a deeply buttressed cloister surrounding a pond. The addition makes no effort to conform with his original design. That he was perfectly capable of designing an extension in the style of the original building is obvious from his additions to the Georgian Temple Dinsley of 1908 and the Jacobean Ashby St. Ledger in 1909. Here the additions are in complete harmony with the older house. But Berrydowne seems to be the only occasion when his additions increased the complexity of an already complex facade.

There were occasions when Lutyens was asked to add to houses of no architectural pretension and in 1897 came such a commission. Cyril Flower, created first Lord Battersea in 1892, owned two seaside villas—red brick of the 1880s—in the small resort of Overstrand in Norfolk. Flower was a typical early Lutyens client, related to that group of people that included the Souls and the Asquith set— rich, talented and much loved. While he was at Cambridge he was adored and as if that were not enough when he was still quite young he inherited a large portion of south London! His wife Constance, Lady Battersea, daughter of Sir Anthony Rothschild in her racy memoirs of 1922, remembers the building of The Pleasaunce. It was in 1888 that Flower bought the villas:

> Anything more unlike what it is now can hardly be imagined. Very commonplace, rather uncomfortable, extremely inconvenient and with little pretence of beauty. . . . It was not long before we agreed that 'The Cottage' would require much alteration in order to make it a suitable country home . . . Mr Lutyens . . . entered fully into my husband's views; between them they evolved out of the old cottage a truly original, but certainly very comfortable homey abode.[64]

What Lutyens evolved with Battersea was certainly very strange, and it seems to have been a number of years abuilding with a considerable amount of alteration while the house was going up. Lady Battersea again:

> Upon my yearly arrivals . . . I would expect to be greeted by some novelty, of which I was not always prepared to be an enthusiastic admirer; thus the first impression of the clock tower and of the cloisters was not a favourable one. Yet now I am quite attached to the tower . . . On one occasion I was startled by the sight of some masons constructing a high brick wall to the balcony of the window in my sitting room, which would effectually have shut out the view from my seat in my favourite corner. I indignantly began to remonstrate, and, in spite of Sir Edwin Lutyens' orders, threw the bricks down to the terrace, to the ill-concealed amusement of the workmen.[65]

Two interesting points come out of these memories: first, normally Lutyens got on very much better with women clients, rather than with men but this doesn't seem to have been the case here; secondly, the house would still seem to have been building after Lutyens was knighted, which was not till 1918. This would suggest that building was still going on twenty years after its first commission, but perhaps the title is a slip of Lady Battersea's pen. Certainly the house as we see it today gives the impression that it was built over a considerable period. But then as we saw at Berrydowne, Lutyens at this time delighted in suggesting a highly complex building history when the whole house was conceived on the drawing board at the same time.

The Pleasaunce is approached from the village street through a splendid Mannerist gate, made of stucco and tiles in a style worthy of Scammozi or any of the most extreme Mannerists. Beyond this to the right there is first a block of stables in red brick and stucco and the drive then opens to form a cloistered yard in the centre of which there is a clock tower with a very pronounced batter in a yellow stucco. Above this there is a strip of window and then a hipped roof, the whole reminiscent of a fantasy of medieval Germany—romantic and rather over prettified. However, we have only to turn around to discover something very different. Here between a curving pair of walls is the entrance porch. A pair of Ionic columns flank the entrance and, above, fully as large as the entrance itself, is a vast carved stone cartouche containing the arms of the newly ennobled owner. On coming through this pompous entrance one finds that one has not in fact entered the front door at all, but is walking down a covered passage, supported with wooden columns on brackets with the same flat Art Nouveau swing that we have noticed at Berrydowne. Above this arcade there is an upper floor, designed rather in the manner of Voysey in white roughcast, with vertical strips of oriel windows, derived from Shaw, but also used by Mackmurdo in the house of Cadogan Gardens. Hardly have we had time to consider this surprising elevation than we have a red-brick block with Neo-Georgian overtones but with mullioned windows (see plate XI). This has a flat roof with a parapet that gives a little kick up at each corner, and beyond this again, but now presumably on one of the original villas, there is a tile-hung gable, and beyond it, still on the same facade, the house builds up to four storeys with a welter of tile-hanging violently thrust out at the bottom and a tall, Surrey hipped gable roof. In the corner of this at the top, is another of the Shavian oriels, and below it one of Lutyens's corner windows. Below this again, the wall sweeps out to form a corner, octagonal, covered summer-house. In this facade alone there are nine different window types and five different building forms thrown together.

The elevation round the corner is, if anything, more complex. There are seven major breaks in the facade, the roofs leap and twist in various directions, there are two gabled bays, one wide with a bay projecting from it. There are two loggias, at different floors and positions, a hipped portion and then at the corner the tall over-sailing tile-hung block with its corner oriels as we have already noticed. But Lutyens has not even finished here, for below the oriel he has built out an octagonal loggia, with a hipped tile roof, supported on stone Doric columns. He repeats this on the other side of the terrace in front of the house as an end to a long roofed promenade. The roof here is supported by stucco-buttressed semicircular arches, which in the roof space support reverse semicircular arches, a delicious piece of solid geometry tucked away under a roof in a garden to an obscure villa on the north coast of Norfolk: at this time there seemed to be no end to Lutyens's invention. Weaver suggests[66] that there was trouble here (and Lady Battersea confirms it), but once again Lutyens overcomes the difficulties and adds something extra in doing it. By a lesser hand it would seem an ill-considered jumble, but somehow Lutyens has been able to pull the whole facade together and create if not a coherent at least a pleasing balance of parts. He has done this because he understands the principles of architectural three-dimensional balance to a degree that few other architects before or since have done. Before the Gothic Revival and Norman Shaw's development of the ideas implicit in High Victorian church design of balanced form, no architect would have considered them. But many of Lutyens's near contemporaries, both 'moderns' such as Frank Lloyd Wright in America and DeKlerk in Holland, or more traditional Arts and Crafts architects in England got involved with this attitude to architectural form, though none of them perhaps approached it with quite the panache of the young Lutyens.

With Lutyens too it was only in just a few buildings, and those were all built in the late 1890s which he designed with the frenzy that we see at Berrydowne or The Pleasaunce. But throughout his career he took pleasure in combining seemingly disparate architectural forms. For instance, the three show elevations of Ednaston Manor in Derbyshire of 1912 are staid Neo-Georgian, but at the rear two large gables thrust their way into the hipped roofs. With Lutyens romantic architecture had at last reached a point when it could rival Stokesay Castle (which he visited with Herbert Baker while he was still with George) or Compton Wynyates in their seeming casualness and romantic balance.

Chapter nine

THE BARN 1897

EVEN after these eccentricities of Lutyens there is little to prepare us for E. S. Prior's Barn at Exmouth. Prior was another of Shaw's brilliant pupils who helped to found the Art Workers' Guild. He was master in 1906 and co-author, with other members of Shaw's office, of *Architecture, a Profession or an Art* published in 1892. This plea that the architect should not become merely a professional was very important in its time and its message is still potent to this day. A great deal of the thinking behind the recent rejection by the rank and file architects of the Royal Institute of British Architect's decision to allow advertising stems from this debate. Most 'art' architects believed that architects were creative artists and that they were beholden to nothing but their own genius. A view as popular then as it is now, it dominated the careers of composers like Wagner and painters like Whistler. It was also to lead to the art for art's sake affectations of the aesthetes which culminated in the affected posings of Oscar Wilde.

For an architect more than for any other artists this attitude must end by being self-defeating. The architect can never be a creative artist as, shall we say, a painter looking at a blank canvas can choose to paint whatever he will, or a composer can write music of his own choice. The architect is more akin to the violinist taking up a composer's score for the first time and considering how he should play the work. The architect must always interpret the wishes of his client and then build within the bounds of the materials with which he chooses to build. It is only when he has satisfied all the physical conditions that he can give any thought to art. Those very architects who seemed to care most about the nature of materials permitting the materials to dominate their architecture—the group of Shaw pupils who circled around Lethaby—were the very architects who believed most passionately in the integrity of the architect as an artist. And it was from these architects, who not unnaturally did not have large practices and therefore had plenty of time for polemics, that these ideas spread, first to Germany and then to the International Modern Movement where it has become one of its standard tenets. To this day young architects leave the schools believing that it is their only duty as architects to foist on the public their generation's ideal of modern architecture, at the expense of the requirements of their clients. Unless they are able to display quite remarkable talents in self-publicity, they soon inevitably come to a rude awakening, though their architecture no doubt improves after the shock.

In 1897 Prior, who had left Shaw's office in 1880, had been in private practice for seventeen years when he came to design The Barn; it cannot therefore in any way be called a young man's job. He had not, however, built much, being as much concerned with writing as with building, and the author of a number of authoritative studies of Gothic architecture. He finally published his *History of Gothic Architecture in England* in 1900, and became Slade Professor of Fine Art in Cambridge in 1912.

By now the High Gothic Revival was well and truly over and the Arts and Crafts Movement which it had spawned was moving into a later and strangely mystical phase. Right from the beginning, influenced by Wordsworth, who found that: 'To every natural form, rock, fruit, or flower, even the loose stones that cover the highway, I gave a moral life: I saw them feel' (*The Prelude*, Book III, line 127–9), and inspired by Ruskin's curious mixture of mysticism and functionalism, the Gothic Revivalists had always had a highly moralistic attitude to the use of natural materials. By the time that first Philip Webb and then W. R. Lethaby had converted the style from Gothic to Vernacular Revivalism, this attitude to natural materials had reached a stage of mysticism that can only be described as slightly mad. The materials of the immediate countryside had, of course, always to be used no matter how expensive that were, but as well as this they had to be used in such a way that the architectural style of the building was overlaid in a sort of crankiness and asymmetry which in some strange way seemed to symbolize the honesty of the building. Although in this way crankiness may have displayed a 'natural' attitude to materials and design it also of course appealed to the High Romanticism which was still very close to the hearts of all designers at this time. In this we can see the seeds of ideas that have run through all parts of modern architecture and are still very much with us. There is a great deal of 'quaintness' in so much of the work of Le Corbusier, the 'New Brutalists' and James Stirling. This style affected such potentially establishment architects as Lutyens and Detmar Blow, but they (unlike those that came after them) soon saw that this quaintness was not suitable for establishment architecture, and in an ambitious drive to the top, which fortunately need not concern us here, by about 1905 they rejected this crankiness on most occasions for a more controlled Neo-Georgian. It must be emphasized, however, that Neo-Georgian in all other aspects than this was as much a child of the Gothic Revival as its more rustic sister.

Prior, however, never saw the need to join the ranks of establishment architects and so he was able within his small *oeuvre* to swing between all the available styles. In the Henry Martyn Hall in the Cambridge of 1887 he was straightforwardly Neo-Gothic and in the School of Medicine of 1900 in the same city there is a touch of Edwardian Baroque, but in his more famous buildings—The Barn, Exmouth, St. Andrew's, Roker, near Sunderland (1906–7) and Home Place, Holt, Norfolk (1903–5)—he uses an extreme Arts and Crafts style. Since in many ways his attitudes are possibly the most extreme of the Arts and Crafts builders of this period and since they have been well encapsulated in a contemporary description in *Country Life* of the building of Home Place (by 'W', presumably Lawrence Weaver), it is worth quoting at length from it. Firstly the writer considers the history of the Gothic Revival as seen in 1909:

. . . no wave of architectural expression has created a larger tempest of controversy than that known as the Gothic Revival. For fifty years and more the fight has raged, and too frequently the ink has been charged with vitriol. Of one thing, however, the observer may be sure—the fashion of imitating mediaeval plans and details has gone forever. Ruskin's plea for pointed windows and his passionate protests against square-headed openings are now regarded with polite astonishment. The Seven Lamps of Architecture have failed to illumine a world which wisely will have none of houses that ape the characteristics of mediaeval churches. While, however, it is easy to see and to smile at the extravagances of the Revival, it would be foolish to decry the weight of its influence. Its general tendency was in the direction of freeing architecture from shackles which had been restraining originality of treatment without ensuring the breadth and balance and refinement of classical art. One aspect of the Revival we can remember with distress and anger—its ruthless tampering with ancient buildings and fatuous satisfaction with Victorian translations of the art which it made haste to destroy. Its good feature was the way it made people think about the qualities which built up the fabric of mediaeval architecture. Whatever the excesses of the age of Restoration, it was then that people became familiar with the ideas of Gothic art. From this knowledge large results were to follow. One of the shackles which fell away was a senseless devotion to symmetrical elevations, which determined the plan instead of evolving from it. Another was the fear of texture and colour, which led to a large devotion to masonry in its most polished form of ashlar and, in the days of economy, to its imitation in cement and paint. Was it not Repton who hated red brick because it set the landscape ablaze? A third was a total ignorance of the right treatment of varying materials and forgetfulness of the traditions of English craftsmanship. It is very doubtful if the movement which took its greatest impetus from the massive genius of William Morris would have got under way with the results so admirable to-day but for the Gothic Revivalists. Opinions will differ as to the comparative merits of Pugin, Burges and others, but not the least notable names among the Revivalists is that of Butterfield, the architect of Keble College, Oxford. To him must be attributed valuable achievement, for he did much for the restoration of red brick to its right position as an honourable material. This was part of his general devotion to many-coloured architecture and of his impatience of mere copyism. His strength lay in the freedom with which he interpreted modern needs in the light of Gothic tradition. Such buildings as Keble College Chapel could never be mistaken by the most ignorant for a work of past days. Not for Butterfield were the miles of thirteenth century mouldings with which Raphael Brandon covered his churches, and even the greater Pearson his cathedral at Truro. He has shaken the dreary spirit of imitation which had suffocated the Revival; he spoke the old language, but in phrases that marked his own abrupt personality. We have referred to Butterfield because he seems in some sort to be the artistic forebear of such workers as Mr. Prior. The latter has shaken off the inessentials of the Revival, but cleaves steadfastly to those underlying ideas which are the essence of Gothic work. Mr. Prior has written that the generative principle of Gothic may perhaps be rightly, if roughly, generalized as economy of material. This is a bald definition to explain the frozen music of spite and pinnacle and flying buttress. It none the less strikes at the root of the matter, if the great mass of mediaeval work is considered as a complete expression of building art of two centuries.

Mr. Prior is a staunch protagonist in the demand that a building shall be racy of the soil it stands on. While his attitude does not stand in the way of importing such small quantities of material from outside districts as are needful to give a touch of variety, it stands firmly for a main construction which shall be purely vernacular. Flint and gravel were the local materials [for Home Place, Holt], and they postulated the use of concrete . . .

Flint, as a building material, demands dressings, for it cannot be squared save at great cost, and then only in small pieces. Norfolk is, perhaps, the poorest county for building stone in England, for practically nowhere, save in the west near Sandringham is there any that can be used for quoins and window dressings. From that district, however, comes a stone of a fine golden brown. . . . The combination of flint and tile is the most characteristic feature of Norfolk wall-building, and the county tradition was followed by roofing with pantiles. The tile for roof and walls were supplied first from a local brickyard, but material ran short, and to ensure the admirable colour and quality the deficiency was made good from Cambridgeshire. In this matter of vernacular building, good principles must not be pressed unreasonably far. The main idea should be to use local materials where possible, but difficulties sometimes arise. In the neighbourhood of Holt the hand-made brick and tile are almost an unknown quantity. The machine-made brick is a useful enough thing for internal building, but for facing work it lacks texture, has generally a poor and even colour, and is of dreary regularity of shape and surface. In such a case it was obviously needful to seek elsewhere for tiles and bricks which would enable the Norfolk tradition of the building to be realised. The folly in such a case would be to introduce a material which was foreign to the district. . . . Mr. Prior's work is governed by the strong conviction that a house should not be a *design* but a *building*, conditioned not only by the needs of the man who will live in it, but by the local expediences of construction. From this follows the disregard of conscious styles and manners. The wisest way of building (so says Mr. Prior) is to use what is most economical in the neighbourhood. Whether the building turns out pleasant and beautiful will depend on the common-sense and good feeling of the man who devises their use. The one thing to be avoided is any capricious following of fashion, for it will destroy sincerity.

. . . Whether Home Place was 'designed' or 'built' must be judged . . . by each reader in accordance with his grasp of the long story of architecture. For ourselves, we think that Mr. Prior, so far from magnifying his office, belittles the effect of his strongly individual design in favour of a way of building which, though admirable in itself, is after all only the material element in the expression of an idea.[67]

We may assume that The Barn at Exmouth, some six years earlier, was built in the same manner and with the same ideals, though flint was not used since the mouth of the River Exe is not flint country. The Barn is similar to Home Place in another way—it is an early example of the 'butterfly plan'. The butterfly plan became popular amongst advanced architects after Shaw had designed his alterations to Chesters in Northumberland in 1891. The plan is formed by wings projecting usually at 45° from the corners of a central hall; thus suggesting a butterfly, impaled on a cloth with its wings outstretched. Four years after Chesters it was Prior who first took up this idea of Shaw's when he exhibited a design for a house in Dorset in the Royal Academy in 1895. This was never built, but the next year Prior built The Barn to a very similar plan. Then in 1900 Detmar Blow built Happisburgh Manor in Norfolk to a butterfly plan; in 1901 Baillie Scott won the *Haus eines Kunstfreundes* Competition with a butterfly plan; and in 1902 Lutyens weighed in with his Papillon Hall, the name echoing the plan. In 1904 Prior returned to the plan with Home Place; in 1910 Wier Schultz built an elaborate tile-hung and gabled butterfly-plan house, How Green at Hever in Kent; and finally Edward Maufe in 1912 at Kelling Hall, about two miles from Home Place, built his first country house also to a butterfly plan. The plan continued after the war though now for rather smaller houses. Gordon Leith, Baker's protégé, built a number of interesting bungalows to this plan in Johannesburg in the 1920s, Oliver Hill built a butterfly-plan house with Tudor elevations in 1937 near Hartley Wintney in Hampshire, while in 1935 Connell Ward and Lucas built an International Modern style house, High and Over, Amersham, to the same plan.

The butterfly plan seems to have appealed to the architects of this period for a number of reasons. Firstly it seemed logical, for from a central core of the hall and staircase the wings pushed out catching the sun and the view. But also, and for architects of this period more importantly, the silhouette created by the plan had the advantage of being symmetrical and romantically complex at the same time. Only the first of these houses, Shaw's Chesters, was Classical, all the others were highly Romantic and most of them were positively cranky in their use of Arts and Crafts building practices. Whether with thatched roofs and extraordinary chimneys as at The Barn; thatched roofs and wonderfully cranky brick and flint-work at Happisburgh Manor; turrets, roughcast and half-timbering at Baillie Scott's *Kunstfreundes* house; roughcast, half-timbering and strictly symmetrical gables and chimneys at Papillon Hall; wildly cranky flint and brick again at Home Place; tile-hung gables crashing into each other all over the place at How Green; knapped flint and brick at the more sober Kelling Hall; or International Modern in Amersham—they all have this overriding crankiness.

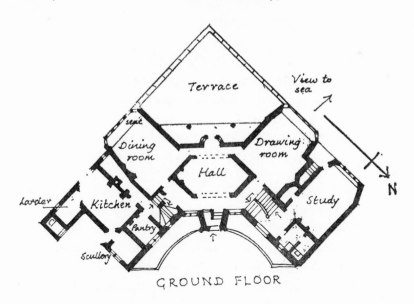

GROUND FLOOR

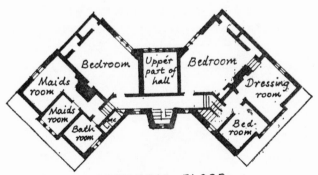

BEDROOM FLOOR

ATTIC FLOOR

The Barn, Exmouth, Devon, E. S. Prior 1897. Plans

The plan of The Barn, though, seems at first sight very logical. At each end of a hexagonal hall, which rises through the first floor, the dining and drawing rooms project at 30°. The staircase is tucked behind the drawing room and beyond this is a study some four steps above the drawing room floor. On the first floor two bedrooms, dressing rooms and maids' rooms are fitted in, and above is a day and a night nursery tucked in under the roof. Since Prior has used a hexagonal hall he has been able to avoid the rather unsatisfactory spaces that often grow into butterfly plans. In this way the plan is vastly superior to his Dorset plan, which has an amorphously shaped hall with complex triangles tucked in behind. The wings also give a nice sense of welcome combined with enclosure on the entrance front. But with a wholly typical perversity, little advantage is taken of the fact that this form of plan means that it is possible for rooms to have windows on three sides. The view to the sea is due west, but the house is orientated in such a way that the drawing room only looks across to the sea, while the dining room only has windows facing south. The opportunity to have two aspects in each of these rooms is lost, and lost for no obvious reason. If the plan has some cranky sense, the elevations carry crankiness beyond all logic. The house was originally thatched, but having been once burnt down it was reroofed in the present slates. Thatch with its rounded edges lends itself more readily to the shapes that Prior envisaged.

The facades are such a combination of forms thrown together in such a seem-

The Barn – perspective of entrance front by Raffles Davison

ingly haphazard fashion that it is difficult to think of the house as a static object—
a home and shelter to return to for rest after a day's work. Here everything seems
to be in movement, it seems almost to be a living being. In the centre of both
fronts, there rises a three-storeyed gabled block, in its middle the front porch rises
in a vertical strip up three storeys until it hits the underside of the tile-hung gable
of the main roof. Immediately under this, to either side, are strips of leaded windows, and then the tile-hanging continues, slightly set back, until it comes to the
roof of the two wings where it stops, cantilevering a considerable distance from the
front wall plane. In the meantime the two-storeyed side wings are forced into the
facade creating what seems to be an almost geological rift in its centre. The impression of violent movement is emphasized by the fact that the ends of these wings
hip down almost to ground level, crouching leopard-like for the spring forward
into the centre. These hips then sweep up to a pair of enormous and strangely
shaped circular chimneys, their caps supported on a ring of balls. There is pre-
cedence for these chimneys in some of the houses on Dartmoor. However, they
were never so large as these and they were never placed in such a prominent
position. The exaggeration of these chimneys, a traditional design in themselves,
is very typical of this type of extreme Arts and Crafts designer. Where Lutyens or
Baker merely took traditional forms and used them in a manner that fitted perfectly
with the countryside around, a man such as Prior had to assert his adherence to
traditional mode, forcing it upon the viewer until all sense of tradition has been
destroyed and all that remains is an awareness of the architect's personality.

The walls are laid in coarsed sandstone alternating with beach pebbles. Although
this is a traditional building technique, Prior has not been content to follow only
local traditions, but has reverted to one of Devey's romantic tricks, by suddenly,
and for no apparent reason, changing his dressed stone for a random unfaced stone
which reduces in scale as it rises up the building. This is contrasted with the most
finely worked stone to the entrance porch. The windows, where they are not
under the eaves, are capped with massive stone lintels.

The garden side continues the eccentricities (see plate X). Here the two outer
wings are gabled and these crash at 30° into the middle gable to create an almost
alpine combination of M-shapes. If this were not enough Prior then shaves off the
corners of these wings so as to add another cant to the facade. In the centre of each
gable, as it were emphasizing the separateness of each block, there is a curved
headed window. This is butted hard against the central group of windows, making
as uncomfortable a relationship as possible. One cannot but feel that in this house,

The Barn – perspective of garden front by Raffles Davison

whatever his client may have desired, Prior was after a Mannerist sense of unease, which is entirely inappropriate in an ordinary small house. But to Geoffrey Hoare and Geoffrey Pyne, in their *Prior's Barn & Gimson's Coxen*:

> The Barn is a very subtle building, intimate in size with the rooves almost growing out of the hillside. The original thatch was destroyed by fire but the variations in the levels of the windows remain and the gentle shifts of line give a feeling that the craftsman worked without a detailed plan. Look, for instance, at the four levels on the study-drawing room wing. On the left of the porch is the semi-venetian window of the study with the bedroom close above. The floor level is actually below the top of the study window. On the right the grand drawing room bay was increased in depth after the fire. Below it lurks the semi-basement window with just a hint of incarceration.[68]

It may be felt that the fact that the ceiling of the study cuts across the top of the Venetian window is a sign that the architect did not just allow his craftsmen freedom from close detailing but was unable fully to understand his plans in three dimensions.

However he did understand about good building craftsmanship and Prior's very high standards can be followed in the record of the building that Hoare and Pyne have extracted from letters preserved in the Rolle Estate Office. His main difficulty seems to have been in getting suitable stones. On 4 March 1896 Prior writes to Mr Chaumier, the Agent for the Rolle Estate: ' "The stone has not come in yet in big enough lumps to be of much use. We want the biggest blocks he can give us at the first. Pieces with some eight or ten cube feet in them. We shall be brought to a stand still next week without them. Your method of blasting breaks the stone all to pieces—no big blocks are being received. . . . [I want] good blocks 18″ high 18″ on bed and some two of three feet long such as can go into our base courses pretty much as they come." ' Later in the year there were problems with the thatch. The Council minutes ' "recommended that the plans submitted by Mr E. S. Prior for Major Weatherall . . . be not passed as they are not in accordance with the Byelaws—the roof being of thatch." '[69] However, after Prior had written to say that he would spray the roof with an incombustible material the Council gave way, though perhaps unwisely as later events were to show. The house was built for a Major Weatherall, who like Prior was an old Harrovian though he was seven years his junior, and cost over £7,000, a high price for a small house in the 1890s. Weatherall sold the house in 1905 and six months later it was totally burnt down (like a number of other thatched houses in this study). However, it was fully insured and the new owners commissioned Prior to rebuild to slightly altered plans, using slates this time. And so it stands today, much altered, but still one of the most picturesque, cranky and quaint of any of the houses of the 1890s, or indeed of any other period.

Chapter ten

STONEYWELL, LEA COTTAGE AND LONG COPSE 1897

OTHER Arts and Crafts architects were not perhaps so cranky as Prior, but they also seem to have been affected by the belief that at least a certain amount of crankiness and straightforward discomfort is necessary for true rural living. The leader of this group was Ernest Gimson. In many ways Gimson is the essential Arts and Crafts intellectual, 'getting back to nature' and enjoying the country crafts. However on every occasion the brilliant quality of the work that he produced and his entirely masculine attitude to life contrast well with that of many of his colleagues and contemporaries. Ashbee, with his affected city ways, his highly refined art work and his attempt to found an artistic colony in the Cotswolds, may possibly be the excuse for mockery; but Gimson and his friends, down the road as it were in another part of the Cotswolds, seemed able to produce work redolent of all that was best in the old crafts tempered still by a quality of design which makes their work far superior to even the products of the Morris workshops. There is none of the intellectual arrogance here that Morris, and so many of his followers such as Prior and Lethaby often display in their works.

In many ways the most creative of this group, Gimson was born in Leicester, the son of the founder of the engineering firm of Gimson and Co., who, like Voysey's father, held advanced religious views and attended the Leicester Secularist Society, to which in 1884 he took his nineteen-year-old son to hear William Morris speak. It was Morris who later advised him to go into Sedding's office. Here he met the Barnsley brothers, also the sons of a practical man, a partner of John Barnsley and Son, builders of Birmingham, who amongst other things had built the Town Hall, to Hanson's designs. Thus the three friends were all sons of business men from the centre of the industrial Midlands, as were Frederick Delius, Ronald Firbank and Edward Burne-Jones, to name but three other romantics who rejected the life of the city. Unlike the aesthetic Francophiles Delius and Firbank, the young architects chose to follow William Morris, himself the son of a successful business man, and to take up handcraftsmanship in the depth of the country, not being concerned too deeply in the making of money or popular success. Before this, Gimson and Sidney Barnsley set up practice for a short time in London at 3 Raymond Buildings, with Philip Webb in No. 1 and Lethaby and Lutyens round the corner in Gray's Inn Square. All but Webb were at the beginning of their practice and finding themselves constantly together, with Baker and Detmar Blow, at meetings of the Art Workers' Guild and SPAB. The marriage of the Arts and Crafts Movement and Neo-Georgian architecture can be said to have started in those early years when this group of talented young architects were in and out of each other's offices before they became famous and went off in their separate ways. Some went like Gimson to relative obscurity in the country, others like Lutyens and Baker to build for the Empire, and others like Lethaby to a life very largely given to the restoration of one building, Westminster Abbey, and to polemics which in the end were to lead architecture away from all the ideals that the others so strongly held.

Although the Sedding pupils went out to the country and made and created and built, unlike Lutyens, Baker and Detmar Blow, they never felt the need to give up and compromise with commercialism and the 'filthy rich' as Morris put it. For the Barnsleys and Gimson it was enough to make furniture in houses that they had built with their own hands and live a life of contentment in the country. They may never have built a Delhi nor a factory but they died in a more contented old age than did Detmar Blow, harassed by the bailiffs and the Duke of Westminster, or Lutyens depressed that his ever more megalomaniac schemes for London would never see fruition. In 1890 Gimson exhibited furniture in the Arts and Crafts Exhibition and with Barnsley helped to found Kenton & Co. Gimson learnt most from this short-lived project and since each partner had only put up £100 and were able to take away several pieces of furniture it was, as Norman Jewson points out in his enchanting book *By Chance I Did Rove*,[70] not an unmitigated disaster when it collapsed. While his friends Weir Schultz and Sidney Barnsley were touring Greece, and studying Byzantine architecture with the results that we have already noted at the church of Sancta Sophia, Lower Kingswood, Gimson toured Italy without becoming enthusiastic about Italian architecture. He did not really settle down until he moved to Pinbury Park, Sapperton in the Cotswolds in 1900 although he had in the meantime learnt both the craft of ladderback chair-making and modelling plasterwork, both crafts in which he was later to become a master, as he was in all matters of furniture-making.

In 1897 Gimson had the opportunity to put his ideals into practice, when he was commissioned by his family to build a group of weekend summer cottages in the Charnwood Forest north of Leicester. It was decided to build the cottages without a contractor, using local craftsmen with Detmar Blow, as foreman and working builder. Blow had been working in an office and attending classes in London at the Architectural Association, then not yet a full-time school of architecture, and at the age of twenty-one on a Continental tour with his mother and Sydney Cockerell he met Ruskin in Abbeville Cathedral. Ruskin was much taken by the young man and his sketches and invited him to bring his mother and Cockerell and to accompany him on a tour of Italy. This he did, and next year he went abroad with Ruskin again, this time alone, and had the unpleasant experience of having to deal with Ruskin's last onset of madness which took place on a Swiss hillside. Ruskin was obviously enchanted by both young men. In 1888 he wrote in a letter: ' "Carlyle [Cockerell] . . . carries my umbrella for me as if he were attending the Emperor of Japan" and "Detmar is as good as gold" '. Later when he had Detmar alone he wrote in his scrappy diary of the period: ' "(Dijon, *29th Aug.* '88)—I had the most wonderful day yesterday I have ever had here . . . (Morez, Jura, . . . 1888, *September 2nd*)—That I ever should have such a happy birthday [his mother's] morning again . . . Detmar sketched a Jura cottage, and I painted it for him yesterday at St. Laurent . . . (Sallenches, *11th Sept.*) . . . I've been up far among the granite boulders of the torrent, breaking stones in my old way. (Merligen, *11th Nov.*)—The gentians I sent you a day or two ago were gathered by Detmar—higher than I can climb now . . ." '[71]

This was to be Ruskin's last foreign tour and his last period of sanity. During the tour he became depressed and vague, he had delusions and fantasies; in December he was taken seriously ill in Paris and he never really recovered. As Sir Kenneth Clark says in *Ruskin Today*: 'For the last eleven years he lived on at Brantwood in a silent coma, unable to write, scarcely recognizing his friends, frequently photographed, a national institution.'[72] In Blow Ruskin had found his last disciple, and to him he passed on all his grandly insane passion for natural forms, but he was not in the short time able to inculcate in him his socialist principles and his intense morality, with the result that when the pressures of the world caught up with Blow he happily threw off the Ruskinian morals for the heady wine of French Baroque. But it was Ruskin who persuaded him to give up a normal architectural training and to apprentice himself to a builder. So Blow went to Newcastle upon Tyne, for some reason, and there apprenticed himself to a mason. Laurence Weaver mentions[73] that Blow had built several farm steadings and cottages in Yorkshire (including Mill Hill at Brandsby) when Gimson asked him to build the Leicestershire cottages. This is important since at this time Gimson had not been much involved in building, except for what he had seen in Sedding's office.

The first thing that is most noticeable about the cottages is their extreme Romanticism, even the most extreme of the Tudor Revival cottages of the inter-war period can hardly outdo them in cranky exaggeration. The second thing to notice is that there is not a touch of style revivalism about them, they honestly attempt to give the impression of a hand-crafted building of any period. Lawrence Weaver has it that 'an old inhabitant of the district, who had been absent some years, greeted Stoneywell on his return with the puzzled observation, "Odd that I should have forgotten this old cottage".'[74] A compliment that all right-thinking architects should cherish.

Stoneywell is the most extreme of the cottages. It was built for Sydney Gimson and is placed half way down a hillside almost into Stoneywell Wood. There is still very little attempt at a garden, just scattered boulders and wild flowers, since this would militate against the sense that this is an ordinary country cottage in no way affected by even the sophistication of an ordinary cottage garden. The cottage is still approached from above through a simple gate beside the road and a lane running across a field, the roof just visible under the brow of the hill. The path leads down to the back of the cottage and you have to walk right round the house to come to the front door. It is surprising how many architects of this period

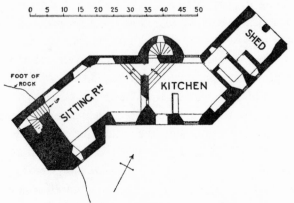

Stoneywell Cottage, Charnwood Forest, Leicestershire, E. Gimson 1897. Ground floor plan

Stoneywell Cottage – perspective by F. L. Griggs

favour this highly romantic approach to their houses. The cottage which is shaped like an open Z in plan, runs down the hillside, the upper floor at the far end being at the level of the ground. The entrance front is a highly effective romantic composition. The gable growing out of the hillside is buttressed by a great stone chimney and from here the roof falls down in a series of drops. In the sweep of the roof is a series of dormer windows, all at different levels. Originally this roof was in thatch and like Groote Schuur and The Barn had to be reroofed with the result that it now has a slightly harsher appearance in its slates. The wall has three windows, all at different heights, with the front door itself a simple hole. This entrance immediately shows that we are in a different world to that of Lutyens's clients, Major Weatherall at The Barn or even for that matter, Voysey's free think-ing radicals. There is no pretension here, not even the pretension of large but simple spaces.

The door opens to the kitchen. There is no porch, and only an oak settle at right angles to the door designed and made by Gimson gives any protection from the draught. Beyond the settle is a great open fireplace for cooking. As Weaver says: 'The lintel over the fireplace is an amazing bit of construction, a single gigantic slab weighing a ton and a half, a rough shard of slate that had lain neglec-ted in an old quarry until Mr. Detmar Blow espied it.'[75] Its great blue abstract shape set against the white wash of the rest of the walls dominates the room. In the centre is a Gimson table and simple ladderback chairs. Although the design is strongly over-simplified there is still a very clear architectural mind at work. The kitchen, because of the odd-angled shape of the house, is of a regular diamond shape, one wall is taken up by the fireplace and the other by the entrance to the larder. Beyond the flat wall, which has a tall window of almost Georgian propor-tions looking out on to the hillside, a series of angled stone steps appear. Four of these steps, made of natural stone not evenly trimmed, rise up to the curving stone staircase which rises in a bulge in the outside wall to the bedrooms. Beyond this the steps continue to turn and rise into the sitting room.

Although this is not a big room it gives an impression of space by the subtle way in which it twists following the slope of the ground outside. Beyond the corner is a wonderful deep ingle with a store for logs and above this a tiny window which penetrates deep into the wall and allows just a trickle of light from the south into this cave which otherwise might have been too claustrophobic. On the far wall a narrow staircase twists its way up to the main bedroom over. This bed-room is an enchanting place; whitewashed beams and roof trusses run up to the roof, the shapes retained, each beam obviously consciously chosen for its purpose. Still in the middle of the room is the oak bed that Gimson designed and made for it. There are no corridors so all the bedrooms are entered one from the other, which explains the two staircases. There is one absurd bedroom lit by a tiny window which can only be approached by a stepladder from a lower bedroom. Of course the whole thing is absurdly romantic and in many ways totally illogical.

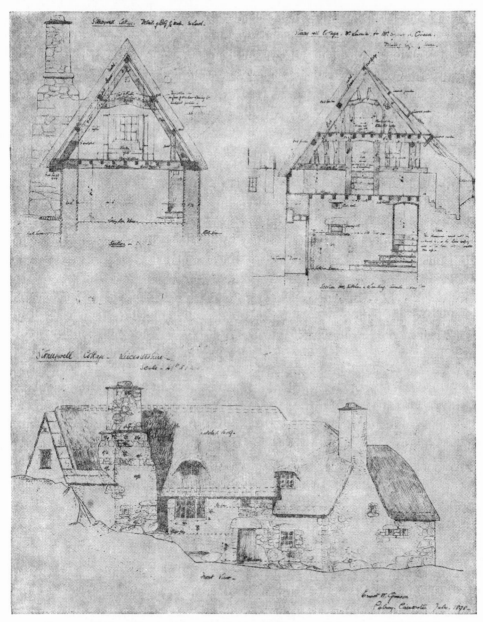

Stoneywell Cottage – working drawing by E. Gimson of elevation and sections

Why for instance should the two secondary bedrooms be approached from the wide central staircase and the main bedroom only be approachable from a very narrow stair out of the living room? But in an extraordinary way what should be only tiresome affectation somehow seems acceptable and to be the only sensible way of building given the set conditions, most of the difficulties of which were created by the choice of site—a steep hillside. The reason for this strange sense of reality can only be the method by which this building was constructed.

We have quite a full description by the indefatigable Lawrence Weaver of the building of one of the other houses on this site, Lea Cottage. Some time ago Lea Cottage, which had not been so well kept up as Stoneywell, looked just like a simple thatched Tudor farm cottage which has been allowed to run down (see plate XIII). There was nothing to suggest that it is a sophisticated exercise in building. Recently, however, it has been restored and extended and has lost some of its quality. This is how Weaver describes its building:

Mr. Blow took with him [from Yorkshire] to Leicestershire his foreman mason and a small band of men, who had worked with him before. The materials to his hand were very promising. They consisted chiefly of rough boulders, loose stones and the materials of old dry walls which the site provided. In the disused quarries of Swithland there were lying the remains of magnificent slate slabs, which lent themselves particularly to the rough and massive way of building that the neighbourhood seemed to demand. The foreman mason was Mr. Frank Green, who came from East Knoyle, Wilts . . . With him worked Henry Shepheard and Jimmy Snook (delightful name!). Three Leicestershire men joined the band. The other two were known simply as 'Harry' and 'William'; and Mr. Detmar Blow writes of them: 'Both dear giants in structure, and totally unlike their comrades being (I grieve to record it) too fond of beer.' The trowels that they brought matched their stature, for they were nearly two feet long.

The walls of Lea Cottage are of solid masonry, and coated within with a thick layer of plaster in order to counteract condensation. The timberwork of the first floor and roof was all made on the same principles that governed the masonry. At Sapperton in Gloucestershire Ernest Gimson had a band of men working at carpentry, furniture-making and other crafts, and they were responsible for the whole of the woodwork at the cottages.

Within, the timbers are not too smoothly wrought; they are of generous strength, and . . . of a natural curve where the need of increased headroom or the disposition of bracings indicate that curved pieces are more practical than straight.

Such irregularities are sometimes created by the solemn farce of cutting timbers which come straight and square from the sawmill into misshapen forms to re-create an old feeling. At Lea Cottage, however, the timbers are rough and sometimes curved, because they were English stuff and grew so . . . , instead of being foreign wood which came already squared from an ordinary timberyard.[76]

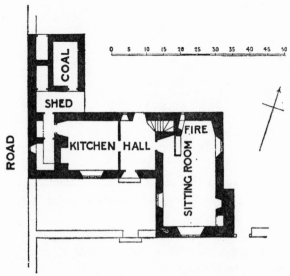

Lea Cottage, Charnwood Forest, Leicestershire, E. Gimson 1897. Plan

The plan of Lea Cottage is slightly more pretentious than that of Stoneywell. Here there is a hall, with a staircase leading out of it, the kitchen divided from it by a light screen in the medieval way. The sitting room is rectangular with a settle screening one of the two ingles, with which, for some reason, this small room is graced. The low ceiling is heavily beamed and from the beams are suspended shelves for books—a trick that Gimson was fond of, repeating it in most of his cottages in Gloucestershire. On the upper floor there is once again great play made of the wavy oak structure, in one place a natural shape having been used to form a truss, a natural or 'found' form of timbering much beloved by such architects as Baker and Lutyens. It is interesting to see that all this timberwork was fabricated

Lea Cottage – perspective of living room by F. L. Griggs

in the Cotswolds some 150 miles away and then transported to the site. It makes one realize that there was considerably more pre-planning and careful design in these cottages than is usually thought.

At about the same time that Gimson and Detmar Blow were building their cottages in Leicestershire, Alfred Powell was creating a similar cottage next door to a Philip Webb house in Ewhurst in Surrey. The two houses make a fascinating comparison. Coneyhurst is a late Webb house. It was built in 1885 so that about twelve years divide the two houses, but they seem to belong in many ways to different eras. At first glance it is the Webb house that seems the more recent. It was built for a spinster, Miss Ewart, and so by Victorian standards it counts almost as a cottage. It is, however, not small being three storeys high and having a large hall, two sitting rooms and a large dining room, as well as the usual tail of kitchens and a staff cottage attached. The most interesting room within the house is the tall hall and the staircase, which rises on one side of it. Between a solid oak frame the staircase runs up while the balusters and railings are formed of a white-

painted trellis, proportioned like Georgian windows. This simple device was something that Lutyens was obviously much taken by since he used it a number of
times in his later houses, notably the children's staircase in the Viceroy's House.
The outside of the house, at least in photographs, has much of the quality of a
Lutyens house, with beautifully laid red brickwork, a complexity of gables and
hips to the tile roofs, and tall unmoulded chimneys with hipped tile caps. Although
there are a number of different window shapes, nearly every window is a sash
window, with small panes with narrow glazing bars of Georgian proportion. The
styles of different periods are mingled to create a coherent whole.

Unfortunately, as with so many of the houses by the architects of the first
generation of the Arts and Crafts Movement, Coneyhurst suffers from a sense of
unpleasant harshness when seen in the brick. It is very difficult to put a finger on
what is wrong. Everything is most carefully done, the bricks are beautifully laid,
the detailing is exact but yet there is a feeling of deadness. It is almost as if the
architect's almost neurotic puritanical exactness has transferred itself to the
carpenter and the bricklayer and the bricklayer's fear of making an error in front
of this strong man has transferred itself into the very brickwork! This is something
that you never get in a Lutyens building; however run of the mill the job is, one
feels that something of the architect's sparkling involvement in life comes through
even in his brickwork. All this may perhaps seem somewhat far-fetched, yet it was
this spirit that informed the socialism of William Morris, though he so failed to
bring it about in his work. As we have seen John Ruskin felt it so strongly that he
sent off a young architect that he felt was the most talented of his generation to
apprentice himself to a stonemason so that he should understand the way in
which a man felt when he was building.

Alfred Powell, another of the small group of friends round Gimson, was also
from Sedding. Just next door to Coneyhurst on a high bank above a lovely valley
stands Long Copse in staggering contrast to Coneyhurst. It is stone built, with a
long roof of thatch and, at the end at right angles, a tiled wing (see plate XII). Like
the Gimson cottages it was originally built as a summer cottage of just two rooms,
joined together at a slight angle with a curving staircase between them. The plan is
obviously derived from the same source as Stoneywell's, though not so sensitively
handled and lacking the brilliant subtlety of the twisting staircase between the two
halves. The house was built for a Mrs Mudie-Cooke and Powell acted as Master
of the Works as well as designing it. He bought all the materials. All the craftsmen,
we are told by Laurence Weaver,[77] were university men, save the plumbers. This

D.H.–G

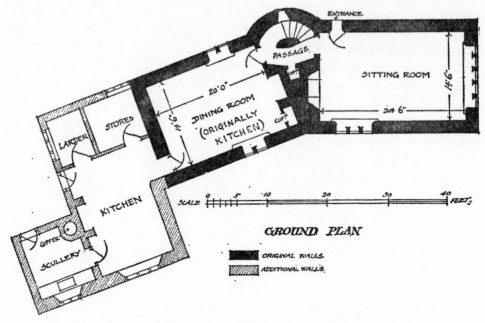

Long Copse, Ewhurst, Surrey, A. H. Powell 1897. Ground floor plan

is very difficult to believe, for the craftsmanship is of the highest quality, the stone laying for instance is firm and neat, without any of the pseudo-quaintness that we saw in Prior's professional work at Exmouth, and the thatch must have been laid by an expert. No doubt in fact the university men acted as labourers during their vacation whilst the real craftsmanship was carried on by professionals. It is, however, interesting that as early as this young men from universities chose to go out to labour during their vacations. The famous Ruskin fiasco at Cowley had a much firmer social significance.

It may, however, have been these students that give this cottage the slightly twee character so lacking at Charnwood Forest. There is the careful display of hand-wrought timber that we have seen in Leicestershire for, as Lawrence Weaver says:

The interior is simple and dignified. Nothing but oak was used for beams, flooring and doors, and the great timbers are rough from the adze. Some of the uprights are left in the round, stripped of bark, but unsquared. This seems just to overstep simplicity and to plunge into the crude . . . The whole of the woodwork construction was arranged so that the timbers could remain exposed. This allowed them to be cut from the green tree and used straightway without seasoning. The trees were chosen to give in their natural shapes the required curves for the roof principals. The walls are whitewashed, and the house is innocent everywhere of both paper and paint.

Once again all this smacks of a little too much refinement and indeed downright silliness. It is difficult to understand how the house has stood up for eighty years if it really was built of green timbers straight from the woods, or why properly seasoned timber was not used. This would certainly not be something that a real building craftsman would have done. Weaver gives the game away—this cottage is really in the end just a matter of playing it rough, with Mrs Mudie-Cooke a latter-day Marie Antoinette—for he goes on to say:

> There is no accommodation in the house for servants, who have their quarters in an adjoining thatched cottage—another aid to the owner's pursuit of perfect quiet. The whole of the upper floor, with its five bedrooms, bathroom etc., is thus available for family and guests.[78]

The wing that sticks out from the house was an addition which was also created because of a need for further comfort. Lawrence Weaver again:

> Mrs. Mudie-Cooke's idea was to have a little country retreat of the purely cottage type, with a single living-room, into which the entrance door gave. This was well enough in summer, but winter brought devastating draughts. . . . An extra room . . . was provided by converting the original kitchen [into a dining room] and building a new kitchen and offices beyond. At the same time there were provided additional bedrooms on the upper floor and a verandah by the outer door of the dining room.[79]

This extension is in the same sandstone, but is tiled in the local Horsham tiles rather than the Norfolk thatch. As Weaver says, himself catching the rather precious atmosphere, 'There is a tenderness about the way the moss and willow weed grow on this stone roof, that seems Nature's benediction of the use of local things.'[80] Yet in spite of all this nonsense when one first sees the house lying at the head of its valley, drowsing of a summer day, and when one enters the cool and perfectly

proportioned interior, all this is swept away in a realization that in spite of everything this is a real house built by real people for real people, an experience that is
alas all too rare.

Like the Charnwood Forest cottages this is achieved because it is the work of
young enthusiasts building the buildings themselves. When a Webb or a Prior
attempt the same look but do not build themselves, the result is always either
eccentric or dead, and sometimes both. However, few architects can afford to
handcraft just one house at a time. It is essential to find some other means to
achieve the same quality, and it was Dawber, Lutyens and Baker who seemed most
able to achieve this, by great attention to detail but at the same time a careful
creation of a building team that followed them from house to house. While
Lutyens and Dawber found their teams ready to hand in rural Surrey and the
Cotswolds, Baker had to create his team from scratch in South Africa.

Chapter eleven

BROADLEYS, MOOR CRAG
AND BLACKWELL 1898

1897 was the year of the Queen's Diamond Jubilee, but by now Edwardian archi-tecture was in full flower, and all the figures that one normally considered to be Edwardian were at work and for most of them 1897 was important. Work was plentiful and there was obviously a feeling that now was the time that experiment could be attempted. This was the year that Lutyens, Ashbee and Prior all designed buildings in which the gables were exaggerated in such a way as to dominate the house. Voysey also seems to have been caught in the mania for thrusting gables in at every possible position. Normally, he contented himself with vast hipped roofs, but in 1897 he built New Place tucked into a bosky hillside above Hasle-mere in Surrey. Here he came the nearest he ever did to a complex roof shape. On the garden front, which drops a whole floor from the entrance, he built a curved three-storey bay window, and balanced on top of it a rather thin gable. The house then sets back, and the ground rises to a block which starts as a gable from which a chimney rises, through a smaller gable. This then continues on the same plane to become a bay window, which turns back towards the roof at the rear, rather unhappily overlooking the roof of another wing which here juts for-ward to end in another gable—altogether a muddled and thoroughly un-Voysey-esque facade. Norney, at Shackleford in Surrey, the other house that he built this year, though not as eccentric as New Place, makes a display of no less than four gables, three of which are different, along its entrance front. It may be that here Voysey is under the influence of Lutyens who was building all around the Shackleford area. If this is so it is the first example of an established architect being influenced by the boy genius of Thursley. In any case it was to be a short-lived influence since after 1897 Voysey relapsed into his hipped style and in future when he used gables they grew inevitably from the main roof form.

In 1898 at Windermere, Voysey was building two important houses: Broadleys for A. Currer Briggs and Moor Crag for Mr and Mrs J. W. Buckley with gardens by Mawson. Of the two Broadleys is marginally the more interesting. Both houses are built of 2-foot-thick stone walls pebbledashed with sweeping slate roofs over, which at least go some way to keeping within Lake District tradition, though in the chimneys Voysey makes no attempt to follow local examples. Like so many of his buildings these houses seem to have been designed in the calm of his Marylebone offices, with little consideration given to the real life of the countryside in which they are placed. Voysey was too fastidious to have become involved in the hurly-burly of ordinary country life, and his houses reflect this; they lie firmly hugging the shapes of the hillside but still seem not to be of the hill. One feels that it is symptomatic of him that his specifications, which were quite short, should have taken up a considerable amount of space in specifying the architect's requirements, whenever he visited the site, for clean towels, water and soap. There is always a touch of the townee who must be always washing his hands about Voysey's buildings. He seems to be the perfect architect for the maiden lady with advanced views. He included many such people in his clientele. It is unfortunate that his houses should give this impression since he seems to know his sites well and he always sites his houses beautifully to take advantage of the land. Moor Crag is particularly well placed (see plate XIV). The main part of the house is on the flat but is set at right angles to a steep slope. Voysey makes use of this slope with the highly romantic treatment of the end gable of the house, which he sweeps right down the slope of the hill to below the main ground level. Otherwise the main facade is all that one would expect in a Voysey house; a pair of gables at each end, between them first a bay from which a verandah grows, which then becomes the roof of a further bay in the centre of the gable. Three thick but completely plain chimneys poke through the roof acting as foils to the great sweep of tiles.

If there is perhaps a touch of the suburban in Moor Crag this can never be said of Broadleys, which is one of Voysey's most exciting houses. If perhaps it suggests a future for his architecture that was never to happen, it is none the less a splendid achievement in its own right and for once makes it possible to speak of Voysey in the same breath as Lutyens or Frank Lloyd Wright. Like so many of these houses it is approached by an almost secret drive from above and to the side, so that suddenly we are on the rear forecourt. The house sits high up above Windermere and so, like Perrycroft and Greyfriars, Puttenham, all the living rooms look away from the entrance, which means that the front door becomes involved within the service area. However, here everything is handled with much more care than at Perrycroft or Greyfriars. The main block faces west across the lake and at right angles to this is the service block, forming an entrance court at the rear of the

Broadleys, Windermere, Cumbria, C. F. A. Voysey 1898. Perspective of entrance front by R. Gradidge

house. Voysey arranges it that the back door is right at the end of this block, forming a completely different drive for deliveries—not a perfect solution but an improvement on his usual bodge.

As one comes up to the entrance court, one sees the bulk of the house with its overpowering roofs to the left; originally this looming quality was increased since the first floor at this end projected out to form a small verandah, supported on simple wood columns. This alas has now been filled in. Beyond the great hipped roof, which comes down to the sill level of the first floor windows, a new hipped roof juts out, supported on a strip of leaded windows on all sides. This is the staircase block. Beside this is an unprepossessing little porch, and then crammed up to the hipped roof is a gable, which dies into the long strip of the service wing, lit below and in the roof with a minimum of windows, the tiny dormers lighting only a passage. This means that the bedrooms it serves face due north, but they have a fine view up the lake to the town of Windermere.

It is, however, the front overlooking the lake which is the more dramatic (see plate XV). Here the enormous roof is allowed to dominate, coming down to just above the sill height of the first floor windows; but through this roof three great curved bay windows, flat-roofed like great barrels, force their way up while the roof sweeps down round them to either side. To the right of these bays an enormous chimney, as wide as the bays and as deep but within the depth of the house, also forces itself up through the roof, and rises to just below the roof ridge,

where it is cleanly cut off with a flat tile capping. Above it four chimneypots protrude dwarfed by the immense size of the large block. Where the service wing
projects there is another vast chimney at right angles to the first, thus helping to
show the turn in the main form. This was the great period for chimneys. Any
architect who had studied the work of Norman Shaw—and all architects of
intelligence had—would have learned from the master how to balance the vertical
of chimneys against the horizontal of the ridge line, the angles demarcated by the
roof gables, and then wished to carry Shaw's ideas well beyond anything he could
have imagined. In Voysey houses in particular chimneys grew to three or four
times the cubic area required. They raise themselves to an immense height over
roofs, which in turn sweep down almost to ground level, their vast eaves supported
on thin brackets. Gables grow from the eaves, and raise themselves to two or even
three storeys up to the highest point of the main roof, whose vast area always
dominates the whole mass of the house. Considering the exaggerations it is
remarkable that there are not more cases in which it does not become merely
ludicrous. But Voysey at least has such understanding of architectural scale that he
in the end retains enough control to avoid the major excesses, and most other
architects working in this style never went as far as Voysey in his use of these
exaggerated symbols of homeliness.

Voysey continues with these symbols in the interior of Broadleys. One enters
through a low porch and turns to the right down a passage which on one side
almost immediately opens on to a tall hall running up two storeys, the passage
roof forming the floor of an open gallery over. To the right is a tall fireplace
running up two storeys, and, looking out across to the lake, the curved stone-
mullioned bay window runs up the full two-storey height of the room. The tall
bay window and the gallery growing out of the hall are very similar to Baillie
Scott's Blackwell which was going up down the road at the same time. The coincidence is surprising since it was rare in 1898 for English architects to plan small
houses in this way, though there are enough Tudor precedents for the plan.
Baillie Scott published an earlier version of Blackwell's plan in his article in *The
Studio* of January 1895, entitled 'An Ideal Suburban House', and this may possibly
have influenced Voysey's plan. If this is so it adds a further coincidence since it
would seem that Baillie Scott was influenced in his design by a project of Voysey's,
which he in his turn had published in *The Studio* in 1894. However, a comparison
of the two halls shows that they are only similar in the most superficial way, and
Baillie Scott's is the more interesting in his use of space. There is always in

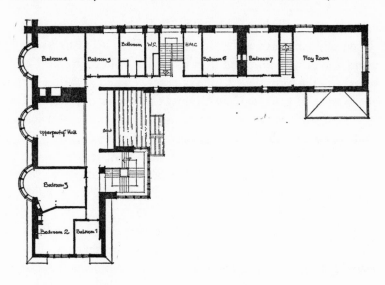

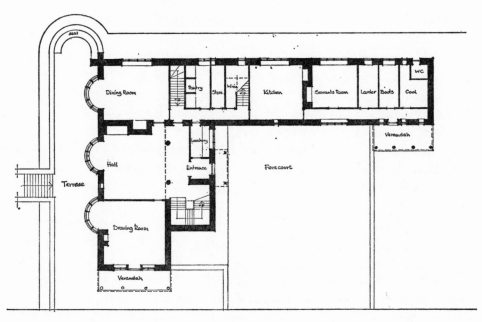

Scale in feet

Broadleys – ground and first floor plans

Voysey's planning an almost French logic, whereas Baillie Scott follows the romantic accretive English traditions of Shaw. In all his plans Voysey is too fond of drawing two parallel lines and then fitting his main rooms between these lines. Each room is of the right size and the windows come where they logically should, but there is none of the spatial excitement that comes from Baillie Scott's looser planning. At Broadleys the staircase, which as we shall see is a splendid thing in itself, far superior to Baillie Scott's, is tucked away in a corner, while Baillie Scott allows his to dominate the room. Where Baillie Scott creates his enchanting ingle and the room over, Voysey allows his fireplace to stand on the wall which rises two storeys, flooded by light from the tall double-storey bay. In Baillie Scott's case the bay windows are carefully kept to the lower parts of the room, so that the light will not flood up on to the ceiling. In the gallery Baillie Scott allows just glimpses of the hall, while Voysey has an open balcony, with a charming little curved projection, for looking down into the hall. However, set against his spatial excitement is Baillie Scott's overriding and rather oppressive Tudory detailing. Voysey, on the other hand is calm and simple, with just plastered walls and plain painted woodwork.

Voysey's staircase rises off the hall in the corner and, like most of his staircases, follows round a square in simple dog-legs. Within this space he has achieved a series of fascinating effects. The lower part of the staircase is panelled, in the simple almost unmoulded oak panelling that Voysey affected. It runs up to the top of the strip window that we have noticed from the outside, the top of which comes just above the sill of the first floor window, so it is only just above eye level at the first step. Thus one does not get a sense of an enclosed tower that one would from windows well above eye level. At each corner of the turn of the stairs there are square balusters which are carried right up to the undersides of the ceiling, where they develop wide, flat-moulded caps, seemingly holding up the ceiling. Similarly stair balusters continue up above half-rail level, rising in slats fretted with elongated heart patterns up to the chair-rail dado level on the first floor, where they run horizontally. This dado is carried right around the first floor; it is, of course, the height also of the balustrade of the passage and also the height of the top of the staircase windows. This use of a continuous horizontal line running remorselessly across, affecting all features, is very typical of Voysey. It is something that he probably picked up from architects such as Street, who also found pleasure in the remorseless logic of his 'vigour', as it was called. It is, of course, something that is much more obvious on the drawing board than it is when used in the building, where it can lead to gross inconvenience and silliness, as it does in the handrails of this staircase, which are both unusable for the purpose for which they were intended and are almost uncleanable. However, this idea was picked up by the creators of modern architecture, always wrongheadedly picking up the least practical aspects of the 'English style', and even to this day architects find a perverse pleasure in lining-up otherwise unrelated elements in a design. This becomes particularly annoying when all the tops of furniture are lined through to achieve a pleasing architectural picture, ignoring the function of each piece. Voysey of course would never have carried matters as far as this and his furniture is always perfectly comfortable to use in spite of its at times rather frenzied proportions. His rooms are always well proportioned and comfortable to live in.

1898 was the *annus mirabilis* for M. H. Baillie Scott, who up till now had been a somewhat obscure architect languishing in the Isle of Man. He had set up practice there in 1889 and for the last eight years had been building a series of relatively undistinguished houses. He was, however, a delightful water-colourist who could create the most charming dream pictures of his own work and he was assiduous in sending these to *The Studio*. Stuck away as he was on the Isle of Man, Baillie Scott seems never to have had much direct contact with the leaders of the profession but he was always able to see what the latest trends would be, and his drawings would often reinterpret these into a more elegant and acceptable style. It was inevitable that sooner or later someone would fall for these ravishing drawings and commission him to build. It is really not surprising that the first important client should have been the highly 'artistic' Grand Duke of Hesse who in 1897 sent an envoy to the Isle of Man to commission him to redecorate and refurnish a drawing and dining room in what must have seemed the dowdy and old fashioned thirty-year-old ducal palace at Darmstadt. Baillie Scott turned to that other highly publicized but little commissioned architect C. R. Ashbee and his Essex House Workshops to make the furniture and light fittings to Baillie Scott's designs. Baillie Scott, like so many architects of his time, believed that he should have total control over the design of every part, both of the architecture, the furnitures and all decorations. As he points out in his book *Houses and Gardens* of 1906,[81] he was never to have this chance, and his only interiors which in any way lived up to his ideal were designed to be fitted into older buildings. Other than that insuperable difficulty he was given at Darmstadt a free hand.

Even Baillie Scott in 1898 designed with darker colours than he would have done a few years later. He intended that the dining room should be dark to contrast

Darmstadt Palace, Hesse, Germany, M. H. Baillie Scott 1897. Perspective of Duchess's day bed
by R. Gradidge

with the white-painted elegance of the drawing room, but the heavy character of
the original German palace got the better of his designs, and the black-and-white
photographs, which are the only record that we have, suggest that the drawing
room is almost as dark as the dining room. There are, however, elegant pieces;
particularly delightful is the sofa in the sitting room, designed like a Byzantine
four-poster bed, with tall columns and triangular capitals of writhing plants holding
up a tester, which projects out over the sofa at picture-rail level. From this are
suspended at one corner a rosary and at the other a sanctuary lamp, though
whether this touch is Baillie Scott's or the Grand Duchess's is not recorded. For this
room Baillie Scott designed some very characteristic furniture, which was made by
Ashbee. Though there was at the time some discussion as to who was responsible
for the designs, and indeed who was in fact originally commissioned, to our eyes
the furniture seems to be completely Baillie Scott and to have none of Ashbee's
hankering after the eighteenth century. Baillie Scott always worked to medieval
precedents, and like Morris and Burges he admired painted furniture. However,
the results are very different to the work of the older men. For this furniture is

covered with light floral patterns, often on oak stained lightly so that the grain shows, or the wood is painted white and is once again stencilled in bright greens or purples, with perhaps from time to time a touch of gold leaf used further to lighten the design.

Morris had of course been in the forefront of the revived interest in naturalistic pattern. His formalized forests of plants swirling in organized arabesques were as popular at the end of the nineteenth century as they are now. Unlike artists today, most designers of the 1890s were consummate artists in pattern design. They had been taught by the Japanese the value of blank spaces and thus their patterns had become attenuated. But where Morris created an overall pattern, they would use just one perfectly drawn plant, a flower perhaps on a stem with its attendant leaves, but placed in such a way that the whole surface is made to relate to this one small design. On his furniture of the period Baillie Scott proved himself to be a master of this style. At Darmstadt is a music cabinet of dark oak. The cupboard doors above the music racks have elaborate silver hinges which end in sculpted lilies, and this motif is repeated in the painting on the doors themselves. Here each door is painted with a single formalized stem, at its head five lilies, the painting just stretching a little above and below the hinges. It is this that gives the design its tension. The edges of the rack have a simple alternating pattern but otherwise there are no mouldings and all the interest is concentrated on the two painted panels. The design reminds one in the end not so much of Pre-Raphaelite Gothic furniture as of the background to Pre-Raphaelite painting. The scarlet hanging panel embroidered with a single stem of lilies which hangs beside Our Lady in Rossetti's 1850 painting of the Annunciation called *Ecce Ancilla Domini*, must have influenced Baillie Scott.

The influence of the Pre-Raphaelites, and in particular Burne-Jones, is also very strong in the furniture designs, particularly in a barrel chair that was made for Darmstadt. This precursor of so many chairs by Mackintosh and Frank Lloyd Wright is clearly taken from furniture used in the foreground of a then famous Burne-Jones tapestry that used to hang in Stanmore Hall. The chairs have backs shaped like barrels, with seats circular on plan. On three sides there are flat splats which run up above the head of anyone sitting down. In Baillie Scott's chair the splats are decorated with a repeated design of heart-shaped leaves; later the splats became plain, or sometimes they were pierced. This type of chair can never have been comfortable for basically it was unfunctional though both Mackintosh and Wright adapted the design for use in dining rooms; but it had the pictorial quality that was so much admired in interior decoration at this time.

Painters have always exerted an influence on architects (when they themselves were not in fact architects, which in the Renaissance they often were), and the backgrounds to pictures have often seemed a valuable source for ideas. However, it was in the 1890s that the idea took root that an interior should be designed to look as much like a picture as possible. It was perhaps a natural development of the picturesque theories of a hundred years earlier which suggested that the landscape should be transformed into a semblance of the work of Claude. For this idea first developed in what would seem to be the intractable field of landscape gardening before it became popular indoors. Baillie Scott with his delightful perspectives, suggesting a Burne-Jones dream fantasy, led the way to this ideal. It was this painterly approach, particularly in his use of colour, that made his interiors so different from the work of the other architects that we have been studying. Neither Lutyens nor Newton seems to have given much thought to interior colour. Morris and Co. was brought in by the client at Bullers Wood, and on only a very few occasions do we find Lutyens thinking about colour schemes. But a Baillie Scott house is nothing without his original colour schemes and furnishings.

Baillie Scott's whole attitude to colour differed from that of most architects who came after Adam, and who had reacted against the Adam brothers' over-designed, interior-decorated interiors. To a certain degree Baillie Scott returned to the

Barrel chair by M. H. Baillie Scott

Adam conception and colour schemes. For Baillie Scott there were three basic colour schemes. The first one was the dark colours that he used in dining rooms. Dark oak would be set off against sombre browns, dark greens, oranges and dark reds, colours not too dissimilar to the colours in common used at that time for dining and billiard rooms. The two other schemes relied on a great deal of white, most of Baillie Scott's furniture design being enamelled white or lightly stained an 'artistic' green. His pure white interiors often rely on a very sharp contrast of golden orange, perhaps combined with a pale blue or light purple and pink. It was these elegant, rather feminine colours that he considered suitable for drawing rooms. In bedrooms on the other hand he tended to use khaki greens, once again set off with intense patches of purple and pink. The palette is always very light and very clean, the watercolour washes seem almost to come straight from the tube without any mixing, and the contrast with the rather heavy colours of even such artistic designers of an earlier generation as William Morris and Norman Shaw is enormous. Mackintosh and Walton seem to have arrived at a similar palette quite separately. They too were wonderful water-colourists, as were most of the alumni of the Glasgow School of Art—and at this time even the more commercial designers were turning to a lighter palette—but Baillie Scott seems to have been the first person to have published such schemes. He suffered the usual fate of a pioneer and very few of his designs were ever used. Now all are lost so we have only his coloured pictures on which to base our ideas of what his interiors would have looked like. If they were only partly as fine as the drawings, and they probably were, then they must have been very exciting to live in.

Blackwell in Bowness-on-Windermere was Baillie Scott's first major commission after the Darmstadt work. It was commissioned by Sir Edward Holt, and James Kornwolf suggests[82] that it may have been the client who stipulated the vaguely manorial style for the outside, though why he should think this is not clear. The house is in fact designed in a careful reproduction of the style of the traditional houses in the neighbourhood. It is built of rendered brick with stone dressing with a modicum of Tudor trim, the tubular chimneys being copied direct from Westmorland originals.

The entrance front is a traditional L-shaped entrance court, with a gabled porch as the main entrance. It is not particularly well handled and has none of the panache of Lutyens or the warm sense of welcome that we find in Voysey's work. The garden fronts are much more interesting. The main front here comprises a group of three gables kicked forward from the main block. The windows in these

Blackwell, Windermere, Cumbria, M. H. Baillie Scott 1898. View of entrance front (top) and from south-west (bottom) by R. Gradidge

gables seem to bear little relation one to the other, one more case of the desire to give the impression of a haphazardly thrown together elevation. The right hand of these gables is the most straightforward with a single window at each level and to the right of it the deep ingle of the fireplace. The central gable has at its base a large bay window, with a low horizontal window over it lighting a smaller bedroom. It has the same sill level as its neighbour and is as wide but only rises to the mullion level. On the third gable all is different again. Here, reflecting the hall inside, there is a small bay pushed hard up against the left-hand side; then half-way between the ground and first floor there is a large window with a tiny window to one side, and above this the second-floor window sill is at the level of the top of the window beside it. After these gables the facade drops back, then right at the extreme left-hand side another bay pushes out. Beyond this there is a garden wall and turning the corner the ground drops down a further floor, the end gable thus running up four floors. At the extreme left-hand side of this there is another deep bay. Unlike the other bays, which are canted, this one is rectangular in plan and made entirely of squared stone mullions, with the leaded lights carried to the outside edge, a direct lift from Voysey's bays. Inside, this bay forms the most enchanting ingle seat.

Although the exterior is effective in its casual-seeming handling of a complex problem of windows and levels, it is in the three-dimensional use of interior space that Blackwell is more interesting. Though not perhaps as Kornwolf in his oddly titled *M. H. Baillie Scott and the Arts and Crafts Movement: Pioneers of Modern Design* would suggest, for he is of the opinion that Baillie Scott's two-storey hall plan with its ingle is completely original and leads, save the mark, to Le Corbusier's 1922 Ozenfant Studio. This use of space is not in fact in itself particularly original for it comes direct from the works of both Ernest George and Norman Shaw.

The entrance porch leads into a cross-passage from which the main hall place is visible through a semi-transparent screen. To the left at the end of the passage is the dining room and to the right is the drawing room, both interesting, but not as spatially exciting as the main hall. This is heavily Tudor-beamed, in a rather overpowering manner, but it is justified here since most of the ubiquitous timberwork is structural and actually holds up the various partitions that divide up the spaces. As one enters the hall from the low passage it suddenly rises to two storeys; to the right a staircase turns in a dog-leg to the framed gallery that forms the first floor corridor, running over the entrance passage. This staircase branches off half-way up and with a sharp turn leads into a delectable little room which is formed over the fireplace, creating a deep ingle for the fire. This ingle is lit by the small bay that we saw outside. The idea of a small room over a fireplace must be taken from Tudor precedent but it was favoured by George who used it a number of times but in particular at W. S. Gilbert's house in Harrington Gardens in South Kensington. Shaw also used it in the dining room of his own house at 6 Ellerdale Road in Hampstead, which he had built twenty-four years earlier for himself.

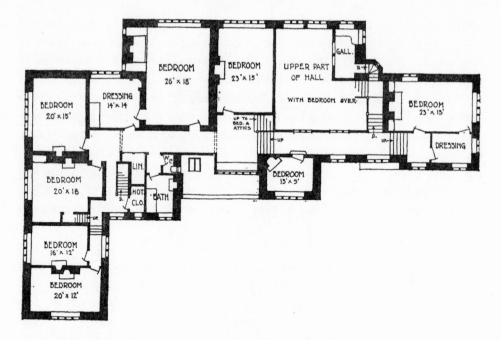

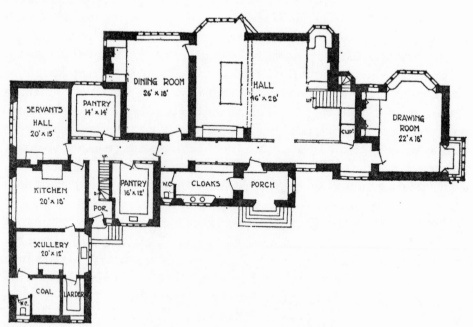

Blackwell – ground and first floor plans

Blackwell – perspective of hall by R. Gradidge

Since Shaw's room was designed to be a secret den he was not able to make use of space in the way that Baillie Scott does. This little room is away from the main hall, but is none the less clearly part of the room. It makes an ideal place for carrying on a private conversation while still being able to feel that one is part of the main company. Baillie Scott has not, however, completed his tricks for this room, for to the left of the entrance the ceiling drops, just where a bay window breaks out, and here there was a billiard table, with the traditional fixed seat tucked in under the gallery. It was odd at this time to give the billiard table such prominence. Even Cecil Rhodes, building himself a bachelor mansion in Cape Town, put the billiard room well away from the main body of the house. It is obvious that Baillie Scott had found in Sir Edward Holt a client who was willing to experiment. In the two other reception rooms Baillie Scott certainly experimented.

The dining room he designed to be very dark, as was his usual practice. It has another wonderful deep ingle, each side of the fireplace lit by two little windows. Architects at this time understood that when you design a small space which grows from a larger space it is essential to light it with separate windows in scale with the smaller room. As well as turning the space from a cave into an area in its own right, this also serves to give its own scale to the smaller room which otherwise would be dwarfed. This trick was, like so many others concerning interior space, pioneered by Shaw. In this dining room Baillie Scott used another Shaw trick—the very deep frieze. A dado runs at about 4 feet above the floor and, since it is just above eye level when one is seated, it gives a sense of enclosure at the dining table. Immediately above this, the wall becomes a stencilled frieze of formalized peacocks coloured in a mixture of greens and oranges. The oak ceiling is divided in square panels with great joists, and the boarded infill has diagonal struts.

In complete contrast to this dark room is the delectable light drawing room, which is one of the few rooms to look out over Windermere (see plate XVII). The house lies quite a way above the water and most of the other rooms face across to the fells that sweep down to the lake. This room was never furnished as Baillie Scott had intended, but it is painted in white enamel as he wished it to be. It is entered through a pair of doors and immediately to the right is the fireplace with its inevitable ingle which once again has its own little window. Immediately above the doors, which are no more than normal height, there runs a deep shelf, which is carried right round the room, except at the windows. This shelf is supported throughout on thin and elegant columns from which bowls of wood branch out at the top, carved with formalized leaves and fruits. At the ingle, and at the bay window, which looks over Windermere, these tree forms group in pairs of threes, to give the impression of a formalized bower. The ceiling of the fireplace ingle carries through no higher than the frieze, and over the fireplace this low ceiling is supported by a little cupboard, with tiny glazed windows. There are fixed seats between the columns, and finely wrought firedogs, using the same formalized tree pattern in the grate. Both bay windows in this room have seats under them, and the great square bay which juts out flush with the side wall is surrounded by the same little tree columns. Baillie Scott has continued this tree motif throughout the house in carving on bosses and screens: 'In the adornment of this house,' he says:

. . . it was specially desired that the mountain ash should form the subject for decoration . . .

In the carved trees, which appear in the staircase screen and on the hall ingle, birds' nests are interwoven in the branches and birds flutter amongst the leaves and fruit. In the brackets to the lower beams and in the bosses to the ceiling various local plants are represented. One is entwined with bryony, another shows the blooms of the wild guelder-rose, while the bloom and berries of the

White Lodge, St Mary's Convent, Wantage, Berkshire, M. H. Baillie Scott 1898. Perspective of entrance front by Baillie Scott

hawthorn and the wild rose are amongst the features of the carving. The same variety of carving occurs in the white drawing room, where, in the capitals to slender columns, the foliage and branches of various trees are represented.

Two of the most important features in the metal-work are the drawing-room grate and hall electric light pendant. In each of these the ironwork is brightened by white enamelled and scarlet berries.[83]

Baillie Scott's work is perhaps a little 'precious', but in these earlier houses, he had developed an ideal and formalized conception of decoration that was very much his own. It was a form of decoration that was to have a more profound effect on the Continent, than in England.

In 1898 Baillie Scott designed another important house, the White Lodge, which he built for the chaplain of Street's St. Mary's Convent at Wantage in Berkshire. Nothing can have been further from Street's immensely grand but somewhat dour work, which had been built only forty years earlier than Scott's elegant little house. Here there is not the slightest suggestion that this house is for a clergyman; it might be an ordinary upper middle-class house in any suburb, the only concession to the client's profession being a small oratory tucked away in the corner of the study. This is an enchanting little vaulted room, with an elegantly cool piece of stained glass, showing a very formalized design of the Virgin and Child in yellows and bright greens. The house is one of Baillie Scott's quietest, though the white-painted and rendered pebbledash walls being set off by the red of roofs in one of his ravishing water-colours, do not, as so often, live up to the romantic ideal in reality. Somehow the dream has some of the harshness of so many rendered Neo-Georgian buildings of the 1930s. It is difficult to see why in the end this house disappoints. It is most carefully detailed; once again the leaded windows, set in stone, are brought right forward flush with the wall. The edge of the roof to the gables is cut off sharp and given hardly any overhang, which is just excusable from a structural point of view when using heavy render, but none the less causes the kind of pattern staining that we are used to in modern buildings which have also had their moulding smoothed away. On the entrance front the downpipes, some of which of course are additions, are very noticeable. However, architects

White Lodge – ground and first floor plans

who have really thought their design through always manage to avoid this solecism.

The plan is Baillie Scott's first really developed 'American' open plan. There can be no doubt that he studied the work of the Shingle School and in particular the work of McKim, Mead and White, whose buildings were often published in England, though it is hardly likely that Frank Lloyd Wright's work would yet have been known to him. Indeed it may be that the chopped-off gables are an attempt to interpret some of the Shingle-School gables. The hall can be opened up with double doors which lead into the dining room, which has a deep ingle. To the other side the hall leads into the study, also deeply ingled, from which leads the oratory; thus the space has been allowed to flow into all the living rooms. It is interesting to see that even Baillie Scott, the great English protagonist of the open plan, did not use this type of plan again for a number of years. It was not until central heating was properly understood here that such plans became at all practical.

Chapter twelve

LE BOIS DES MOUTIERS
AND ORCHARDS 1898

FINALLY we turn to two magnificent houses that Lutyens built in 1898. One is a suburban house and the other a house in northern France, near Dieppe. Le Bois des Moutiers has never been discussed in any study of Lutyens's work, though it is difficult to see why not, since this large house with its lovely garden by Gertrude Jekyll is one of the most imaginative of his early designs. However, it does not easily fit into any of those patterns so beloved of academics, which suggests that Lutyens's career moved from the simple English Vernacular Revival to High Classicism with hardly a consideration of any other style. In fact like many other architects of this period, in the 1890s he was questing for a style which took the English Vernacular as a basis only. He built in any number of different styles but still within the Arts and Crafts tradition. This could lead to the Baroque on the one hand and the crankiest of structural honesty on the other. Lutyens tried most of these styles during this period. It would seem that it was only after both Gertrude Jekyll and his wife's aristocratic family had come to dominate him that he forsook this quest and turned to the Neo-Georgian Vernacular that had been pioneered by Philip Webb, though he never forgot his early delight in complex ideas and forms.

Le Bois des Moutiers can be looked upon as the culmination of one of these styles, just as the exactly contemporary Orchards is the first completely satisfactory example of Lutyens's Old English Vernacular style, a style which he had taken from Shaw but had sophisticated and mixed with the true tenets of the Arts and Crafts Movement to create something entirely his own. It is this style of his that is still most admired today. The two houses are quite different; neither is better than the other, they both display to a high degree the quite staggering Lutyens imagination and sense of architectural form which in those early days this amazing twenty-nine-year-old seemed able to pour out with unceasing abundance.

Before we consider Le Bois des Moutiers in detail, however, it will be as well to go back to 1896, to one of the earliest commissions that Lutyens got through

Gertrude Jekyll: the extension to the inn at Roseneath in Dunbartonshire which he designed as a guest house for HRH Princess Louise, daughter of Queen Victoria, no less, and wife of the future Duke of Argyll. I mention this background since this was Lutyens's first aristocratic client and one might have suspected that for this reason he would have been particularly uncontentious in what he designed. However, the commission was only for an extension to the local pub, adding a bar with bedrooms, so perhaps he felt that he could design in a more experimental manner than would have been possible had he been altering the ducal home. There is an early sketch by Lutyens of the pub extensions in the RIBA Heinz Gallery which shows a highly romantic Art-Nouveau design which Hussey scathingly calls a 'half-hearted adaptation of Surrey picturesque to Scottish baronial in the local material'.[84] The completed design was a toned down version of this scheme but is still very close to Scottish Art Nouveau which was developing just then in nearby Glasgow. With his darting architectural imagination Lutyens was certainly more interested in the experiments going on up there than he made out in his letters to Lady Emily. Perhaps also it was that he was a long way from Surrey and the implacable 'Bumps'. It is noticeable that all his experimental buildings of this period are those furthest from Godalming—Overstrand in north Norfolk, Rose- neath in Dunbartonshire and most experimental of all, Le Bois des Moutiers, across the Channel near Dieppe. It is almost as if he felt that at this distance he could move at least a little away from the path of good taste and establishment respecta- bility that all those elderly ladies had mapped out for him. Certainly he always had a sneaking regard for all the new things going on, and he was quite considerably swayed by fashion over the years. He attended meetings of the Art Workers' Guild and knew the wild men such as Ashbee, Prior and Lethaby. It is, for instance, noticeable that although, in a letter of this period to Lady Emily, he wrote of: ' "Surroundings prompted by the New Art Glasgow School . . . White rooms with black furniture, black rooms with white furniture" ',[85] it was in fact he him- self who first used this colour combination in a fashionable house, when he set up home in Bloomsbury in 1897 with his new bride.

For whatever reasons then his extension to Her Royal Highness's inn are somewhat surprising. The inn itself (it has since been pulled down leaving only the Lutyens bit) was a typical square Georgian building in the local grey stone. To this Lutyens added a long block bearing little relation to the original design. Lutyens's roof is steeply pitched whereas the original building has a flat-pitched roof under ordinary sash windows. In the extension the lower part is of rubble stone into which are punched mullioned windows. Directly above these there is a straightforward Classical cornice and from this a plastered wall jetties out— Tudor, Vernacular and Classicism happily mixed. There is a great stone porch with a Voyseyesque curving sweep to its roof and beside it is a tall trio of attenuated Tudor chimneys which balance the facade. On the first floor the windows run from the porch to the chimney in a band of leaded lights, but beyond this and around the corner they become a series of stumpy oriels, such as we saw at The Pleasaunce, tucked under the sharply curving eaves, with two corbels to hold up the eaves at the extreme edge of the building. It is difficult to find the precedent for this wild use of oriels, which became very popular with advanced architects within the next few years. Initially it derives from Shaw's Old Swan House, Chelsea Embankment, of 1875, but little was seen of these oriels again until Lutyens started to use them in his more obscure buildings, which certainly were not known to the general public. Then in the same year, 1896, Mackintosh used them in his Glasgow School of Art and in 1899 Mackmurdo built 25 Cadogan Gardens with a facade which seems to comprise nothing but these oriels.

By that time Lutyens had taken his use of these oriels much further in his Le Bois des Moutiers, which even Hussey, ever ready to absolve his hero from any taint of the new art, recognizes as: 'one of the rare instances in his work . . . of *nouveau-art* modernism', and goes on to say that it is another instance of that hesitation in his development which, 'if pursued, might have transformed the course of English architecture in the Edwardian decade'.[86] That was written in the late 1940s when it looked as though modern architecture was sweeping all before it and shamefacedly Hussey was trying to bring even Lutyens into line with the standard view of the history of modern architecture. Now that 'modern' architecture is dead and the doctrinaire views of the 1930s are dying we can perhaps see this whole period in a clearer light. The fact is that Lutyens toyed with these ideas, saw them for the eccentricities that they were, presumably found that they were not popular with his clients, or certainly his patrons, and so turned to giving his clients what they wanted.

Le Bois des Moutiers was built for 93,000 francs for the French Protestant Anglophile banker Guillaume Mallet and it is still lived in by the Mallet family, for whom Lutyens designed a series of buildings over the years and in 1910 also built for them at Varengeville a small butterfly-plan Neo-Georgian, or Neo-Mansart guesthouse. Like so many of his clients the Mallets became firm friends and it was Madame Mallet who in 1908 introduced Lady Emily to theosophy, which was to

Les Bois des Moutiers, Varengeville-sur-Mer, France, E. L. Lutyens 1898. Perspective of entrance front by R. Gradidge

have such a dire effect on the Lutyenses marriage. Although Varengeville-sur-Mer is a seaside village, just a few kilometres from Dieppe, Le Bois des Moutiers is not a seaside house. It is built on the cliffs some distance from the sea, which can just at times be glimpsed through the trees in the garden. The entrance is right on the village street, a wall is cut back to display a quite long formal avenue with a brick path between herbaceous borders, clipped hedges and tall poplars leading up to the house. This entrance is French and formal. As the path arrives at the house it develops into a brick-paved, circular court which is crossed at right angles by a path leading through voussoired arches in the rendered side walls. To the left this path ends in a formal rose garden. There are beds of roses in a pavement surrounded by clipped yew hedges. The hedges on plan are curved at the end away from the house to become semicircular backs to stone benches, the seats of which form a somewhat impractical full circle. These circles are exactly reflected in the plan of

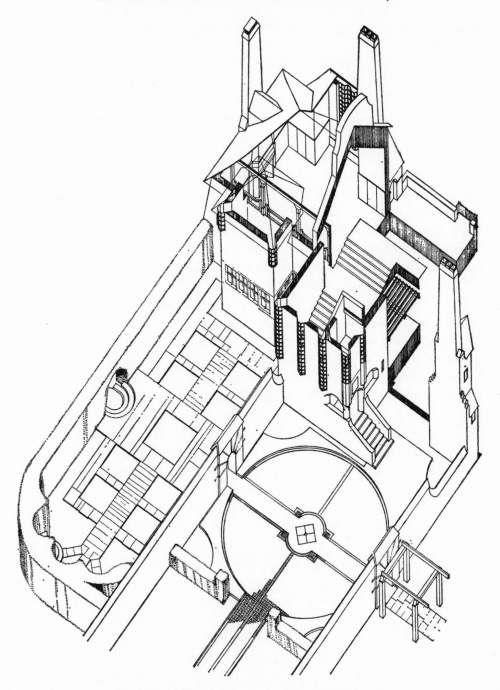

Les Bois des Moutiers – axonometric of entrance court

the circular steps which drop down through an arch in the hedge on a line with the cross axis.

On this axis, at the other side of the entrance court, there is a pergola which runs beside a croquet lawn, the vista ending in the distance with a small temple-eyecatcher-cum-garden-house. The formality of this part of this garden in France is, perhaps not surprisingly, much greater than in the Lutyens–Jekyll work in England of this time. Both the gardens of Overstrand and Orchards have architectural elements but they do not seem to be tied together with so much Classical logic, a logic which is none the less mixed with the formal informality of Norman Shaw's house planning and the High Romanticism of the landscape garden as it had developed to culminate some sixty years earlier in the gardens of Repton and Nash. This entrance at Varengeville is the first of the grand line of the romantic formal Lutyens–Jekyll gardens which were to culminate thirty years later in the magnificent architectural water gardens at the Viceroy's House, New Delhi.

This combination of English informality and Gallic formality is continued at the front door. One can find in so many of the plans of houses of this period an unwillingness to accept the full implication of a centre line. Front doors never enter directly on to the main central spine of the house, however formal the elevations may be. Almost always on entering the front door one is turned to one side, before it is possible to enter the main rooms. At Le Bois des Moutiers Lutyens, seemingly worried about too much formality in the garden, has broken the main centre line before even one gets to the front door. For at the point where one would expect to find the front door it is necessary to turn a pace to the right and then to the left again, then to climb a few stairs at right angles to the entrance. The steps lead into an arch where one must turn right again to come to the front door. All highly perverse.

The arches of this entrance porch are built into the corner of a wing which projects forward from the main body of the house (see plate XVI). This wing, which is covered with a great hipped roof kicked up sharply at the bottom, has four oriels, like the Roseneath oriels but very much longer. The oriels here run from immediately under the eaves to just below the top of the arch. Once again the two outer oriels come in the corners and seem to be supporting the roof. Behind the porch projection, which contains the staircase, the rest of the house runs through as a flat-faced block, with leaded mullion windows under a great tiled roof. This smoothness is soon broken by a great chimneybreast which projects forward to form an enclosure to the entrance court. This form of court, with a porch pushed into one corner balanced at the other side by a strong vertical emphasis, is almost identical in form with Butterfield's otherwise very different, entrance court to All Saints, Margaret Street, London. Most surprising of all, this tall chimney, which seems to serve ingle-nooked fireplaces at two different levels, is an almost complete sham since at both the main floors it faces on to passages, and the seeming ingles are in fact cupboards!

A great deal of the oddity of this treatment can be explained by the fact that it is the encasing of an existing house. The whole music room wing, and the entrance porch and the projections to the east front are additions to what was originally a simple block. The old house though has been so subtly cased by Lutyens that we may treat it as a completely new-minted design. Here there is little of the obvious crankiness created by using old buildings that we find in his contemporary work at Overstrand. Immediately to the left of the entrance block the facade drops back and the roof eaves are lowered. But this block also has a wing with a hipped roof jutting forward, with shorter oriels in the corners pushed up under the eaves, just like Roseneath the slight drop in scale of the whole unit elegantly balancing the entrance wing. Above all this complexity of form tall chimneys sail, most of them of traditional shape, but the two at the ends of the main block have great curved tops suggesting gable ends rather than chimneys; whether they reflect something in the original house it is now hard to say.

It is surprising that this elevation of Lutyens's is not better known (the only analysis to date is in the November 1977 edition of the French magazine *Architecture Mouvement Continuité*, No. 43) for it is one of Lutyens's finest displays of asymmetrical balance—the kind of imaginative balance for which Norman Shaw was so justly famous. The porch has details taken from Shaw's porch for 180 Queen's Gate of 1883–5, combined perhaps with Stevenson's side entrance to 1 Lowther Gardens, Kensington Gore of 1877–8. The massing under a series of long roofs at slightly different levels reminds one perhaps more of a church like Shaw's All Saints, Richards Castle, Shropshire of 1889–93, though asymmetrical balance of this kind was common enough in manor house design from the time of Salvin, and architects such as Devey, influenced no doubt by Compton Wynyates, often attempted similar massing, though they were perhaps never as subtle as Lutyens at his best.

Round the corner, however, Lutyens suddenly changes course. No longer are we in the Neo-Tudor world of Devey but in the Neo-Baroque of the last phase of Shaw, which was contemporary with Le Bois des Moutiers. As we have seen the

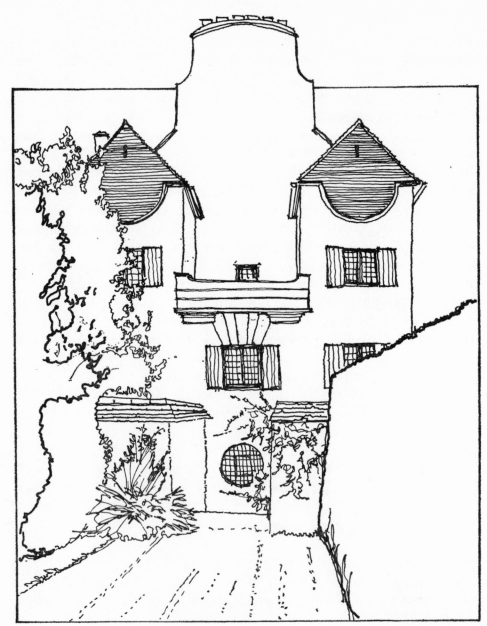

Les Bois des Moutiers – perspective of side elevation by R. Gradidge

main roof is terminated by a curved chimney, shaped like a gable end, on this, the east, elevation it runs up two storeys offering a blank face. Beside it two small gabled wings jut forward. Until now the house has been built of the simplest materials, pebbledash to the walls, with tile cappings and creasings. However, these gables, and only these gables, have tile-hanging, which is stopped with a projecting stone cornice curving down in a semicircle. Below this odd detail, which seems to be entirely original, there are oak-mullioned leaded windows, with oak shutters. Between the two gables at ground-floor window height is a balcony striped with red tile courses and beneath this a stone cornice with great Michelangelesque voussoirs over another oakmullioned window, below which is a circular window which looks into the cellar. This is an early example of Lutyens's more extreme Mannerism, comparable to the work of Beresford Pite of exactly this date.

We turn the corner to the garden front, and here find another Lutyens, an altogether calmer man, at least for most of the facade, though perhaps here in this rather bland elevation we can see the original house, as it were, grinning through. This facade is almost Neo-Georgian in its proportions, a line of nine mullioned windows, in two tiers with dormers in the roof over. But there are oddities here. Firstly the rhythm of the dormers is strange. From left to right, there is a pair, then one unequally spaced, then a group of three and then one by itself. Below, the fenestration follows the dormers; first a pair of windows, then a narrower gap, another window and then an oval window. Below this oval window, on the main floor (because the ground slopes there is a basement on this side), a porch projects. It is a surprisingly heavy affair with rendered columns and Art Nouveau caps, old friends from Overstrand and Berrydowne. From here a grand flight of steps leads down into the garden.

To the right of the main facade, and slightly lower, we are suddenly presented with a new element—and this is an addition to the existing house—the new music room. Although the main roof runs through with the rest, there is a slight projection and this has gables which sweep down low on either side. At the bottom of the wing there is an enormous cyclopean arch punching through the buttressed wall. Above, voussoirs shoot up to support the tall studio windows which run up two storeys. This window is one of the most delightful that Lutyens ever created. It seems to have been formed by taking two of the long oriel strips which we saw in the entrance front, and joining them together with flat strips of window, to create a wavy form on plan, and to give a sparkle as the seaside sun glitters from the myriad panes at different angles (see plate XVIII).

D.H.–H

After the excitement of the exterior, most of the rooms are rather disappointing, for Lutyens did little to the main rooms in the centre of the house, and they remain, what they always were, simple boxes. Though most of the rooms have his fire-places, some of the best are in a form of highly sophisticated Mannerism reminis-cent of Webb's fireplaces at Standen. It is in contrast to these rooms that the Lutyens additions stand out. The staircase is perfectly splendid; solid steps mount easily through a tall room, lit by the long mullions that we saw on the entrance. Nearly at the top of the stairs there is a landing and this leads on to the minstrels' gallery of the music room. This great room is lit to the south by the glittering window that looks over the garden and down the sloping lawn, through a wood to the sea. Under the gallery there is a lower, private, area, with its own bay window which looks over the rose garden. The lower part of this room is panelled in oak, which is broken by a stone Classical fireplace running right up to the heavily decorated plaster ceiling. This music room is the culmination of that whole series of hall rooms so beloved of Norman Shaw and of Lutyens's master Ernest George. Unlike those rooms, which were always related to the main living space of the house, and often also had a staircase running through them, this is tucked away to one side and is of a much simpler shape.

All in all Le Bois des Moutiers is a house of considerable originality. It displays Lutyens's remarkable ability to combine panache with architectural form in a way that was perhaps not to flower again for another thirty years when he built his war memorials, not too far away on the battlefields of northern France: the battle-fields where the children of many of his clients were to fall, and where the safe world of middle-class security was to be destroyed for all time. But in 1898, few people could have foreseen the carnage that was to come, even if the Boer War was showing how nasty modern war could be. To Lutyens in that year came the chance to build one of the most perfect of his dream houses.

Orchards was a house built on a virgin site near Munstead Wood outside Godalming in Surrey for a typical Lutyens client—rich with second generation money, and artistic. Lady Chance has described how Lutyens came to be com-missioned to design Orchards, the first case that has come down to us of his getting a job after another architect had been appointed. At least in this case Lutyens does not seem to have been in any way responsible for the change. 'Passing through a sandy lane', Lady Chance remembered, 'we saw a house nearing completion, and on top of the ladder a portly figure giving directions to some workmen. The house was a revelation of unimagined beauty and charm, we stood entranced and gazing until the figure descended and we found ourselves, after due explanation, being welcomed as future neighbours.'[87] The house was Munstead Wood and the portly figure Gertrude Jekyll. Directly Gertrude Jekyll heard that the Chances were about to build nearby she made every effort to get the job for her young protégé. Unfortunately Halsey Ricardo, a family friend, had already been commissioned to do the job and he had designed a Tudor house, which he had exhibited at the Royal Academy in 1898. Nicholas Taylor thinks that Mrs Chance (as she then was) was dissatisfied with Ricardo's design before she saw Munstead, and Gertrude Jekyll realized that this was the opportunity that Lutyens needed, for he had recently become engaged to Lady Emily Lytton and had been forced by his future father-in-law to take out an excessive life insurance, to guarantee his future wife's security. It was this life insurance that was to mean that for many years afterwards he was forced to chase after every job going, and it was unfortunate that his first victim should have been as good an architect as Halsey Ricardo who was himself always in financial difficulties. Lutyens confessed in a letter that it would be awful if he were ever supplanted as Ricardo had been.

As so often happened, however, when Lutyens got the job he went on to produce the kind of wonderful building that could not be equalled, let alone bettered, by his competitor, and at Orchards he had found in the Chances ideal clients. Sir William Chance was a member of the family who manufactured Chance Glass, and a radical who wrote pamphlets on monetary reform and working-class housing. His wife, Julia, was an artist-sculptor, who sculpted garden ornaments of some quality. She was a Strachey, her brother being St Loe Strachey, editor of the *Spectator*, a cousin was Lytton Strachey. Thus they belonged to that group of artistic and rich radicals from whom in the next generation the Bloomsbury Group sprang—a group who had little time for Lutyens and his romantic conservatism.

Like Munstead the house was the result of a careful collaboration with an older artistic lady—two in this case since Gertrude Jekyll was continuously involved from the beginning. Here Lutyens could not play any of his design tricks, or pull any of his architectural long noses. Orchards is set on the brow of a hill, but unlike most of the houses that we have been looking at, it is approached by a short drive leading straight up to the entrance. None the less the first view reminds us of so many of the other dream houses. First we see a long barn to our left and what appears to be the main part of the house, with a tall, oak-leaded bay window, spreading out in front of us. We are in fact looking at one side of the stable court, and in

Orchards, near Godalming, Surrey, E. L. Lutyens 1898. Perspective of entrance front by R. Gradidge

front is the northern wing of the entrance court. The bay window lights not the drawing room but a studio. The stable wing that stretches to our left once had an arch in it; this has since been blocked which lessens the effect that (as in an old-fashioned manor farm) we are entering the main part of the house only after we have passed the dung yard of the functional farm buildings. Thus even Lutyens, following Voysey and Webb in this house, takes us past the service quarters to get to the main entrance. It is something that would have been considered a most serious planning solecism at any time in the work of a sophisticated architect before the 1890s.

Lutyens almost certainly knew Webb's Standen well and it is interesting to compare Webb's much grander house plan with that of Orchards. We enter the Webb house by first passing the old cottages that he saved, with the service area projecting forward, forming an L-shaped entrance enclosure not dissimilar to that of Orchards. But while Orchards stands on the top of a hill, and presents with its glittering bay window a sense of welcome, the entrance at Standen is almost medieval in its defiance, set as it is in a secluded dell. None the less Lutyens learned much from Webb's clever visual planning, and as on so many other occasions he seems to have taken Webb's still ponderous Gothic Revivalism and turned it into something both more homely and architecturally pure. Lutyens's architecture could not have existed without the Gothic Revival, but none the less he could never have accepted anything so humourless nor doctrinaire, any more than later he was able to accept the equally humourless and doctrinaire modern architecture.

This entrance also reminds us a little of Halsey Ricardo's Fox Oak, which he built just south of Weybridge in 1887, and then extended in 1892. Could it be that Lutyens was paying a subconscious compliment to the architect that he supplanted? The tall and slightly spidery Tudor chimneys and stone walls of Ricardo's Surrey Vernacular house have a lot of the character of these early Lutyens houses. But of course all these architects were influenced by the same sources—the vernacular farm buildings of the then still rural neighbourhood. The roof of the barn at Orchards, with its walls supported by buttresses, continues round in a single sweep across the entrance to end in a hip at the right that runs almost down to ground level. Just before this point the great bay window projects, running the full height of the wall and covered with its own hipped roof, which thrusts forward from the main plane. To the left of the bay, in the centre of this wing, the walls angle slightly back to form a covered entrance to the main court, and above this there is a dormer lighting only the main roof trusses. This dormer is the only punctuation above the eaves to the smooth sweep of the roof.

It might seem that we have lingered rather too long on this rather simple entrance, but as Ian Nairn remarks in his description of the house in *The Buildings of England: Surrey*: 'In most of the [early] houses Lutyens was obsessed or dominated by a spatial idea . . . The idea is that of an immensely sophisticated entrance approach, deliberately calculated from the moment one turns into the drive, and an inner kernel of space, a courtyard or quadrangle, using the same motifs and sophisticated balance for the benefit of the static observer as the entrance does for the moving one.' As Nairn continues: 'The sensation of walking through to the quad, which lies beyond [the entrance arch], is like entering a fairy palace with a union of buildings, exterior space, and landscape as miraculous in its way as anything the Baroque produced in uniting buildings, interior space, and painted decoration.'[88] Through the arch, in front across the court, is the main porch with a stone arch with the slightest of Tudor mouldings round the opening. This porch is two storeys high and has strips of leaded windows running round all

Orchards – perspective of entrance court by R. Gradidge

three sides under a lightly timbered gable. These windows continue on in a strip
under the eaves, breaking slightly forward in two places. It is a very early example
of a device much liked by Frank Lloyd Wright, though only used once by him
before 1898, in the Heller House in Chicago of 1896. From Lloyd Wright this
idea was taken up by the Modern Movement and became one of the favourite
clichés of the 1930s, in which these strip windows were spread across facades
without any consideration of where partitions came or what was behind. At
Orchards there are no partitions since these windows light one enormous Lutyens
corridor, the slight projections reflecting in one case a radiator and in another a
seat. To the right of this facade there is a long cloister made up of **three** arches
which bound down the side in great semicircular leaps, leading to Lady Chance's
studio the great window of which we saw as we came in. At the junction of this
cloister there rises a very typical Lutyens chimney. From a stone rectangular block
built well above eaves level two slender brick chimneys tower to the same height
again. They are echoed by another pair on the other side of the roof.

Architects of this period, such as Voysey and Prior and in particular Lutyens,
were deeply concerned with pure form. Since the simple Vernacular style that all
these architects used was so nearly styleless it became possible to concentrate on
form rather than other more decorative elements. Orchards is in many ways the
supreme masterpiece of this styleless architecture, as Lawrence Weaver says: here
Lutyens was still working in the spirit of Munstead Wood, 'but with greater facility

in the handling of materials, and with a readiness to let the mass and outlines of the building develop a natural rather than a contrived picturesqueness. The grouping of the house with its attendant and attached offices and walled gardens shows the same spirit as that which animated the sixteenth-century Englishman when he built, in native style, a house in which to dwell in native manner. Precisely the same careful attention to line and proportion, apt choice of fitting materials and right adaptation of features to their purposes are apparent round the whole compass of the buildings.'[89] In this way and in this way only was Lutyens copying period styles at this time.

The plan is masterly in most aspects, only in the service quarters is there a slight hiccup. The main view is to the south-east, so all the main rooms are laid out looking south, with the entrance to the north. Like Munstead Wood, but unlike most houses of this period, the house was designed to be worked in during the day by a husband who wrote and a wife who was a sculptor, so this meant that there would have, as it were, to be two axes. One revolved around the normal reception rooms, with their tail of service rooms, and the other, the study and the studio, arranged to be slightly away from the main body of the house. Lutyens placed the study on the east end of the main block and then joined it with the cloister to Lady Chance's two-storeyed studio. The courtyard thus perfectly symbolizes the dual nature of the house.

The main entrance leads, as is so common in Lutyens houses, on to a wide passage that runs right across the house; to the right is the main staircase and a considerable distance to the left is the entrance to the drawing room, where visitors would normally be shown. Beyond this through a door the passage continues to the service areas. Thus the dining room, which was just beyond the drawing room to the left, could have been reached only through the drawing room. The studies and studios of the owners are beyond the staircase. Lady Chance had two studios, one was above Chance's study and approached in part by the main staircase and in part by a separate stairs, nicely symbolizing its character. It is slightly separate from the house, and appropriately dark, with an ingle fireplace. The overmantle is a tiled map of the garden. Possibly this was another slight nod in the direction of the usurped Halsey Ricardo who was of course much given to the use of tiles, as he was to long cloisters.

The staircase is very splendid, if without any of the spatial tricks that we have seen in Baillie Scott's work and in such later Lutyens houses as Little Thakeham. It rises in easy stages, each step solid oak, with the same moulded underside that

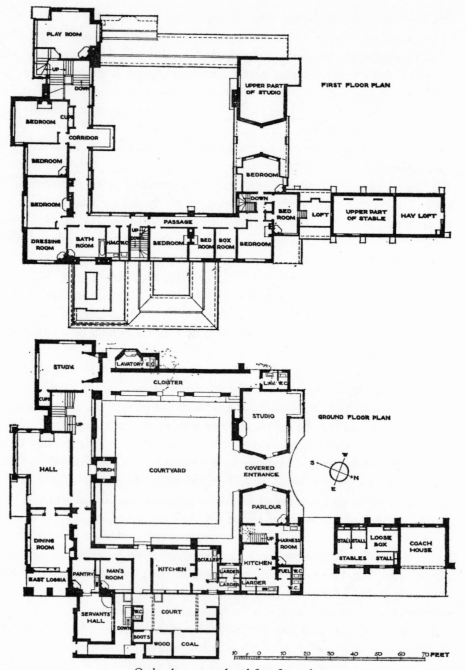

Orchards – ground and first floor plans

Baker used at Groote Schuur. The first two flights run up normally within the main walls of the house, then the wall kicks forward, and at the second landing the new studio staircase starts, turning on its own dog-leg and paralleling the course of the main stairs. At the top of the stairs there is a typical Lutyens trick. A simple thing that shows his continuous attention to the smallest details coupled with a fluid and witty mind. The rise of the last step is omitted and in its place the ceiling joists from the ceiling below jut through the open gaps. Just to make quite sure that we realize that this is not just a piece of casual accident, each joist end is carved to form a recessed panel. The upstairs passage is another of Lutyens's circulation spaces which are designed as much for living in as they are for walking through. The walls are continually jutting forwards and backwards, making different enclosures, and in the centre the corridor projects out over the porch to form a space 10 feet deep with windows all around it—a delightful sitting-out room which looks over the entrance court.

Lady Chance's studio away from the house is two storeyed with a tall, open timber roof. Running up one wall for the full height there is a gigantic brick and tiled chimneypiece, tricked out here and there in Classical detail. As Nicholas Taylor has suggested, this is an example of 'Lutyens's habit of slipping in elements of the sublime in unexpected places'. The tall oak and leaded bay that we saw at the entrance making a perfect north light to the studio contrasting in its tudor style with the classical fireplace. Sublimity mixed with practical good sense.

The drawing room is a delightful low room panelled with a deep bay which looks over the garden. This is linked to the dining room which is again panelled in oak, the frames barely a quarter of an inch proud of the bed. There are oak-mullioned leaded windows, pushed as far as possible to the outer face of the wall. An oak Doric column supports the long span of the window, from lintel to sill, making a contrast in its austere Classicism, with the Tudor leadwork of the windows—a trick that Lutyens used a year earlier in the angled corner bays at Fulbrook. However, here the columns are used to more purpose for at the door to the drawing room there was a sideboard, designed to display a collection of pewter. In one of his typically enchanting details Lutyens designed the sideboard to act as a frame to the main door, repeating the Doric columns, and supporting them on little oak plinths, which he rusticated. On the returns by the door he tucked in bookshelves and below the display shelves there are cupboards, made in the simplest Arts and Crafts manner, following the lines of the panelling. The whole partition between the drawing room and the dining room was alas taken out in 1939 to create one enormous living room, destroying a great deal of the quality of both rooms in the process.

The gardens and the garden front are if anything finer than anything that we have yet seen. The south front is probably the most controlled of all Lutyens's highly complex romantic compositions. Here he is dealing with a much longer elevation than for instance that at Munstead, and he has allowed more elements to come into play, but, perhaps because of the Jekyll influence, there is here none of the excited jamming together of diffuse elements that we have so often seen in other houses of his of this period.

Taking this garden facade from left to right, on the left the roof sweeps down from a gable to just above the study window, and from this a pair of linked tile-hung dormer windows rise, the sill of the left higher than that of the right. The right-hand dormer in fact forms a small bay, the windows carried round, lighting the staircase to the second studio. Beyond this and set back on a stone wall rise a pair of tall brick chimneys. Then a gabled stone bay projects making a contrast, in its solid stonework, to the lightness of the first set of gables. In this bay the lower windows light the drawing room, and the upper main bedroom. While the drawing room windows are a horizontal strip between buttresses, the bedroom windows are taller in two sets of frames, the upper frames projecting in ears above the lower windows. A trick taken from vernacular architecture, where it is some-times used in barns, no doubt to help in the packing of the upper roofs, it seems to have little practical purpose in the bedroom of a country house, though used as it is here it adds just that lift to the elevation which would otherwise have been a little bland. Beyond this wing, the eaves of the roof run in a straight line above the heads of the first floor windows; the walls are of the dressed rubble stone of the district—the same warm cream that we have seen at Munstead. Contrasted with the silvery grey of the oakwork are the soft warm red of the tile-hanging and the sharp red of the tall brick chimneys. Lutyens's use of natural materials at this time was almost faultless. As Butler says of Munstead in the *Memorial Volumes*:

The English have known for some centuries how to fashion the materials at hand; and Lutyens merely made a synthesis of those earlier wisdoms. He played tricks with them. The result is that the very *stuff* of the house is as telling as the arrangement of its lines for appearance. Looking at the walls, we can almost feel their texture; and our eye delights to stroke the tiled roofs for their protective look of warmth and velvety coating. Internally too, the stretched parchment flatness of plaster and the lumbering toughness of oak are impressions quite as strong as those given, for instance, by the proportions of that gallery or the subtle curvature and tapering of the roof-truss members. In fact we sense the structure throughout and, at the same time, perceive the architect's understanding of the real nature and qualities of the constituents.[90]

On this facade the elements may not seem to be of any particular interest—indeed many a suburban house can show similar combinations—but it is only when their position and form are closely analysed that the subtleties become obvious. It is this subtle approach to what are in the end banal forms that gives the impression that the building has grown organically over the years. On this garden front the part to the left seems to belong to an early and more naive and cranky period than the suave architecture of the right-hand two-thirds. Neither of course could be separated without damage to the weave of the whole. Although the immediate impression is that of simple naivety, this facade is in fact extremely carefully proportioned. The tall chimneys come exactly one-third of the way along the facade and are exactly twice the height of the wall from the ground to the eaves, though this is not immediately obvious since the stone plinth on which the brickwork of the chimneys rests is much higher than the eaves. Most surprising of all the single gable is precisely the same width as the paired gables to the left. All this is reflected in the plan. On most occasions Lutyens began to plan using a simple grid, with walls then moved forward and backward off the main lines, but often the partitions between rooms were retained on the original grid lines. It is the position of these partitions, projected as it were vertically on to the elevations, which dominates the facade here, the plan and the elevations being entirely integrated. This can be most clearly seen in the paired dormers. The main staircase is set back behind the tall chimneys, which actually serve fireplaces at right angles to the chimney, but the right-hand gable with its dropped sill lights both this staircase and the secondary staircase which winds up to the second studio which is lit by the other dormer window. The whole game, and in particular the distorted position of the chimneys is outrageous, but it uses natural materials with such assurance that we accept it with delight and with none of the reservations that we give to earlier displays of romantic nonsense.

The strange but successful orientation of the house becomes more obvious when we turn the corner to the east front (see plate XIX). It is the east front that has the view, which means that not one of the important rooms of either floor has it. On the first floor only dressing rooms, bathrooms, minor bedrooms and even a box-room look out on to the Surrey hills. This does seem perverse and on the ground floor this perversity is carried further for here no rooms look east, though the morning sun originally penetrated to the dining room through the loggia. The servants' hall, which could have had east-facing windows (in a retrogressive step that smacks of the Regency) is placed down low and windowless on this side, its only light coming from an inner court. (This has since been changed for in the alterations of 1939 the servants' hall was turned into the dining room with windows looking east.) The reason for the Chances' self-denial is no doubt quite conscious. When one lives in a house with a magnificent view one does not need it thrust on one from every window, as it is for instance at Fulbrook, where interestingly Gertrude Jekyll was not involved in the garden or the setting of the house. A view is much more exciting if it merely appears in glimpses and from specific places from the garden. Orchards is a house where the garden and the house were conceived as one and the view was quite consciously used as only one of the factors that made up the totality of the design. Equally important were the gardens, the woods, the garden ornaments and the house itself. The view is appreciated from the garden and the garden is appreciated from the house.

The east front deserves careful analysis since here once again Lutyens is at his most picturesque. The long line of the roof is brought to an end with a simple gable, under is the main dressing room window, catching the morning sun and the view and then below this is a loggia, which leads out into the most architectural part of the garden. The plan of the wall of the gable is run on to form a solid base for another of the great chimneys which rises to make a perfect termination to the main part of the house. However, at this point the roof has turned right and continues in a long straight line to end at a hip at the entrance arch. Below this roof runs a long line of leaded windows, but just after this line of windows has got started they are abruptly punctured with another tall chimney, the twin of the first. To the rear of the first pair of chimneys and at right angles to them are the block of four chimneys that we have already seen at the entrance: these two sets of chimneys, in twin pairs and four, play a constant pattern one with the other as we walk around the facade.

Up till now all the chimneys have been of the same type—basically Tudor, hexagonal brick chimneys rising from a stone base. But now, and for no obvious functional reason in the middle of this secondary roof ridge, Lutyens suddenly

Orchards – view from lower garden by R. Gradidge

throws in a new element—a chimney in a completely different style. In contrast to
the earlier chimneys, this rises from its base-square in one single plane to the top.
The face is of indented panels and just near the top there are louvres. Then it
carries a little hipped roof and above this are low chimney pots, where there is
none on the other chimneys. It is based on Philip Webb's Standen chimneys but
moulded like Nesfield's at the Lodges at Kinmel and Kew Gardens. This is an early
example of a form that Lutyens was to use in his Neo-Georgian designs although
here it symbolizes the kitchen flues, with their slightly different function. Much
more important than this is the way in which it controls the wing which otherwise
might seem endless. A chimney in the same style as the others would not have
made a firm enough halt to the flow of the roof and windows. The elevation
perhaps reminds one of a Bruckner movement. It opens after a misleadingly simple
tutti, with a vast opening theme, which is then after only a short interval repeated
exactly; then comes the long main working out, to be interrupted towards the end
by another beautiful but seemingly unrelated theme, which finally gives way again
to the main fabric of the movement, but now we know that the great mass is drawing to its close, which it does without any more excitement.

The garden grows directly from this front. To the south side there is just a

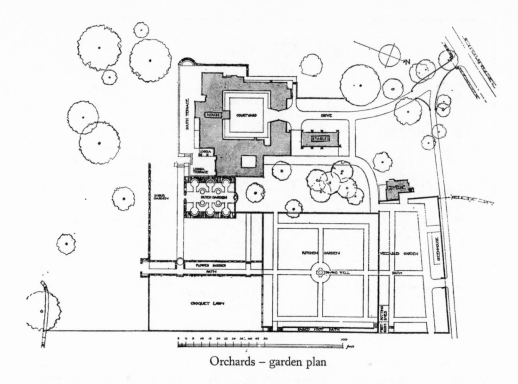

Orchards – garden plan

simple terrace and beyond it a lawn of rough grass and the woods. The terrace continues round, and in front of the loggia Lutyens and Gertrude Jekyll concocted an architectural garden exactly contemporary to the quite different garden at Varengeville. This is the point where it is quite impossible to decide where one left off and the other began. Probably the conception of an architectural garden was Gertrude Jekyll's. She was the more sophisticated and knew the Italian gardens well, and to her also, of course, must be given the romantic planting. However, Lutyens was almost certainly responsible for the geometric forms which they take. Indeed it is in these garden designs that he first developed the passion for geometry that in his later years was so to dominate his architecture. But at Orchards this is still very subdued, though there are considerably more garden works here than at Munstead Wood, even more so than at the 1895 (pre-Jekyll) gardens at Woodside, Chenies. Here Lutyens designed a geometrical architectural garden, with a line of formal terraces and paths which meet at an octagonal pergola over a circular pond, from four of whose sides octagonal beds are formed, with steps between.

By the time we get to Orchards things have become more complex. From the loggia there is a wide terrace from which nine curved stone and tile steps drop down to a long cross-walk. This is grassed, and from it to either side are semi-circular seats, the central of these on the loggia side being formed of the lower three curved steps. At the north end is the wall to the kitchen and this has in it a circular basin with a wall fountain built in the same horizontal tiles that we have seen over the windows, and which are also repeated in the upstands to the steps. Here there is a lion-head fountain designed by Lady Chance. From this formal area close to the house, the garden drops down in a series of terraces. Appropriately by the kitchen there is a large, walled kitchen garden, designed to be seen through arches from the rest of the garden. At either end of the east wall of the kitchen garden there are steps leading to a raised walk running along by the top of the wall. Although the formal garden area is small, the combination of formality and freedom has meant that one gets all the emotional pleasures that one might expect in a much larger garden. This sense of a much greater size is enhanced by the subtle way in which the outlying landscape has been incorporated into the garden, from the woodland to the south and the magnificent view to the east.

EPILOGUE

JUST nine years after Bullers Wood, by 1899, the new Vernacular-Arts and Crafts-Neo-Georgian style (call it what you will) had arrived, a style that was to influence architects in England for sixty years until the war that had started in 1914 concluded its second phase in 1945. During the years that the style survived numberless minor masterpieces were produced, particularly by the architects whose work we have considered, Lutyens's work, of course, dominating that of his contemporaries. But there were many architects who at this time could design in this style and could create minor but carefully thought out buildings which people were, and still are, happy to use every day. It is in the design of such buildings rather than in the attempt to build inhumane masterpieces that the truly creative architect should be concerned. A small comfortable house is an infinitely more difficult problem than a vast palace; only Lutyens succeeded with both in a way that no other architect has ever done before or since. But where Lutyens led many others followed and lucky is the person who owns a house by one of his followers. However, the character of the period is probably best summed up not in a building but in a composition—*The Enigma Variations*—the work which in 1899 the 42-year-old Edward Elgar finally, after years of provincial obscurity, burst upon the public. In an extraordinary way his 'portrait of my friends pictured within' seems to capture the quality of precisely the artistic upper and middle classes for whom architects were building at this time.

Near to Malvern, where the Elgars lived, was Madresfield Court, the ancestral home of the Lygons—Earls of Beauchamp. In the 1860s the fifth Lord Beauchamp had commissioned the son of Philip Hardwick (of Euston Arch) P. C. Hardwick, to extend considerably the Elizabethan Madresfield, which he did with some style. In the 1890s there lived at the Court the young and musical sister of the seventh Earl, Lady Mary Lygon. In 1897 she helped Elgar to found the Worcestershire Philharmonic and it was through her that Elgar came to know the aristocratic and

artistic people of the neighbourhood, whom otherwise, whatever his wife's pre-
tensions, it is unlikely that the son of a Roman Catholic piano-tuner would have
met. Lady Mary was Lady of the Bedchamber to Princess Mary of Teck, the
future Queen Mary, and it was through her that Elgar, remarkably early in his
career, had got to know Edward VII, still of course then Prince of Wales.

The Lygons were High Church and artistic and when Mary Lygon's brother
married the sister of the richest man in England, the second Duke of Westminster
(a gentleman who was to figure in an unpleasant way in the later careers of
Lutyens and Detmar Blow as he was in the career of his distinguished brother in
law, Lord Lygon, whom he was later to hound from the country for his homosexuality), she, as a wedding present to her new husband, remodelled the chapel
at Madresfield. Work started in 1902 and went on until 1923. For this she called
in Arthur Gaskin and the highly artistic, Arts and Crafts workers of the Birmingham Guild of Handicraft, to create an elegant dream world. The altar triptych is
by the great Birmingham architect W. H. Bidlake, and the chapel is painted overall
with flowers and pretty children surrounding the kneeling figures of Lady
Beauchamp in her wedding dress and Lord Beauchamp in his coronation robes,
in a formalized but none the less lifelike manner by Henry Payne.

Evelyn Waugh knew Madresfield Court well in the 1920s. He took the chapel
as his model for the chapel in the house of Brideshead in *Brideshead Revisited*,
though the remainder of the house is based on Castle Howard, which also, as it
happens, has an Arts and Crafts chapel of a slightly earlier date. He describes the
chapel with sparkling accuracy, only altering a few details and the sex and religion
of the donor, and in that way perhaps subtly altering the character of the building,
for in the book it is given by the Roman Catholic Lord Marchmain to his wife as
a wedding present. As Waugh describes it:

The whole interior [of the chapel] had been gutted, elaborately refurnished and
redecorated in the arts and crafts style of the last decade of the nineteenth
century. Angels in printed cotton smocks, rambler-roses, flower-spangled
meadows, frisking lambs, texts in Celtic script, saints in armour, covered the
walls in an intricate pattern of clear, bright colours. There was a triptych of
pale oak, carved so as to give it the peculiar property of seeming to have been
moulded in plasticine. The sanctuary lamp and all the metal furniture were of
bronze, hand-beaten to the patina of a pockmarked skin; the altar steps had a
carpet of grass-green, strewn with white and gold daisies.[91]

At the same time that the chapel was being created, C. R. Ashbee and his Guild of Handicraft from Chipping Campden were asked to work on the library which leads to the chapel. Here in contrast to the camp glitter and gold of the chapel, there is unstained carved oak and marvellously made oak inlaid doors which contrast with the hand-wrought steel light fittings. Waugh's description of the metalwork of the chapel perhaps better fits the Campden work that it does the chaste work of Arthur Gaskin and his followers.

In 1899 Madresfield, tucked under the Malvern Hills, seemed a haven of artistic and aristocratic sensibility to Elgar and his wife. Some of Elgar's other friends whom he portrayed in the *Variations* might perhaps not have fitted into such a precious atmosphere. They were boisterous and a little vulgar; like W. M. Baker, banging and crashing around or G. R. Sinclair and his rather tiresome dog. Two of the variations represent Elgar's remarkable wife—both her strength of character and charm. Here, perhaps, surprisingly, Elgar used what was to become known as his 'nobilmente' style—the style of the *Pomp and Circumstance* marches. Although she was as much in love with Elgar the composer as in Elgar the man, it is possible she represented to him something of the philistine, almost Prussian side of English upper-middle class life of that time. For the new upper-middle classes, who were such important clients for architects, were by no means always as liberal and cultured as the middle-class Beals of Standen or the aristocratic Lygons of Madresfield. It was Elgar's ability to straddle both these strands of English society that makes him seem so similar to Lutyens. Both of them combine the sensitive Pre-Raphaelite dream of the Arts and Crafts ideal with the brass splendour of Empire. As indeed did Kipling, who with Burne-Jones as an uncle and with Morris and all his set around him as a child, was more closely linked through birth to the Arts and Crafts Movement than anyone else that we have considered.

After the Great War, when the country was torn by its losses, it was Elgar, in the Cello Concerto and Lutyens in the Cenotaph who both in 1919 seemed best able to interpret this barren sense of lost perfection. This quality dominates the Cello Concerto but is prefigured in the *Enigma Variations*, particularly in the great Nimrod theme and the ravishing thirteenth variation. This variation is said to represent the throbbing of the liner which took Lady Mary Lygon off to Australia, accompanying her brother who had been sent out to govern New South Wales, some years before Hilaire Belloc had made that post seem not entirely desirable. None the less, Elgar's intensity of feeling seems rather absurd in the portrait of an acquaintance off for a trip which many would have delighted in. But it is the same almost overpowering nostalgia welling out from the most ordinary of occasions that is present in so much of Lutyens's architecture of this period. If they are dreams they are dreams of a world of lost perfection, which even as they are dreamt the dreamer knows is of a future that is not to be.

With the advantage of hindsight it seems that it was Lutyens and Elgar who had the most subtlety in expressing their realization that there might be something wrong with English society—that it had in some way lost its cohesiveness. The establishment was pulling apart in a way that it had not done since the Glorious Revolution had destroyed the old Tories. The aristocratic liberal families, heirs to the Whig oligarchs, suddenly found that the civilized, if deeply dishonest, society that they had inherited was collapsing from within. In 1899 the Boer War started. With the war came the 'Pro-Boers', the first of so many upper-class liberals who since then have believed that treachery to their country is preferable to treachery to an ideal. The Pro-Boers were soon followed by the upper-class suffragette movement. It was these people who were already tearing the fabric of English society apart well before the Great War; indeed the war seemed on the whole to have a cohesive effect. Although by the end of the war propaganda suggested that liberal ideals had triumphed, the whole selfconsciously civilized society that supported these by now somewhat tawdry beliefs had received its death blow.

Both Lutyens and Elgar were shattered by the war, not just by the loss of life but by the destruction of the society in which they had succeeded in achieving an honoured place. Elgar died in 1934 and Lutyens lived on for another ten years but neither of them felt anything but dismay at what occurred after 1914. Elgar, who had lost his wife at about this time, practically gave up all composition and Lutyens turned to a harder and more mathematical architecture. Their world seemed dead. Certainly the bright intellectuals of the 1920s and 30s, inspired by the refugees from the High Romanticism of Nazi Germany, thought of them, and their art as dead. But now, after another forty years, and after the disasters that have been inflicted on this country in the name of the Modern Movement, perhaps now that modern architecture has in its turn been rejected, we may turn back to what little there is left of the Arts and Crafts Movement bitten into by the intellectuals on one side and the philistines on the other, and try to salvage at least some of the ideals that for just a few years seemed to suggest that Morris's dream of honest craftsmanship and fine design could come true. A dream perhaps, but a dream that is just possibly still within our grasp. As Rossetti's friend Arthur O'Shaughnessy put it, in lines that were to be set by Elgar just before the Great War:

> For each age is a dream that is dying,
> Or one that is coming to birth.[92]

REFERENCES

1. P. Morton Shand, *The Architectural Review*, **80** (1936), 218.
2. Peter F. Anson, *Fashions in Church Furnishings 1840–1940* (London: Faith Press, 1960), 280–1.
3. Gavin Stamp, 'AD Profile 13: London 1900', *Architectural Design*, **48** (1978), 363.
4. Robert MacLeod, *Charles Rennie Mackintosh* (London: Country Life, 1968), 52.
5. P. G. Konody, *The Art of Walter Crane* (London: Bell, 1902), 93.
6. Christopher Hussey, 'The Making of "Country Life"', *Country Life*, **141** (1967), 53, 54.
7. *Ibid.* pp. 53–4.
8. *Ibid.* p. 54.
9. Pamela Maude, 'Portrait of a Perfectionist: Edward Hudson, the Founder of Country Life', *Country Life*, **141** (1967), 60.
10. Quoted by Stanley Weintraub, *Beardsley: A Biography* (London: W. H. Allen, 1967), 23.
11. *Ibid.* p. 47.
12. *Ibid.* p. 70.
13. Isabel McAllister, *Alfred Gilbert* (London: A & C Black, 1929), 104.
14. Quoted by Isabel McAllister, *ibid.* p. 107.
15. *Ibid.* p. 107.
16. Nikolaus Pevsner, *The Buildings of England: Berkshire* (Harmondsworth: Penguin Books, 1966), 284.
17. Quoted by Isabel McAllister, *op. cit.* p. 133.
18. Quoted by Isabel McAllister, *op. cit.* p. 134.
19. Quoted by Michael Kennedy, *Portrait of Elgar* (London: Oxford University Press, 1968), 15–16.
20. *Ibid.* p. 41.
21. *Ibid.* p. 42.
22. H. J. L. J. Massé, *The Art-Workers' Guild 1884–1934* (Oxford: Shakespeare Head Press for The Art-Workers' Guild, 1935), 54, 57.

23. Quoted by Alan Crawford in his re-creation of the Masque for the Victorian Society's Arts and Crafts Conference, 1978.

24. H. J. L. J. Massé, *op. cit.* p. 58.

25. Wilfrid Blunt, *England's Michelangelo: A Biography of George Frederick Watts, O.M., R.A.* (London: Hamish Hamilton, 1975), 223.

26. *Ibid.* pp. 224–5.

27. Mrs G. F. A. Watts, *The Word in the Pattern: A Key to the Symbols on the Walls of the Chapel at Compton,* 2nd edn (London: Astolat Press, n.d. ?1905), 11.

28. Wilfrid Blunt, *op. cit.* pp. 225–6.

29. William Godfrey Newton, *The Work of Ernest Newton, R.A. and a Critical Appreciation* (London: Architectural Press, 1925), 4.

30. *Ibid.* p. 8.

31. Mark Girouard, *The Victorian Country House* (Oxford: Clarendon Press, 1971), 168–71.

32. *Ibid.* p. 171.

33. *Ibid.* p. 171.

34. Andrew Saint, *Richard Norman Shaw* (New Haven and London: Yale University Press, 1976), 326–31.

35. James D. Kornwolf, *M. H. Baillie Scott and the Arts and Crafts Movement: Pioneers of Modern Design* (Baltimore and London: Johns Hopkins Press, 1972), 71–5.

36. Nikolaus Pevsner and David Lloyd, *The Buildings of England: Hampshire and the Isle of Wight* (Harmondsworth: Penguin Books, 1967), 86.

37. H. S. Goodhart-Rendel, 'Architectural Memories, 1905–1955', *Architectural Association Journal,* 71 (1957), 147–8.

38. See Sir James Richards' preface to Duncan Simpson's *C. F. A. Voysey* (London: Lund Humphries, 1979), 7.

39. C. F. A. Voysey, 'Ultra-modern architecture', *Architects' Journal,* 81 (1935), 408.

40. John Newman, *The Buildings of England: West Kent and the Weald* (Harmondsworth: Penguin Books, 1969), 159.

41. Ernest Newton, *A Book of Country Houses* (London: Batsford, 1903), [1–2].

42. Thomas H. Mawson, *The Art and Craft of Garden Making,* 2nd edn (London: Batsford, 1901), 2–3.

43. Betty Massingham, *Miss Jekyll: Portrait of a Great Gardener* (London: Country Life, 1966), 80.

44. Quoted by Christopher Hussey, *The Life of Sir Edwin Lutyens* (London: Country Life, 1950), 75.

45. William H. Jordy, *American Buildings and their Architects,* vol. 3 (New York: Anchor Books, 1976), 70.

46. *Ibid.* p. 343.

47. H. Allen Brooks, *The Prairie School: Frank Lloyd Wright and his Midwest Contemporaries* (University of Toronto Press, 1972), 78–9.

48. Frank Lloyd Wright, *An Autobiography* (London: Faber, 1945), 103.

49. Christopher Hussey, *The Life . . .* , *op. cit.*

50. Betty Massingham, *op cit.* p. 68.

51. Quoted by Betty Massingham, *op. cit.* p. 61.

52. Gertrude Jekyll, *Home and Garden* (London: Longman, Green & Co., 1901), 1–3.

53. *Ibid.* pp. 3–5.

54. Quoted by Betty Massingham, *op. cit.* pp. 69–70.

55. Gertrude Jekyll, *op. cit.* pp. 6–10.

56. Gertrude Jekyll, *op. cit.* pp. 12–13.

57. Gertrude Jekyll, *op. cit.* pp. 13–21.

58. Herbert Baker, *Cecil Rhodes by his Architect*, 2nd edn (London: Oxford University Press, 1938), 19.

59. *Ibid.* p. 22.

60. Illustrated in *Groote Schuur: Residence of South Africa's Prime Minister* (Pretoria: Department of Information, 1970), 19.

61. *Ibid.* p. 20.

62. *The Lutyens Memorial*: A. S. G. Butler, *The Architecture of Sir Edwin Lutyens*, 3 vols; Christopher Hussey, *The Life of Sir Edwin Lutyens* (London: Country Life, 1950).

63. Laurence Weaver, *Houses and Gardens by E. L. Lutyens* (London: Country Life, 1913), 21.

64. Constance Battersea, *Reminiscences* (London: Macmillan, 1922).

65. *Ibid.*

66. Laurence Weaver, *op. cit.* p. 51.

67. [Laurence] W[eaver?], *Country Life*, **26** (1909), 634–638.

68. Geoffrey Hoare and Geoffrey Pyne, *Prior's Barn & Gimson's Coxen* (published by the authors, 'Selforth', Little Knowle, Budleigh Salterton, 1978), [14].

69. *Ibid.* pp. [22–5].

70. Norman Jewson, *By Chance I Did Rove* (2nd edn, published privately, 1973), 18.

71. Quoted by E. T. Cook, *The Life of John Ruskin*, vol. 2 (London: George Allen, 1911), 525, 526, 527.

72. Kenneth Clark, *Ruskin Today* (Harmondsworth: Penguin Books, 1967), 14.

73. Laurence Weaver, *Small Country Houses of To-Day*, vol. 1, 3rd edn (London: Country Life, 1922), 34.

74. Laurence Weaver, *Small Country Houses of To-Day*, vol. 2, 2nd edn (London: Country Life, 1922), 20.

75. *Ibid.* p. 18.

76. Laurence Weaver, *Small Country Houses of To-Day*, vol. 1, 3rd edn (London: Country Life, 1922), 35–7.
77. *Ibid.* pp. 25–6.
78. *Ibid.* pp. 28–9.
79. *Ibid.* p. 27.
80. *Ibid.* p. 28.
81. M. H. Baillie Scott, *Houses and Gardens* (London: George Newnes, 1906), 235.
82. James D. Kornwolf, *op. cit.* p. 188.
83. M. H. Baillie Scott, *op. cit.* p. 167.
84. Christopher Hussey, *The Life* . . . , *op. cit.* pp. 72–3.
85. Quoted by Christopher Hussey, *The Life* . . . , *op. cit.* p. 74.
86. Christopher Hussey, *The Life* . . . , *op. cit.* p. 85.
87. Quoted by Christopher Hussey, *The Life* . . . , *op. cit.* p. 74.
88. Ian Nairn and Nikolaus Pevsner, *The Buildings of England: Surrey* (Harmondsworth: Penguin Books, 1962), 322–3.
89. Laurence Weaver, *Houses and Gardens by E. L. Lutyens*, *op. cit.* pp. 23–4.
90. A. S. G. Butler, *op. cit.* vol. 1, p. 23.
91. Evelyn Waugh, *Brideshead Revisited* (London: Readers Union/Chapman & Hall, 1949), 28.
92. Arthur William Edgar O'Shaughnessy, Ode: *We are the Music Makers.*

BIBLIOGRAPHY

1. *General studies* (alphabetically by author)

ADAMS, MAURICE B., *Artists' Homes* (London: Batsford, 1883).

—, (ed.), *Modern Cottage Architecture* (London: Batsford, 1904; second enlarged edn, 1912).

ALLEN, GORDON, *The Cheap Cottage and Small House* (London: Batsford, 1912).

BARRON, P. A., *The House Desirable* (London: Methuen, 1929).

BROOKS, H. ALLEN, *The Prairie School* (University of Toronto Press, 1972).

CAVALIER, JULIAN, *American Castles* (Cranbury, New Jersey: A. S. Barnes and Co., 1973).

CONDIT, CARL W., *The Chicago School of Architecture* (University of Chicago Press, 1964).

DAVISON, T. RAFFLES, *Modern Homes* (London: Bell, 1909).

DARLEY, GILLIAN, *Villages of Vision* (London: Architectural Press, 1975).

DIXON, ROGER AND STEFAN MUTHESIUS, *Victorian Architecture* (London: Thames and Hudson, 1978).

FERRIDAY, PETER (ed.), *Victorian Architecture* (London: Jonathan Cape, 1978).

GIROUARD, MARK, *The Victorian Country House* (Oxford University Press, 1971); revised and enlarged edn (New Haven and London: Yale University Press, 1979).

GOODHART-RENDEL, H. S., *English Architecture Since the Regency* (London: Constable, 1953).

GREGORY, EDWARD W., *The Art and Craft of Home-Making* (London: Murby, 1913).

HITCHCOCK, H. R., *Architecture: Nineteenth and Twentieth Centuries* (Harmondsworth: Penguin Books, 1958).

HOLME, CHARLES (ed.), *Modern Domestic Architecture and Decoration* (London: The Studio, 1901).

JENNINGS, H. J., *Our Homes, and How to Beautify Them* (London: Harrison and Sons, 1902).

JORDY, WILLIAM H., *American Buildings and their Architects*, vols 3 and 4 (New York: Doubleday, 1972).

MACARTNEY, MERVYN (ed.), *Recent English Domestic Architecture*, 4 vols (London: The Architectural Review, 1908–11).

MARTIN, ARTHUR, *The Small House: Its Architecture and Surroundings* (London: Alston Rivers, 1906).

MASSÉ, H. J. L. J., *The Art-Workers' Guild 1884–1934* (Oxford: Shakespeare Head Press for the Art-Workers' Guild, 1935).

MUTHESIUS, HERMANN, *Die Englische Baukunst der Gegenwart*, 2 vols (Leipzig and Berlin: Cosmos, 1900).

—, *Das Englische Haus*, 3 vols (Berlin: Wasmuth, 1904–5; 2nd edn 1908–11); reprinted in an English translation, *The English House*, edited with an introduction by Dennis Sharp (London: Crosby Lockwood Staples, 1979).

PICTON-SEYMOUR, D., *Victorian Buildings in South Africa* (Cape Town; A. A. Balkema, 1977).

SCULLY, VINCENT J., *The Shingle Style* (New Haven: Yale University Press, 1955; revised 1971).

SERVICE, A. S. D. (ed.), *Edwardian Architecture and its Origins* (London: Architectural Press, 1975).

—, *Edwardian Architecture* (London: Thames and Hudson, 1977).

—, *London 1900* (London: Granada, 1979).

SHAW, R. N. AND T. G. JACKSON (eds), *Architecture, a Profession or an Art: Thirteen Essays on the Qualifications and Training of Architects* (London: John Murray, 1892).

SPARROW, W. SHAW (ed.), *The British Home of Today* (London: Hodder & Stoughton, 1904).

—, *Flats, Urban Houses and Cottage Homes* (London: Hodder & Stoughton, 1907).

—, *The Modern Home* (London: Hodder & Stoughton, 1906).

STAMP, GAVIN, *London 1900* (London: Academy Editions, 1978).

STATHAM, H. H., *Modern Architecture* (London: Chapman and Hall, 1897).

STEVENSON, J. J., *House Architecture*, 2 vols (London: Macmillan, 1880).

SUMMERSON, SIR JOHN, 'British Contemporaries of Frank Lloyd Wright', in *Studies in Western Art* (Princeton University Press, 1963).

—, *The Turn of the Century: Architecture in Britain Around 1900* (Glasgow University Press, 1975).

TAYLOR, JOHN RUSSELL, *The Art Nouveau Book in Britain* (London: Methuen, 1966).

WEAVER, LAWRENCE, *Small Country Houses of To-day*, First Series (London: Country Life, n.d. ? 1910 and 1912); Second Series, 3 vols (vol 3. by R. Philips) (London: Country Life, 1922–5).

—, *Small Country Houses: Their Repair and Enlargement* (London: Country Life, 1914).

—, *The 'Country Life' Book of Cottages* (London: Country Life, 1913).

WILLMOTT, ERNEST, *English House Design* (London: Batsford, 1911).

WRIGHTON, PRISCILLA (ed.), *The Small English House* (London: B. Weinreb Architectural Books, 1977).

2. *Specific architects and designers*
(titles are arranged chronologically within subject)

C. R. ASHBEE
Ashbee, C. R., *A Book of Cottages and Little Houses* (London: Essex House Press and Batsford, 1906).
—, *Craftsmanship in Competitive Industry* (Campden, Glos.: Essex House Press, n.d. ?1908).

M. H. BAILLIE SCOTT
Furniture Made at The Pyghtle Works, Bedford by John P. White, designed by M. H. Baillie Scott (Derby: Bemrose and Sons Ltd, 1901).
Baillie Scott, M. H., *Houses and Gardens* (London: Georges Newnes, 1906).
Kornwolf, James D., *M. H. Baillie Scott and the Arts and Crafts Movement* (Baltimore and London: John Hopkins Press, 1972).

HERBERT BAKER
Reilly, C. H., 'Sir Herbert Baker', in *Representative British Architects*, chap. 3 (London: Batsford, 1931), 40–53.
Baker, Herbert, *Cecil Rhodes by his Architect* (London: Oxford University Press, 1934).
—, *Architecture and Personalities* (London: Country Life, 1944).
Grieg, Doreen E., *Herbert Baker in South Africa* (Cape Town: Purnell, 1970).
South Africa, Department of Information, *Groote Schuur* (Pretoria, 1970).

JOHN BELCHER
Squire, Sir John, *The Hall of the Institute of Chartered Accountants in England and Wales* (Moorgate Place, London: privately published, 1937).

J. F. BENTLEY
L'Hôpital, Winefride de, *Westminster Cathedral and its Architect*, 2 vols (London: Hutchinson, 1919).
Scott-Moncrieff, W. W., *John Francis Bentley* (London: Ernest Benn, 1924).
Butler, A. S. G., *John Francis Bentley, the Architect of Westminster Cathedral: An Essay* (London: Burns & Oates, 1961).
Ricardo, Halsey, 'John Francis Bentley', in P. Ferriday (ed.) *Victorian Architecture* (London: Cape, 1963), 289–300.
Richards, J. M. (ed.), 'John Francis Bentley', in *Who's Who in Architecture* (London: Weidenfeld and Nicolson, 1977), 36–7.

FRANK BRANGWYN
Shaw-Sparrow, Walter, *Frank Brangwyn and His Work* (London: Kegan Paul, 1910).

Furst, Herbert, *The Decorative Art of Frank Brangwyn* (London: John Lane, 1924).

Belleroche, William de, *Brangwyn Talks* (London: Chapman and Hall, 1944).

Brangwyn, Rodney, *Brangwyn* (London: William Kimber, 1978).

R. A. BRIGGS

Briggs, R. A., *Homes for the Country* (London: Batsford, 1904).

BASIL CHAMPNEYS

Guppy, Henry, *The John Rylands Library, Manchester 1899–1924* (Manchester University Press, 1924).

CROUCH AND BUTLER

Crouch, Joseph and Edmund Butler, *The Apartments of the House: Their Arrangement, Furnishing and Decoration* (London: Unicorn, 1900).

GUY DAWBER

Reilly, C. H., 'E. Guy Dawber', in *Representative British Architects*, chap. 4 (London: Batsford, 1931), 80–7.

ALFRED GILBERT

Hatton, Joseph, *Alfred Gilbert R.A.: His Life and Work* (London: The Art Journal, 1903).

McAllister, Isabel, *Alfred Gilbert* (London: A & C Black, 1929).

Bury, Adrian, *Shadow of Eros* (London: Macdonald & Evans, 1954).

ERNEST GIMSON

Lethaby, W. R. and others, *Ernest Gimson: His Life and Work* (Stratford on Avon: Shakespeare Head Press, 1924).

Carruthers, Annette, *Ernest Gimson and the Cotswold Group of Craftsmen* (Leicester Museum Publication no. 14, 1978).

W. CURTIS GREEN

Reilly, C. H., 'W. Curtis Green', in *Representative British Architects*, chap. 8 (London: Batsford, 1931), 99–110.

W. Curtis Green R.A. (London: Green, Lloyd and Adams, 1978).

T. G. JACKSON

Jackson, Basil H. (ed.), *The Recollections of Thomas Graham Jackson, Bart, R.A.* (London: Oxford University Press, 1950).

GERTRUDE JEKYLL

Jekyll, Gertrude, *Home and Garden* (London: Longman, Green & Co., 1900).

Jeykll, Francis, *Gertrude Jekyll* (London: Jonathan Cape, 1934).

Massingham, Betty, *Miss Jekyll: Portrait of a Great Gardener* (London: Country Life, 1966; 2nd edn, Newton Abbot: David and Charles, 1973).

ROBERT LORIMER

The Work of Sir Robert Lorimer (London: Country Life, Architectural Supplement, 27 September, 1913).

Hussey, C., *Sir Robert Lorimer* (London: Country Life, 1931).

EDWIN LUTYENS

Weaver, Lawrence, *Houses and Gardens by E. L. Lutyens* (London: Country Life, 1913).

—, *Lutyens Houses and Gardens* (London: Country Life, 1921).

Lutyens, Robert, *Sir Edwin Lutyens: An Appreciation in Perspective* (London: Country Life, 1942).

Butler, A. S. G., *The Architecture of Sir Edwin Lutyens*, 3 vols (London: Country Life, 1950).

Hussey, Christopher, *The Life of Sir Edwin Lutyens* (London: Country Life, 1950).

Reilly, C. H., 'Sir Edwin Lutyens', in *Representative British Architects*, chap. 10 (London Batsford, 1931), 126–41.

Lutyens, Robert, *Notes on Sir Edwin Lutyens* (London: Oriel Press for The Art Workers' Guild, 1970).

Richardson, Margaret (ed.), *Lutyens. Catalogue of the Drawings Collection of the Royal Institute of British Architects* (London: Gregg, 1973).

Gradidge, Roderick, 'Edwin Lutyens: the last High Victorian', in J. Fawcett (ed.), *Seven Victorian Architects*, chap. 7 (London: Thames and Hudson, 1976), 122–36.

Saint, Andrew, 'Sir Edwin Landseer Lutyens', in J. M. Richards (ed.), *Who's Who in Architecture* (London: Weidenfeld and Nicolson, 1977), 190–2.

Inskip, Peter, *Edwin Lutyens* (London: Academy Editions, 1979).

O'Neill, Daniel, *Sir Edwin Lutyens: Country Houses* (London: Lund Humphries, 1980).

Gradidge, Roderick, *Edwin Lutyens: Architect Laureate* (London, Scolar Press, 1980).

CHARLES RENNIE MACKINTOSH

Howarth, Thomas, *Charles Rennie Mackintosh and the Modern Movement* (London: Routledge and Kegan Paul, 1952).

Bliss, Douglas Percy, *Charles Rennie Mackintosh and the Glasgow School of Art* (The Glasgow School of Art, 1961).

Young, Andrew McLaren, *Charles Rennie Mackintosh (1868–1928)*, Catalogue of Centenary Exhibition (Edinburgh: Scottish Arts Council, 1968).

MacLeod, Robert, *Charles Rennie Mackintosh* (London: Country Life, 1968).

Charles Rennie Mackintosh (Scottish Art Review Special Number, vol. 11, no. 4, 1968).

Pevsner, Nikolaus, 'Charles Rennie Mackintosh', in *Studies in Art, Architecture and Design*, vol. 2, chap. 9 (London: Thames and Hudson, 1968), 152–75.

Jordan, Robert Furneaux, 'Charles Rennie Mackintosh', in J. M. Richards (ed.), *Who's Who in Architecture* (London: Weidenfeld and Nicolson, 1977), 193–6.

A. H. MACKMURDO

William Morris Gallery, Walthamstowe, *A. H. Mackmurdo and the Century Guild Collection*, Catalogue (London, 1967).

The Minories, Colchester, *The Eccentric A. H. Mackmurdo 1851–1942*, Catalogue of Exhibition (1979).

Pevsner, Nikolaus, 'Arthur H. Mackmurdo', in *Studies in Art, Architecture and Design*, vol. 2, chap. 7 (London: Thames and Hudson, 1968), 130–9.

JAMES MACLAREN

Service, Alastair, 'James MacLaren and the Godwin Legacy', in *Edwardian Architecture and its Origins* (London: Architectural Press, 1975), 100–18.

MCKIM, MEAD AND WHITE

A Monograph of the Work of McKim, Mead & White 1879–1915, 4 vols (New York: The Architectural Book Publishing Co., 1915–20; revised edn with new essay and notes on plates by Leland M. Roth (New York: Benjamin Blom Inc., 1973).

Reilly, C. H., *McKim, Mead and White* (London: Ernest Benn, 1924).

Baldwin, Charles C., *Stanford White*, revised edn with an introduction by Paul Goldberger (New York: De Capo Press, 1976) (first published 1931).

Roth, Leland M., 'McKim, Mead & White', in J. M. Richards (ed.), *Who's Who in Architecture* (London: Weidenfeld and Nicolson, 1977), 206–8.

T. H. MAWSON

Mawson, T. H., *The Art and Craft of Garden Making* (London: Batsford, 1901).

BERNARD MAYBECK

Cardwell, Kenneth H., *Bernard Maybeck* (Santa Barbara: Peregrine Smith, 1977).

WILLIAM DE MORGAN

Gaunt, William and M. D. E. Clayton-Stamm, *William de Morgan* (London: Studio Vista, 1971).

ERNEST NEWTON

Newton, Ernest, *A Book of Houses* (London: Sprague, 1890).

—, *A Book of Country Houses* (London: Batsford, 1903).

Newton, William Godfrey, *The Work of Ernest Newton, R.A.* (London: Architectural Press, 1925).

PARKER AND UNWIN

Parker, Barry and Raymond Unwin, *The Art of Building a Home* (London: Longmans, Green & Co., 1901).

E. S. PRIOR

Hoare, Geoffrey and Geoffrey Pyne, *Prior's Barn & Gimson's Coxen* (published by the authors, 'Selforth', Little Knowle, Budleigh Salterton, 1978).

Grillet, Christopher, 'Edward Prior', in A. Service (ed.), *Edwardian Architecture and its Origins* (London: Architectural Press, 1975), 142–51.

C. H. B. QUENNELL

Quennell, C. H. B., *Modern Suburban Homes* (London: Batsford, 1906).

E. A. RICKARDS

Bennett, Arnold, *The Art of E. A. Ricketts* (London: Technical Journals, 1920).

Warren, John, 'Edwin Alfred Rickards', in A. Service (ed.), *Edwardian Architecture and its Origins* (London: Architectural Press, 1975), 338–50.

RICKETTS AND SHANNON

Calloway, Stephen, *Charles Ricketts* (London: Thames and Hudson, 1979).

Calloway, Stephen and Paul Delaney, *Charles Ricketts and Charles Shannon*, Catalogue of Exhibition (London: Borough of Richmond on Thames, 1979).

ROBERT WEIR SCHULTZ

Ottewill, David, Robert Weir Schultz', *Acrhitectural History*, vol. 22 (1979), 88–115.

RICHARD NORMAN SHAW

Blomfield, Reginald, *Richard Norman Shaw R.A.* (London: Batsford, 1940).

Pevsner, Nikolaus, 'Richard Norman Shaw', in P. Ferriday (ed.), *Victorian Architecture* (London: Jonathan Cape, 1963), 237–46.

Saint, Andrew, *Richard Norman Shaw* (New Haven and London: Yale University Press, 1976).

—'Richard Norman Shaw', in J. M. Richards (ed.), *Who's Who in Architecture* (London: Weidenfeld and Nicolson, 1977), 296–9.

PHILIP TILDEN

Tilden, Philip, *True Remembrances* (London: Country Life, 1954).

CHARLES HARRISON TOWNSEND

Service, Alastair, 'Charles Harrison Townsend', in A. Service (ed.), *Edwardian Architecture and its Origins* (London: Architectural Press, 1975), 162–82.

C. F. A. VOYSEY

Brandon-Jones, John, *C. F. A. Voysey: A Memoir* (London: Architectural Association, 1957).

—, 'C. F. A. Voysey', in P. Ferriday (ed.), *Victorian Architecture* (London: Jonathan Cape, 1963), 269–87.

Pevsner, Nikolaus, 'C. F. A. Voysey', in *Studies in Art, Architecture and Design*, vol. 2, chap. 8 (London: Thames and Hudson, 1968), 140–51.

Betjeman, Sir John, 'Charles Annesley Voysey', in A. Service (ed.), *Edwardian Architecture and its Origins* (London: Architectural Press, 1975), 152–60.

Gebhard, David, *Charles F. A. Voysey: Architect* (Los Angeles: Henessy & Ingalls, 1975).

Symonds, J., *C. F. A. Voysey. Catalogue of the Drawings Collection of the Royal Institute of British Architects* (London: Gregg, 1976).

Richards, J. M. (ed.), 'Charles Francis Annesley Voysey', in *Who's Who in Architecture* (London: Weidenfeld and Nicolson, 1977), 338–40.

Brandon-Jones, John and others, *C. F. A. Voysey: Architect and Designer, 1857–1941* (London: Lund Humphries, 1978).

Simpson, Duncan, *C. F. A. Voysey, an Architect of Individuality* (London: Lund Humphries, 1979).

GEORGE WALTON

Pevsner, Nikolaus, 'George Walton', in *Studies in Art, Architecture and Design*, vol. 2, chap. 10 (London: Thames and Hudson, 1968), 176–88.

G. F. WATTS and MARY WATTS

Watts, Mrs G. F., *The Word in the Pattern: A Key to the Symbols on the Walls of the Chapel at Compton* (London: Astolat Press, 1900; 2nd edn, ?1905).

Blunt, Wilfrid, *England's Michelangelo* (London: Hamish Hamilton, 1975).

PHILIP WEBB

Lethaby, W. R., *Philip Webb and his Work* (London: Oxford University Press, 1935).

Brandon-Jones, John, 'Philip Webb', in P. Ferriday (ed.), *Victorian Architecture* (London: Jonathan Cape, 1963), 247–65.

Jack, George, 'An appreciation of Philip Webb', in A. Service (ed.), *Edwardian Architecture and its Origins* (London: Architectural Press, 1975), 16–25.

Richards, J. M. (ed.), 'Philip Speakman Webb', in *Who's Who in Architecture* (London: Weidenfeld and Nicolson, 1977), 343–4.

C. C. WINMILL

Winmill, Joyce M., *Charles Canning Winmill* (London: Dent, 1946).

EDGAR WOOD

Archer, John, 'Edgar Wood and J. Henry Sellars', in A. Service (ed.), *Edwardian Architecture and its Origins* (London: Architectural Press, 1975), 372–84.

Manchester City Art Gallery, *Partnership in Style: Edgar Wood & J. Henry Sellars*, Catalogue of Exhibition (City of Manchester Cultural Services, 1975).

JAMES WILLIAMS

Williams, James, *Sketches of Village Buildings* (London: Richard Bentley, n.d. ?1898).

FRANK LLOYD WRIGHT

Frank Lloyd Wright: Ausgeführte Bauten und Entwürfe, with an introduction by C. R. Ashbee (Berlin: Wasmuth, 1911); revised edn, *Frank Lloyd Wright: The Early Work*, with an introduction by E. Kaufman Jr (New York: Horizon Press, 1968).

The Life-Work of the American Architect Frank Lloyd Wright, with an introduction by H. Th. Wijdeveld, 7 vols. of *Wendingen* (Santpoort, Holland: C. A. Mees, 1925).

Wright, Frank Lloyd, *An Autobiography* (London: Faber and Faber, 1945).

Manson, Grant Carpenter, *Frank Lloyd Wright to 1910* (New York: Van Nostrand Reinhold, 1958).

Storrer, William Allin, *The Architecture of Frank Lloyd Wright* (Cambridge, Mass.: MIT Press, 1974).

Hoffman, Donald, 'Frank Lloyd Wright', in J. M. Richards (ed.), *Who's Who in Architecture* (London: Weidenfeld and Nicolson, 1977), 350–4.

INDEX

Buildings appear both under their architects and under their names or locality. Churches and Commercial and Public Buildings are also listed under these headings.

Page references to illustrations are given in italics. Plans have the abbreviation 'Pl.' before the page number.